The Birth Lottery

Values and Ethics Series, Volume 5

The Birth Lottery
Prenatal Diagnosis and Selective Abortion

Judith A. Boss

Foreword by Dr. Mark Waymack

Loyola University Press
Chicago

Loyola University Press
3441 North Ashland Avenue
Chicago, Illinois 60657

Cover design by Mary O'Connor

Library of Congress Cataloging-in-Publication Data

Boss, Judith A., 1942–
    The birth lottery: prenatal diagnosis and selective abortion / by
Judith A. Boss; foreword by Mark Waymack.
        p.   cm.
    Includes bibliographical references and index.
    ISBN 0-8294-0740-5
    1. Prenatal diagnosis. 2. Abortion, Theraputic—Moral and ethical
aspects. I. Title.
    [DNLM: 1. Abortion, Eugenic. 2. Ethics, Medical. 3. Prenatal
Diagnosis. WQ 225 B745b]
    RG628.B67 1992
    179'.76—dc20
    DNLM/DLC
    for Library of Congress
                                                    92–49738
                                                         CIP

This book is dedicated to all children,
especially to my children,

Kathy, Alyssa, and Greg

and my new grandson,

Jonathan

Table of Contents

List of Illustrations

List of Tables

Foreword

In recent years, the scientific community has taken some significant steps toward understanding human genetics. It is now possible to identify several diseases and birth defects with particular genetic markers. And our knowledge in this area will grow exponentially in the next decade as work on the "Human Genome Project," encouraged and financed by the National Institutes of Health, progresses.

At the same time, the medical community has developed the technological means whereby genetic material from a fetus can be collected and screened during pregnancy. Amniocentesis was the first such procedure developed—a technique employed around the sixteenth week of pregnancy. A few years ago, chorionic villus sampling was developed, in which fetal cells are collected around the eleventh week of pregnancy. And now it is possible to isolate fetal cells from a sampling of maternal blood as early as the first month of pregnancy.

Needless to say, there has been a great deal of ethics literature generated concerning moral issues raised by the combination of this genetic knowledge and the ability to perform fetal genetic screening. The moral optimists write about a future in which genetic anomalies may be located *in utero* and corrected. Children who would have been born with Down syndrome or Tay-Sachs or sickle cell anemia or trisomy 16 will, in this wonderful future, be born without those undesirable, genetically caused problems.

The moral pessimists write of a "brave, new world" where genetic diversity has been replaced with homogeneity.

The moral optimists and pessimists, however, have both focused their thoughts upon what still remains but a remote future possibility—our ability to alter a fetus's genetic make-up early enough in the pregnancy to alter the growth and development of that fetus.

What Judith Boss does is to remind us of the moral issues that we face *right now:* What are parents and physicians to do when faced with the knowledge that a fetus has a genetic anomaly and the knowledge that we cannot correct it? The primary motivation behind having such genetic screening done during pregnancy is to decide whether or not to have an abortion. Faced with our inability to genetically alter the impaired fetus, the "cure" chosen is abortion.

Many of us, when we are faced with a child with a significant genetic impairment, feel sorrow and regret. We wish that things could have been otherwise. We may well, in many cases, feel revulsion. And we may even feel that it is worse to live like that than to have never been born. But what does it mean to say that a fetus would be better off not being born? What is in a fetus's best interests?

Whether we are eager to acknowledge it or not, we may see such unfortunate children as regrettable burdens upon their parents, their siblings, and their society. What does it say about us, in a moral sense, if we are willing to balance the inconvenience a genetically impaired child might pose upon us against its very chance for life?

As the reader will come to discover, Boss provocatively argues that it is morally misguided to abort fetuses on the grounds of some genetic impairment. But even someone, such as myself, who is not wholly in agreement with her arguments and conclusions, will benefit from reading this book. For Boss will not allow us to turn a blind eye. Rather, she forces each of us to confront just what is at stake in the "birth lottery."

Mark H. Waymack

Acknowledgments

Many people contributed to the writing of this book. First and foremost I would like to express my deepest appreciation to my dissertation adviser and mentor, Robert Neville, dean of religious and theological studies at Boston University, for his time, support, and invaluable suggestions in the preparation of this manuscript. George Annas, of the Boston University School of Medicine and Public Health, also assisted by proofreading most of the medical portions of the manuscript. I would also like to thank John Howard Yoder of the University of Notre Dame for his input during the early planning stages.

Fritz Wenisch, professor and past chair of philosophy at the University of Rhode Island, was endlessly encouraging as well as helpful in many small but important ways. I will be forever indebted to him. Norma Schrock of the University of Rhode Island also assisted with the word processing, for which I am grateful.

I cannot begin to express my gratitude to my own children who remained supportive throughout this project, especially to my daughter Alyssa, also a philosopher, who provided helpful feedback and assisted with the proofreading of the text.

Even though preparing a manuscript for publication can be tedious at times, everyone at Loyola University Press was wonderful in making the publishing experience an enjoyable one. I am especially thankful for the cheerfulness, support, and persistence of Father Joseph F. Downey, editorial director of Loyola University Press, and to Erin Milnes, project manager, and her assistant, Amy Norton, for the patient and caring attention they gave to the final editing of the text.

Lastly, I would like to use this opportunity to thank all the librarians, medical professionals, and colleagues who took time to answer my many research-related questions, and to express appreciation to those writers and publishers who so kindly gave me permission to use their work in this book.

Half of the royalties from this book will be donated to the Meeting Street School in Providence, Rhode Island.

Introduction

What's at Stake in the Selective Abortion Controversy?

Each year in the United States, more than 250,000 infants, representing about 7 percent of all births, are born with physical and/or mental disorders of varying degrees of severity. Prenatal diagnosis provides direct information about certain genetic and chromosomal abnormalities in the fetus. Although 95 percent of all prenatal diagnostic tests yield negative results, the overwhelming majority of pregnancies in which the fetus is diagnosed as having a genetic disorder are terminated by selective abortion.

The rapidly growing use and availability of prenatal diagnosis in the past decade, and the recent Supreme Court decision that returns some power to the states to regulate abortion, gives the issue of the morality of selective abortion based on prenatal diagnosis a new urgency. Acceptance of the practice of selective abortion based on prenatal diagnosis is influenced by prevailing political, cultural, and legal norms, especially those relating to abortion in general, as well as people's perception of the moral principles involved in the controversy about selective abortion. Unlike elective abortion, in which the pregnancy itself is unwanted, in selective abortion it is that particular fetus, rather than the pregnancy, that is unwanted. While only about 25 percent of Americans believe that abortion on demand is morally acceptable, 87 percent approve of abortion if the fetus has a genetic disorder (Lamanna 1984, 4). This discrepancy cannot be attributed solely to a belief that the fetus has no or limited moral rights. Instead, there seems to be a widespread belief that the very presence of a genetic disorder justifies abortion.

It is not the purpose of this book to discuss the pro–abortion rights position, which condones abortion for any reason as long as it is the woman's decision. Instead, this book will deal with the issue of the abortion of a fetus with a genetic abnormality or other "undesirable" genetic traits under conditions where the fetus would otherwise come to term.

Factors Influencing Attitudes toward Selective Abortion

Several factors, in addition to the availability of safer abortion procedures and more reliable methods of prenatal diagnosis, have worked together in the past few decades to positively influence attitudes toward the practice of selective abortion based on prenatal diagnosis. These factors include changing attitudes toward child rearing, an emphasis on technology as a solution to social problems, the growing stress on individual autonomy and the right to privacy, and, of course, the legalization of abortion.

Changing Family Structure

When the United States and other Western countries were mainly agrarian, children were viewed primarily in terms of their economic value. Quantity of children, rather than quality, was most important. With modernization and the removal of children from areas of economic production and with the declining size of the family, children have come to be valued more in terms of the quality of their physical and mental "normalcy" (Kenen 1981, 68). Some people have gone even further, claiming the right to be "well born" as a basic right of the unborn (Cole 1971, 68).

Technology and Genetic Control

The recent development of technology to diagnose fetal abnormalities has given parents and physicians the ability to make decisions regarding childbearing that were previously left to "God" or chance. Parents are now able, and often expected, to exercise quality control in family planning.

The strong cultural bias of the Western world toward techno-logical control of our environment and destiny offers "quality control" not only as an option but, for some, also as an obliga-tion. Our ability to control our reproductive destiny, it has been suggested, creates a new responsibility on the part of parents to be accountable and responsible for the human life that they cre-ate (Engelhardt 1982b, 186). Joseph Fletcher (1979), one of the most outspoken proponents of the quality-of-life philosophy, argues that to intentionally give birth to, rather than to abort, a child who is known to have a defect, such as Down syndrome, is to inflict a "grievous injury" on the child (126). Fletcher goes on to advocate the use of social control in the form of laws to pre-vent the birth of children who fall below a "minimum standard" (123–24).

While few people would find Fletcher's proposed solution acceptable, most parents are well aware of the awesome respon-sibility that accompanies the ability to diagnose birth defects prenatally. When parents are questioned about their reasons for seeking prenatal diagnosis, the reason most frequently men-tioned is "a parental responsibility to ensure the health of their children and the security of their families" (Hollerbach 1979, 205). This attitude is reflected in the growing number of "wrongful life" suits in recent years and the expectation that physicians should ensure parents that they will have a healthy baby (Elias and Annas 1987, 109).

While prenatal diagnosis and selective abortion are presently directed primarily toward the avoidance of the birth of children with serious genetic disorders, some people question the poten-tial misuse of this new power to control our genetic destiny. They warn that prenatal diagnosis, coupled with selective abor-tion, opens up the possibility of the "custom-made" child

(Holmes, Hoskins, and Gross 1981). This possibility raises the concern about who should decide what sort of people we ought to be (Hauerwas 1986, 205). Pro-life philosophers, such as Paul Ramsey (1978) and Richard Sherlock (1987), and many of the members of the current pro-life movement (Callahan and Callahan 1984) reject the quality-of-life reasoning as a threat to the concept of the worth and equal dignity of all humans.

Autonomy and the Right to Privacy

The philosophy that espouses social control over our genetic destiny, whether in terms of compulsory selective abortion or prohibitions against abortion, has been countered by the Anglo-American legal tradition that gives priority to individual over societal rights. In the past few decades, there has emerged a pervasive attitude regarding the right to privacy and autonomy as an absolute right.

This attitude has been especially strong as regards the issue of parental autonomy and the right to make one's own procreative choices. The right to procreative privacy was first spelled out in U.S. Constitutional law with the 1965 *Griswold v. Connecticut* case regarding a couple's right to use contraception. There has since been an increasing acceptance of selective abortion as a matter of personal choice, as well as a decline in the number of physicians who require women to commit to the abortion of a fetus with a disorder before prenatal diagnosis.

In keeping with this emphasis on autonomy, "most Americans view any systematic interference with reproductive freedom or traditions of parenthood as a serious moral violation" (Fletcher and Wertz 1987a, 306). Medical ethicists John Fletcher and Dorothy Wertz (1987a) believe that this policy of noninterference is an essential feature of a pluralistic society (306). For many Americans, "individual privacy"—"the right to be left alone"—has become the "primary human value" (Elias and Annas 1987, xiii).

Because of this emphasis on parental autonomy, physicians involved in prenatal diagnosis, particularly in the United States, are cautioned by their mentors to be "nondirective" and not to impose their values on the women or couples they counsel (Milunksy 1986, 8; Lebel 1978, 28–31). Susan Johnson and Thomas Elkins (1988) write: "The model of genetic counseling most widely accepted is that of nondirective counseling. The ethical basis of this model would seem to be that of promoting autonomous decision making by the responsible parties, in most cases the parents" (410).

Selective Abortion and the Law

The relaxing of abortion laws in the United States and throughout most of the world has provided a greater measure of reproductive liberty, particularly regarding selective abortion because of a fetal deformity.

Before 1973, the majority of the American public supported legalized abortion only in situations in which the health of the mother or fetus was perceived to be threatened or compromised in some way or when the circumstances of the pregnancy violated cultural norms (that is, rape and incest). Abortion was also prohibited in nearly two-thirds of the world's countries, except when the woman's life was threatened by the pregnancy (Lampe 1973).

At present, about 39 percent of the world's population live in countries that allow abortion on request (Sachdev 1988, 484). Most of the countries that still have restrictive abortion laws allow abortion for fetal deformity (ibid., 16–24). Worldwide, about one-third of all pregnancies now end in abortion. The present abortion rate in the United States is slightly below this figure (Tietz and Henshaw 1986, 43). The most favorable attitudes toward abortion are found in the former Soviet Union, where two-thirds of pregnancies end in abortion (Sachdev 1988, 5). China, with its single-family policy, is a close second regarding the total number of abortions performed (ibid.). Cuba, the former Yugoslavia, Bulgaria, and the Republic of Korea also have high abortion rates (ibid., 16–19; Tietz and Henshaw 1986, 29).

The thalidomide tragedy in Europe in the early 1960s, in which thousands of infants with severe limb deformities were born to women who had taken thalidomide during early pregnancy, and the rubella epidemic in the United States in the mid-1960s, which resulted in about 4,800 abortions (Tietz and Henshaw 1986, 83), led to the loosening of restrictions on selective abortion in the United States, England, and a few other nations.

In 1967, Colorado became the first state in the United States to revise its abortion laws to permit abortion if the physician believed there was a "substantial risk . . . that the child would be born with grave physical or mental defects" (Mecklenburg 1973, 37). By 1971, ten other states (Arkansas, Delaware, Georgia, Kansas, Maryland, New Mexico, North Carolina, Oregon, South Carolina, and Virginia) had adopted similar laws (Cole 1971).

Approval/Disapproval of Selective Abortion

With the 1973 U.S. Supreme Court *Roe v. Wade* ruling, selective and elective abortion became legal in all states. Support for selective abortion, although not as high as support for abortion when the life and health of the mother is endangered, has always been stronger than support for abortion on demand.

The Effect of *Roe v. Wade*

A 1991 Gallup Poll showed that 17 percent of Americans took a pro-life stance, 32 percent accepted the pro–abortion rights position as put forth in *Roe v. Wade*, and 50 percent approved of abortion only in certain circumstances (Gallup 1992, 118). Approval of selective abortion in the United States increased from 52 percent in 1962 to 69 percent in 1970 to 82 percent a few months after *Roe v. Wade* was passed in 1973 (Hollerbach 1979, 201). A 1988 Gallup Poll showed a drop in the approval rate with only 60% of those polled stating that they approved of abortions in cases in which "there is a chance the baby will be deformed" (Gallup 1989, 208). However, approval of selective abortion drops by 10 to 20 percent when it involves a second-trimester abortion (ibid., 5). This discrepancy in approval rates most likely reflects a general lack of knowledge regarding the timing of selective abortions, the overwhelming majority of which are carried out during the second trimester.

Demographic Factors

The level of approval of selective abortion is also strongly influenced by religious affiliation, economic status, and ethnic group.

As regards religious affiliation, the two groups most accepting of selective abortion are Jews and people with no religious affiliation (95 percent in 1975 for both groups). Catholics are the least likely to approve of selective abortion. In a study of the relationship between religion and the family's acceptance of a retarded child, G. H. Zuk (1959) found that "Catholic mothers were more accepting than non-Catholic mothers" (144). At the same time, the most dramatic change in the rate of approval of selective abortion has been among Roman Catholics—from 33 percent in 1962 to 77 percent in 1975 (Hollerbach 1979, 202).

Whites (85 percent) are more likely to approve of selective abortion than are blacks (69 percent) (ibid.). Education level and income are also positively correlated with approval of selective abortion (ibid.). Although single people are no more likely to approve of selective abortion than are married people (ibid., 203), they are less likely to refuse prenatal diagnosis than are married people, perhaps because married people are more secure and capable of raising a child with a handicap (Berne-Fromell et al. 1984, 688). Also, single women are much more likely to seek an abortion for any reason. Single women abort almost twice as many pregnancies as those they carry to term, while married women are ten times more likely to give birth than to abort a pregnancy (Henshaw et al. 1985, 92).

In the United States, geneticists have generally adopted the dominant morality of the culture in formulating their views about prenatal diagnosis and selective abortion (Fletcher and Wertz 1987b, 305). In a 1977 survey of 457 physicians, 87.4 percent of surgeons and 91.1 percent of pediatricians responded that "abortions of genetically defective infants, as determined by amniocentesis," should not be outlawed; 9.4 and 6.4 percent, respectively, said they should be outlawed; and the remainder did not respond (Shaw et al. 1977, 596).

Parents, on the other hand, have been slower to accept selective abortion as a means of so-called pregnancy management. For example, a 1991 study showed that only 40 percent of parents of children with cystic fibrosis said they would "choose abortion if their fetus was diagnosed as having cystic fibrosis" (Wertz et al. 1991, 992). A 1984 Swedish study found that 62 percent of the women who declined maternal serum alpha-feto-protein (MSAFP) testing, a prenatal screening process, did so because they were ambivalent about or opposed to legal abortion; 36 percent of the women who underwent voluntary MSAFP testing were ambivalent about abortion. Active participation in a religious organization was also found to be a major factor in a woman's refusal to undergo prenatal diagnosis (Berne-Fromell et al. 1984, 690).

In their research on the effects of selective abortion on families, Bruce Blumberg and his colleagues (1975) found that 77 percent of families who had had a previous positive diagnosis followed by a selective abortion responded that they would repeat the procedure (807). However, while "these families have accepted selective abortion and its attendant problems as preferable to the birth of a defective child" (ibid.), it is not clear from the study how many actually repeated the prenatal diagnosis/selective abortion experience. The hesitancy to repeat the emotional trauma associated with the procedure and their ambivalent attitudes toward childbearing following the abortion, in many cases seems to override parents' original decision. John Fletcher (1972), for example, found that some parents who underwent the selective abortion experience vowed to make it "the last time" (463).

Another study, however, reported that 94 percent of the women surveyed who had undergone amniocentesis said they would repeat the procedure should they become pregnant again (Finley et al. 1977, 2378). However, only 5 women of the 157 respondents to their questionnaire had had a selective abortion as a result of the amniocentesis. Unfortunately, their responses are not recorded separately. In a study of women who were carriers of hemophilia, seven of the nine women interviewed who had a positive test result had a selective abortion or spontaneous miscarriage. One to five years after the experiences, only 59 percent said they would consider having prenatal diagnosis again (Tedgard et al. 1989). Another study found that while 96 percent of women who had a favorable (negative) test result following amniocentesis said they would repeat the procedure in future pregnancies, only 77 percent of the women who underwent selective abortion following an amniocentesis said they would be willing to do so again (Blumberg et al. 1975, 807).

Selective abortion is a traumatic experience for most families, independent of the experience of prenatal diagnosis. The experience of selective abortion involves the loss of a wanted pregnancy and is most appropriately viewed as an experience of bereavement (DeSpelder and Strickland 1977, 267–69). John Fletcher (1972) found that almost all parents who have chosen selective abortion suffered from what he terms "cosmic guilt" (471). He notes that "added to the guilt associated with being a carrier of genetic disease was the realization that their experiment to get a healthy child failed" (457).

Despite the fact that the majority of people claim that they approve of the practice of selective abortion, this support does not seem to translate into active support for those who have undergone the experience. The lack of understanding on the part of the larger community is often keenly felt by those who have had selective abortions. Many couples report that people did not understand or were not supportive of their choice; others expressed a "sense of isolation" after the experience (Blumberg et al. 1975, 808). Parents of children with genetic disorders have also experienced social disapproval, which tends to exacerbate the guilt they may already feel at being a "carrier" (McCormick 1974). Thus, in many ways, it seems to be a no-win situation for parents who are at risk for having a child with a genetic disorder.

Parents' complete sense of self-worth may be threatened by their perceived inability to live up to the societal norm of producing a normal, healthy family (Blumberg et al. 1975, 806). There is an increased frequency of marital separation before or after a selective abortion (ibid.). However, family disruptions as well as depression and guilt are also more common after the birth of a child with a serious disorder (Cohen 1984, 188). The "genetic guilt" following the birth of a child with a serious disorder is probably more acute than that following a selective abortion (Blumberg et al. 1975, 806).

Because of the great concern for children free from disability, together with our strong cultural bias toward control of our environment and mastery of our biological destiny, it is possible that these societal attitudes, which are now held in check by the present emphasis on autonomy, might someday lead to the ostracization of those who fail to take steps to prevent the birth of a child with a congenital abnormality (Hollerbach 1979, 202).

Abortion for Sex Selection

Selective abortion is not always performed because of the presence of a genetic disorder as such. There is a clear trend, worldwide, toward approval of selective abortion for sex selection, although the reasons given vary from country to country. In some underdeveloped countries, such as China, where a son is the best form of social security in one's old age, sex selection is a common reason for selective abortion (Dickens 1986, 144). In some areas of China, the male to female sex ratio is over 120:100 because of the prevalence of abortion for sex selection (Sachdev 1988, 102).

In the United States and most Western countries, approval of abortion for sex selection, where the choice of sex is unrelated to sex-linked disease, has always been low. However, the declining size of the American family and the preference for sons as first-born or only children, as well as the stress on autonomy, is leading to a modification of this attitude.

A 1975 survey of genetic counselors in the United States indicated that only 1 percent would perform amniocentesis for sex selection (Fletcher and Wertz 1987b, 300). A more recent international survey of physicians from the United States and nineteen other countries reported that 32.2 percent would perform prenatal diagnosis for sex selection, and another 28.4 percent, although they would not perform the diagnosis themselves, would refer the woman to another physician who would (ibid., 301). In 1990, only a few years later, the same researchers reported that 42 percent of the physicians surveyed said they would agree to perform prenatal diagnosis for sex selection (Wertz et al. 1990).

Of the nations surveyed in a 1987 study, the United States was one of the three in which the majority of geneticists surveyed (62 percent) said they would perform prenatal diagnosis for sex selection, giving as their primary reason "respect for the woman's autonomy" (Wertz and Fletcher 1988, 815, 823). On the other hand, 52 percent of geneticists from India approved of prenatal diagnosis for sex selection but gave as their reason social pressures to limit population and the possible harm to unwanted girls (ibid., 825).

As a consequence of this emphasis on autonomy and the right to privacy in the United States, the current public debate over the morality of selective abortion is often superseded by the issue of who should make the decision (Fletcher and Wertz 1987a, 310). This, unfortunately, has too often led to an attitude of uncritical acceptance of the practice of selective abortion without sufficient examination of the relevant moral arguments or the assumptions underlying them.

Relevant Moral Principles

The majority of Americans who take a moderate position regarding abortion believe that there are moral justifications for the abortion of a fetus with a genetic disorder that override the normal prohibition against taking the life of a fetus. "The decision to abort a severely defective fetus," according to this position, "can be viewed as qualitatively different than the decision to abort a healthy fetus. . . . The interest of the mother to be free to choose to terminate her pregnancy is significantly increased when the fetus she is carrying is discovered to be defective" (Rush 1983, 134–36).

As a consequence of this type of reasoning, the discussion of selective abortion has more often centered around who should decide, with the final decision generally resting with the mother, rather than the more basic question of whether the decision should be made at all and, if so, under what conditions or within what limitations. This bias, philosopher John Arras (1984) believes, stems in part from "intellectual laziness" rather than well-thought-out arguments (25).

First, the relevant moral principles must be ascertained; in other words, which standards should guide or inform our decisions? French geneticist Jerome Lejeune (1970), who was a pioneer in the field of diagnosing chromosomal disorders, believes strongly that geneticists (and one might add ethicists) should no longer "play Pontius Pilate and wash their hands saying, 'The parents will choose.'"(123) Instead, it is imperative that involved professionals assume the duty to establish moral guidelines (ibid.). Although parents are deeply involved emotionally, they are not cytogeneticists, he points out, and are not in a position to make an informed judgment.

Equality and Nondiscrimination

In establishing moral guidelines, respect for the equality of all humans and, hence, nondiscrimination against humans with genetic disorders is an obvious concern and the primary moral principle used by many writers who are opposed to the widespread use of selective abortion (Lejeune 1970; Lebacqz 1972; Kass 1973; Sherlock 1987). It was also the guiding principle behind the Reagan administration's stand against the euthanasia of newborns with handicaps. The principle of nondiscrimination mandates that humans not be denied benefits or equal treatment for morally irrelevant reasons, such as sex or skin color. In this context, one must ask whether there is "the real possibility that there may well be morally significant differences between handicapped and normal children (and fetuses) that justify differential treatment" (Arras 1984, 26). If so, what are these morally significant differences?

Some ethicists maintain that we cannot judge the morality of selective abortion exclusively on the basis of one value, such as human equality. Two other important principles that must also be considered in the selective abortion controversy are (1) respect for parental autonomy and (2) nonmaleficence, or noninfliction of harm on individuals and families.

With the addition of these two principles, the consequences for the individuals involved, the families, and society as a whole all must be considered (Fletcher 1986, 821–22).

Beneficence

Frank Chervenak and Laurence McCullough (1985 and 1990) take a somewhat stronger position than does John Fletcher. Although they agree that respect for autonomy is an important value, they regard the positive obligation of beneficence—actively helping others—as one of the two major values involved in obstetric care. Both the physician and the mother, as the moral fiduciary of the fetus, have an obligation to "protect and promote the best interests of the mother and the best interests of the fetus and the child it will become" (1985, 442), rather than merely avoiding the infliction of harm. Therefore, parental responsibility for the well-being of the fetus/child, as well as the physician's professional responsibility to the fetus as patient, must be considered.

Chervenak and McCullough believe that these beneficence-based obligations, although equal in importance to respect for autonomy, may in some circumstances override the woman's right to autonomy. They propose that decision making regarding the management of third-trimester pregnancy be based on a continuum of beneficence-based obligations according to a classification scheme based on the degree of fetal abnormality. When there are no beneficence-based obligations, such as with an anencephalic fetus, the physician should recommend abortion or nonaggressive management of the pregnancy.

Other physicians and ethicists regard the moral obligations created by the possibility of selective abortion not just in terms of the welfare of the fetus and family but as extending to society at large. The principle of nonmaleficence in regard to society, they claim, creates a moral obligation to "prevent genetic diseases and their impact on future generations in the absence of successful genetic therapies" (Fletcher and Wertz 1987b, 295). Preservation of precious medical and financial resources must also be considered. On the other hand, the threat to valued societal beliefs, such as human equality and nonabandonment of those in need, also needs to be considered in deciding whether a fetus with a genetic disorder should live or die.

Conclusion

Prenatal diagnosis and selective abortion are not morally neutral procedures; they must be justified. Each of the principles mentioned above needs to be ordered and balanced in the debate over the morality of selective abortion based on prenatal diagnosis. In doing so, it should be kept in mind that scientific progress does not necessarily mean moral or social progress. Good ethical reasoning, however, must also be based on a sound grasp of the medical and scientific facts involved. In the past, well-meaning people have too often misapplied moral principles, such as nonmaleficence ("Do no harm") without first checking out the relevant facts. For example, in the early 1950s, more than two-thirds of physicians infrequently or never told their patients of a diagnosis of cancer (Oken 1961, 1120). Withholding the truth was seen as an act of kindness based on the mistaken belief that knowledge of their fatal conditions would send the patients into such a state of despair and depression that they would give up all hope and perhaps even commit suicide. Now that studies have revealed that cancer patients who know the truth actually do better, physicians almost always tell the cancer patient about their condition. The principle of nonmaleficence remained the same—the "facts," as they were perceived, altered how this principle was applied in each case.

Thus, while ethical principles are independent of the scientific advances in the field of diagnostic genetics, the application of these principles to the field depends on a sound grasp of the relevant medical and scientific facts.

1

Prenatal Diagnosis and Genetic Disorders

Prenatal diagnosis is the offspring of eugenics—the science that deals with the genetic influences that affect the expression of certain characteristics in offspring. The eugenics movement began in the late nineteenth century with Francis Galton who, in 1865, lamented:

> If a twentieth part of the cost and pains were spent
> in measure for the improvement of the human race that
> is spent on the improvement of the breeds of horses,
> and cattle, what a galaxy of genius might we not
> create (quoted by Lebel 1978, 1).

The science of eugenics can be subdivided into two branches: positive and negative. Positive eugenics is concerned with increasing the incidence of genes that result in "desirable" human qualities, while negative eugenics deals with preventing or limiting the number of or birth of people with "undesirable" human qualities. Prenatal diagnosis, when used as an antecedent to selective abortion, falls into the category of negative eugenics. Thus, the term *prenatal diagnosis* implies more than just the neutral scientific diagnosis of the fetus's genotype. It also entails a value judgment on what is desirable and undesirable and what is normal and abnormal in a human being. This value judgment can now be implemented through the use of prenatal diagnosis followed by selective abortion of "undesirable" or "abnormal" fetuses.

History and Background

Genetic counseling was introduced in Britain and North America in the 1940s. The main concern at that time was reporting risks rather than providing medical care. After World War II, with the horrors of Hitler's eugenics program still fresh in their memories, people became temporarily disenchanted with the eugenics movement. Although the foundations for prenatal diagnosis as a specific discipline were laid in the decade following World War II, it wasn't until after the mid-1960s that prenatal diagnosis became a widely accepted practice. The increasing reliability of prenatal diagnostic techniques and the Supreme Court *Roe v. Wade* decision in 1973 were two major contributors to the acceptance of prenatal diagnosis.

The success of prenatal diagnosis depends on predictability in human inheritance. The basic principles governing Mendelian inheritance were put forth by Austrian monk Gregor Mendel more than a century ago. However, our knowledge of what genetic material actually looks like or how it works is relatively recent. The first catalog of genetic disorders was published in 1956. It included 412 entries (Lebel 1989, 215). Thirty-two years later, the eighth edition of the same catalog listed some 4,344 genetic disorders (McKusick 1988, xi).

It has only been since 1956 that the correct number of human chromosomes has been known. Before this, it was believed that humans had forty-eight rather than forty-six chromosomes.

Chromosomes, rod-shaped bodies found in the nuclei of cells, contain DNA, which stores and transmits genetic information. Normal human cells (somatic cells) contain twenty-three pairs of chromosomes, or forty-six chromosomes total. This is referred to as the diploid number. Germ cells or gametes (sperm and ova) contain only half of each pair, or twenty-three chromosomes total. This is known as the haploid number. The process by which gametes are produced is called meiosis or gametogenesis.

Each of the twenty-three chromosome pairs has been assigned a number from one to twenty-three. The first twenty-two pairs, which are the same for both males and females, are called autosomes. The two chromosomes making up each of these pairs are homologous, that is, similar in fundamental structure. The twenty-third pair contains the chromosomes that determine a person's sex and are referred to as sex chromosomes. A female normally has two X chromosomes, and a male has one X and one Y chromosome. A normal female karyotype (i.e., her arrangement of chromosomes) is designated as 46, XX and a normal male karyotype as 46, XY.

Amniotic fluid is one of the major sources of fetal chromosomal material for prenatal diagnosis. Physicians have been drawing fluid from the amniotic sac for more than a century to relieve pressure from polyhydramnios, an excess of amniotic fluid in the bag of waters surrounding the fetus. The modern technique of amniocentesis was developed in the early 1950s to study the problem of rhesus (Rh) immunization. During pregnancy, the fetus sheds cells from his or her skin and bladder into the surrounding amniotic fluid. Fetal cells appear in the amniotic fluid by fourteen weeks' gestation, with the number of cells increasing as the pregnancy progresses.

Prenatal diagnosis using chromosomal material from the amniotic fluid was first accomplished in 1955 when Fritz Fuchs and Povl Riis (1956) determined the sex of a fetus through an examination of the X chromosomes in the amniotic fluid cells. Amniotic fluid was first used to diagnosis hereditary disorders in 1960 (Fuchs 1971). Six years later, a technique was developed by Mark Steele and W. Roy Berg (1966) whereby the cells from the amniotic fluid could be grown in a culture. Preparations derived from these cells were then used for karyotype (chromosomal) analysis. While direct examination of the amniotic fluid without cell culture can provide some information about the sex and biochemistry of the fetus, direct examination of the fluid is not as reliable nor does it allow for more detailed chromosomal analysis. Thus, Steele and Berg's contribution greatly advanced the usefulness of prenatal diagnosis for parents at risk of having a child with a chromosomal abnormality.

The process of cell cultivation and chromosomal analysis is called cytogenetics. During cell division, at the metaphase stage when the chromosomes are in the process of lining up, it is possible to see individual chromosomes microscopically. This picture is called a chromosomal spread.

Individual chromosomes may be seen more clearly by staining, which involves impregnating the chromosomes with pigments so that their parts are visible under a microscope. Stain produces patterns of light and dark horizontal bands on each chromosome, known as banding patterns. New banding procedures, using different types of stains, that facilitate clearer identification of different regions of the chromosome, are constantly being developed. Individual chromosomes can now be identified using size and banding patterns. After staining, the chromosome spread is magnified about 6,500 times and photographed. The pictures of the individual chromosomes are then arranged in pairs according to standards set by the 1971 Paris Chromosome Conference. By examining the karyotype, or chromosomal spread, a skilled cytogeneticist can determine the sex of the fetus and identify any chromosomal abnormalities. The entire process takes ten days to four weeks after the collection of the amniotic fluid, depending on the technique used.

Chromosomal Disorders

The incidence of major chromosomal abnormalities among newborns is about 0.65 percent, or 1 in every 156 live births (Hsu 1986, 116). About half of these newborns will have multiple congenital defects and/or mental retardation or phenotypic changes (changes in physical appearance) later in life. At least 12 percent of severely mentally retarded children have a chromosomal disorder (Berini and Kahn 1987, 46). Most concepti with chromosomal abnormalities do not reach maturity. An estimated 50 percent of all first-trimester spontaneous abortions involve abortuses with chromosomal defects (Boué et al. 1975). Consequently, couples who experience recurrent pregnancy losses are often advised to seek genetic counseling for subsequent pregnancies, as their risk of having a child with a

Figure 1a

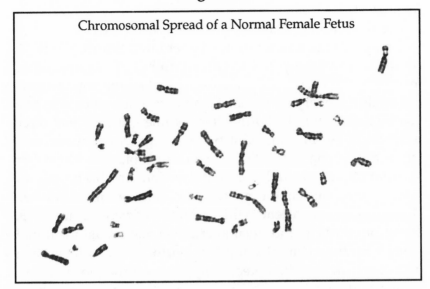

Chromosomal Spread of a Normal Female Fetus

Figure 1b

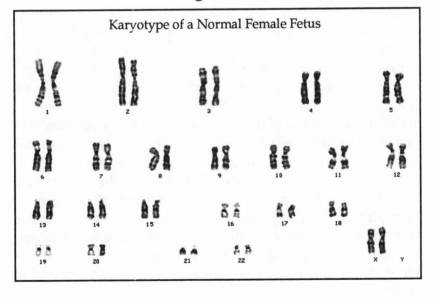

Karyotype of a Normal Female Fetus

chromosomal disorder is significantly higher than normal (Drugan et al. 1990).

The first verified chromosomal abnormality, trisomy 21, or Down syndrome, was confirmed by Jerome Lejeune in 1959. A person with trisomy 21 has three number 21 chromosomes instead of the normal two. Interestingly, Lejeune regarded the use of his discovery for prenatal diagnosis followed by selective abortion as unethical. Shortly after Lejeune's discovery of three number 21 chromosomes in people with Down syndrome, Jacobs and Strong (1959) discovered that people with Klinefelter syndrome had an extra X chromosome. Ford and his colleagues (1959), about the same time, reported finding only forty-five chromosomes in patients with Turner syndrome. Since 1959, scores of other chromosomal aberrations have been identified along with their clinical symptoms. Virtually all chromosomal disorders can now be detected by prenatal diagnosis. Chromosomal disorders can be classified into three types: aneuploidy, unbalanced translocation, and balanced translocation.

With aneuploidy, there is an actual change in the number of chromosomes; both Down syndrome and Klinefelter syndrome are examples of this type of disorder. In partial trisomy or unbalanced translocation, there is a break in a chromosome, and part of the extra chromosome is transmitted in the gamete or part of it is lost during meiosis or the division of chromosomal material in the nuclei of the sperm and egg. Balanced translocation, on the other hand, involves an exchange of material between nonhomologous, or unpaired, chromosomes.

Translocations are generally inherited from the parents and thus, theoretically, can be detected during prepregnancy genetic counseling. Balanced translocations usually have few, if any, pathological consequences. In other words, while the genotype or genetic makeup of a person may be abnormal, with a balanced translocation the abnormality is not usually expressed or evident in the phenotype.

Changes in the amount of chromosomal material can result from the addition of a complete set of haploid or single set of unpaired chromosomes (polyploidy) or in the loss of chromoso-

Table 1

Common Chromosomal Disorders That Have Clinical Consequences

Name	Karyotype formula	Frequency in liveborns
Trisomy 21 (Down syndrome)	47, +21	1 : 700
Klinefelter syndrome	47, XXY	1 : 900
XYY syndrome	47, XYY	1 : 1,000
XXX syndrome	47, XXX	1 : 1,000
Turner syndrome	45, X	1 : 2,500
Trisomy 13 (Patau syndrome)	47, +13	1 : 6,000
Trisomy 18 (Edwards syndrome)	47, +18	1 : 8,000

Sources: Sherman Elias and George J. Annas, *Reproductive Genetics and the Law* (Chicago: Year Book Medical Publishers, 1987), 16–25. Vincent Riccardi, *The Genetic Approach to Human Disease* (New York: Oxford University Press, 1977), 41–52.

mal material. Occasionally, all twenty-three pairs of chromosomes are affected, and an embryo, instead of having the normal two sets of chromosomes, may have only one set of chromosomes, three sets of chromosomes (triploidy), or even four sets of chromosomes (tetraploidy). Although it has been estimated that polyploidy occurs in 2 to 3 percent of fertilized ova, it is unusual in live births and is incompatible with postnatal life (de Grouchy and Turleau 1984, 412).

In most cases of chromosomal abnormality, only one pair of chromosomes is affected. Aneuploidy usually takes the form of the addition of an extra chromosome (trisomy) or, less commonly, the loss of a chromosome (monosomy). It may involve the sex chromosomes or one of the other twenty-two sets of chromosomes known as the autosomes.

Sometimes, chromosomal abnormalities manifest in only some cells. Mosaicism occurs when a cell culture produces cells with different karyotypes—some normal and some abnormal. For example, a child who is mosaic for Down syndrome would have a karyotype of 46/47, +21. In other words, some of the cells have the normal complement of forty-six chromosomes, while others have forty-seven chromosomes, with the extra chromosome being a number 21 chromosome. True mosaicism is unusual, although not rare. When mosaicism is found in a cell culture, the tests are usually repeated to verify the diagnosis.

Mosaicism presents a problem in prenatal diagnosis. While other types of chromosomal abnormalities may have a fairly wide range of prognoses, with mosaicism it is impossible to predict the phenotype of the newborn, as the chromosomal abnormality is present in only some of the cells. In a study of 395 cases diagnosed prenatally as chromosomal mosaicism, noticeable phenotypic abnormalities were found in only 34.8 percent of abortuses and liveborns with autosomal mosaicism and in only 8.4 percent with sex chromosome mosaicism (Hsu 1986).

Aneuploidy is the most frequently seen chromosomal disorder with severe clinical consequences. Sex chromosomal aneuploidies, such as 45, X (Turner syndrome), 47, XXY (Klinefelter syndrome), 47, XYY (XYY syndrome), and 47, XXX (XXX syndrome), are the most common. Their combined frequency in newborns is one in five hundred (Riccardi 1977, 50). They also account for at least 25 percent of spontaneous abortions (ibid.).

Klinefelter syndrome, the most common of these disorders, is characterized by failure of the testicles to develop normally, although sex drive appears to be unimpaired. Abnormally long legs or learning disabilities may also be present. Klinefelter syndrome often goes undetected until adulthood, when a couple seeks help for infertility (Cohen 1984, 60).

Turner syndrome is sometimes diagnosed at birth, though it may not be diagnosed until puberty, when secondary sexual characteristics fail to develop and menstruation does not occur. About 20 percent of the cases of Turner syndrome are the result of mosaicism (X/XX) (*Dictionary of Medical Syndromes* 1981, 819). Many, if not most, of the signs and symptoms of mosaicism, which include webbed neck, short stature, and learning disabilities, may be absent. The management of Turner syndrome includes estrogen replacement starting at puberty.

Unlike people with Turner and Klinefelter syndromes, XYY males are usually phenotypically normal, although they are generally above the ninetieth percentile in height (Cohen 1984, 62).

Table 2

Signs and Symptoms of Turner Syndrome

Webbed neck
Short stature (105–30 cm)
Wide chest with laterally displaced nipples
Absent or rudimentary ovaries and the lack of development of secondary
  sexual characteristics
Cardiovascular malformations (10 to 40 percent of cases) and/or renal
  abnormalities
Skeletal anomalies
Auditory defects
Average or slightly below average intelligence—often showing space-form
  deficiency, although verbal skills are usually good

Sources: *Diseases and Disorders Handbook* (Springhouse, Pa.: Springhouse Corp., 1988), 430. Daniel Bergsma, ed., *Birth Defects Atlas and Compendium* (Baltimore: National Foundation–March of Dimes, 1973), 810–11.

The prognosis surrounding the XYY syndrome has created a great deal of controversy since it was first reported in 1961 (Sandberg et al. 1961, 488). In the mid-1960s, a link was found between aggressive and/or mentally retarded criminals and the incidence of the XYY syndrome (Jacobs et al. 1965, 1351). This finding led some people to speculate that there may be a "criminal gene" and that it might be possible to weed out the violent criminals through prenatal diagnosis and selective abortion. As recently as 1981, the *Dictionary of Medical Syndromes* (1981) stated that with XYY males, "institutionalization for delinquency [is] frequently required" (878). However, data from long-term studies of boys with the XYY karyotype have not shown consistent aggressive tendencies, although XYY males do tend to be more easily frustrated and impulsive—traits that may lead to an above average incidence of violent behavior (Cohen 1984, 62). This aggressive behavior is usually directed at objects rather than people; rarely is bloodshed involved (de Grouchy and Turleau 1984, 398–99).

Table 3

Signs and Symptoms of XYY Syndrome

Above average height
Acne during adolescence
Poor social integration
Low-normal to normal intelligence
Learning difficulties
Below normal motor coordination
Behavior problems, such as tantrums
Low frustration threshold and impulsive behavior
Aggressivity
Abnormal electroencephalogram and electrocardiogram

Sources: Felissa Cohen, *Clinical Genetics in Nursing Practice* (Philadelphia: J. B. Lippincott Co., 1984), 62. *Dictionary of Medical Syndromes*, 2nd ed. (Philadelphia: J. B. Lippincott Co., 1981), 877–78. Jean de Grouchy and Catherine Turleau, *Clinical Atlas of Human Chromosomes*, 2nd ed. (New York: John Wiley and Sons, 1984), 398–99.

It was once believed that the 47, XXX genotype, also known as the triple X syndrome, had few clinical effects, because, as with the 47, XYY syndrome, significant phenotypical abnormalities are often absent. However, it has since been linked to mild mental retardation, learning disabilities, and other congenital malformations of varying degrees of severity (Tennes et al. 1975). Girls with the triple X syndrome also tend to be somewhat taller than their peers. Although they are generally fertile and have normal offspring, menstrual irregularities and premature menopause are common.

Autosomal Chromosomal Aneuploidies

Autosomal chromosomal aneuploidies tend to have more drastic clinical effects than sex chromosomal aneuploidies. Trisomy in most autosomal chromosomes leads to spontaneous abortion in the early embryonic stage.

The most common autosomal chromosomal disorder among liveborns, occurring in about one of every seven hundred births (de Grouchy and Turleau 1984, 338), is trisomy 21, or Down syndrome. About 96 percent of all cases of Down syndrome involve trisomy of the twenty-first chromosome (Volpe 1984, 25). A small percentage of Down syndrome cases are caused by a translocation between chromosomes 21 and usually 14, or mosaicism.

Down syndrome is easily diagnosed at birth, although it becomes more apparent later. The syndrome is diagnosed by the presence of a number of physical characteristics, including distinctive facial features, most of which may be found as single traits in "normal" infants (hence the term *syndrome*). Moderate to severe mental retardation is present in the great majority of cases. However, not all of the traits will be present in every child with Down syndrome. The degree of severity and the range of prognosis tend to be fairly wide. About one-third of children with Down syndrome die before the age of ten years (*Diseases and Disorders Handbook* 1988, 236).

Table 4

Signs and Symptoms of Down Syndrome

Moderate to severe mental retardation—IQ usually between 35 and 50, although it may be in the low-normal range in a few cases
Distinctive craniofacial appearance—epicanthic folds, broad flat nasal bridge, short neck, small malformed ears, down-curved mouth, small white spots on the iris (Brushfield's spots), large protruding tongue, short head, and mild microcephaly
Short extremities with short stubby hands with an incurved fifth finger (clinodactyly) and a single transverse palmar crease (simian crease)
Poor muscle tone (hypotonia) and impaired reflex and motor development
Anomalies of the internal organs, such as cardiac abnormalities and duodenal obstruction
Poorly developed genitalia and delayed puberty—males are infertile
Increased susceptibility to respiratory infections and leukemia
Premature aging
Normal affective and social ability

Sources: Ruth Berini and Eva Kahn, *Clinical Genetics Handbook* (Montvale, N.J.: Medical Economics Books, 1987), 60. *Diseases and Disorders Handbook* (Springhouse, Pa.: Springhouse Corp., 1988), 237. Jean de Grouchy and Catherine Turleau, *Clinical Atlas of Human Chromosomes*, 2nd ed. (New York: John Wiley and Sons, 1984), 343–44.

Congenital heart defect is the most common cause of early death. At one time, about 50 percent of all children with Down syndrome died by the age of five years, and the average life span of the survivors was only thirty years (*Dictionary of Medical Syndromes* 1981). Recent advances in therapy have resulted in a major improvement in the life expectancy. Children with Down syndrome are usually happy and affectionate. As adults, many people with Down syndrome are able to live in group homes and work in a sheltered workshop or hold a regular job.

Other well-known chromosomal disorders include trisomy 18, also known as Edwards syndrome, and trisomy 13, or Patau syndrome. Both of these conditions, with few exceptions, result in death within the first year of life (de Grouchy and Turleau 1984, 230, 296).

Fifty percent of infants with Patau syndrome die within the first month of life (Cohen 1984, 51). This syndrome is associated with severe congenital anomalies, such as microcephaly (an abnormally small head) and microphthalmia (abnormally small eyes), heart and kidney disease, cleft palate and lip, and extra fingers and toes. There is severe mental retardation due to incomplete forebrain development.

Edwards syndrome, which is sometimes confused with Patau syndrome, is likewise characterized by microcephaly and extreme mental retardation, congenital heart and kidney disease, and failure to thrive. Infants with Edwards syndrome are often so weak that they have great difficulty crying and sucking. Although the reasons are unclear, Edwards syndrome is three times more common in females than males (Cohen 1984, 51). Females born with the disorder also tend to live much longer than males (Elias and Annas 1987), suggesting that the discrepancy in the sex ratio at birth may be due to more female fetuses with the syndrome surviving until birth.

The risk to a couple that has had a child with Patau or Edwards syndrome of having a second child with either these or another chromosomal disorder is between 1 and 2 percent (Hamerton et al. 1982).

Figure 2

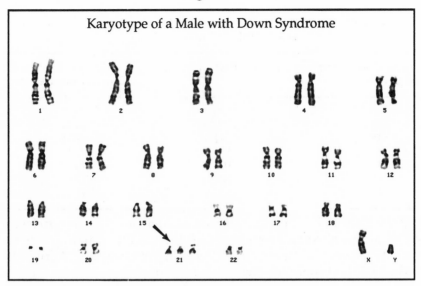

Karyotype of a Male with Down Syndrome

The Etiology of Chromosomal Disorders

Trisomy and other chromosomal abnormalities are usually the result of some accidental occurrence during gametogenesis, the development of the ovum and sperm cells, in one of the parents—usually the mother. The frequency of chromosomal abnormalities increases with maternal age.

About 85 percent of amniocenteses are performed solely because of advanced maternal age, which is arbitrarily set at age thirty-five years or older (Verp and Simpson 1985). While only 5 percent, approximately, of all pregnancies occur in women aged thirty-five years or older, 20 percent of all infants with Down syndrome are born to women in this age group (Knight et al. 1988, 306). One possible explanation for this is that trisomy results from the failure of some chromosomes to move to the opposite pole during the anaphase of cell division in the aging oocyte—the immature ovum (Polani 1982). With increasing maternal age, opportunities for such mishaps increase. It has been speculated that the correlation between maternal age and chromosomal defects in the fetus might also be due to the

Table 5

Risk of Chromosomal Abnormalities in Liveborn Newborns
as a Function of Maternal Age

Maternal Age, years	Risk of Down Syndrome (Trisomy 21)	Total Risk for Chromosomal Defects
20	1/1,667	1/526
25	1/1,250	1/476
30	1/952	1/384
35	1/385	1/204
40	1/106	1/65
45	1/30	1/20
49	1/11	1/7

Adapted from Ernest Hook, Philip Cross, and Dina Schreinemachers, "Chromosomal Abnormality Rates at Amniocentesis and Live-born Infants," *Journal of the American Medical Association* 249 (April 15): 2034–38. © 1983 American Medical Association.

ovum's having more time to be exposed to and damaged by environmental toxins (Verp and Simpson 1985, 23).

The second most common indication for seeking prenatal diagnosis is a previous child with a genetic or chromosomal disorder or the presence of a genetic disorder in the family. Amniocentesis may also be performed because of a past history of miscarriages or stillbirths, exposure to radiation or other environmental teratogens (substances that can cause birth defects), or simply to relieve parental anxiety.

Genetic (Monogenic) Disorders

Mendelian or monogenic disorders (hereafter referred to simply as genetic disorders) are the most common type of inherited disorder and the second major class of birth defects. Between 1958 and 1975, the number of known monogenic traits increased from 412 to 2,336 (McKusick 1975). As of 1988, more than 3,000 monogenic abnormalities had been cataloged (Williamson and Murray 1988, 270).

Genetic defects can be divided into three categories: autosomal dominant disorders, which are found in about 7 of 1,000 births; autosomal recessive disorders, found in about 2.5 of 1,000 births; and X-linked disorders, which occur in about 0.5 of 1,000 births (Milunsky 1986, 1). Genetic defects are responsible for 80 percent of cases of mental retardation, 33 percent of all patients in pediatric wards, and 25 percent of all chronic illnesses (Robinson 1986, 1137).

Each human chromosome, with the exception of the Y chromosome, contains one to two thousand ultramicroscopic structures called genes (Jones 1989, 10). Genes are molecules of DNA, which are composed of different combinations of four types of amino acids, known as nucleotides, arranged in a double-helix form. The average chromosome has about 150 million base pairs of DNA, making a total of about 3 billion divided among the twenty-three pairs of chromosomes. While an average gene has about 10,000 nucleotides, very large genes can have up to 2 million (Williamson and Murray 1988). A single gene disorder can involve as few as one of these 3 billion nucleotides or a large span of nucleotides on a given gene.

For each autosomal chromosome pair, genes containing specific inheritable traits occupy corresponding positions (loci) on each of the chromosomes. Matching pairs of homologous genes are called alleles. If the trait(s) represented by the allele is dominant, that is, "expressed in the offspring even though it is carried on only one of the homologous genes" (*Taber's Cyclopedic Medical Dictionary* 1989, 524), it is represented by a capital letter. If the gene is recessive, that is, not expressed in the presence of a dominant allele, it is represented by a lowercase letter.

While each person has about three to five deleterious genes (Hilton 1972), most are recessive and, therefore, not expressed in the phenotype. When both genes at a given locus are the same (both dominant or both recessive), the person is said to be homozygous for that given trait. When the alleles are different (one dominant and one recessive) the person is said to be heterozygous.

Table 6

Select Genetic Disorders

Disorder	Mode of Inheritance*	Frequency in Liveborns
Albinism	AR	1: 15,000–1: 40,000
		1: 85–1: 650 (American Indians)
Cystic fibrosis	AR	1: 2,000–1: 2,500 (whites)
Sickle cell anemia	AR	1: 400–1: 600 (American blacks)
Tay-Sachs disease	AR	1: 3,600 (Ashkenazi Jews)
		1: 360,000 (others)
Achondroplasia (dwarfism)	AD	1: 10,000–1: 12,000
Huntington disease	AD	1: 18,000–1: 25,000 (U.S.)
		1: 333,000 (Japan)
Polydactyly (extra finger or toe)	AD	1: 100–1: 300 (blacks)
		1: 630–1: 3,300 (whites)
Polycystic renal disease (adult)	AD	1: 250–1: 1,250
Color blindness (red/green)	XLR	8: 100 (white males)
Duchenne muscular dystrophy	XLR	1: 3,000–1: 5,000 (males)
Fabry disease	XLR	1: 40,000 (males)
Hemophilia A	XLR	1: 2,500–1: 4,000 (males)
Lesch-Nyhan syndrome	XLR	1: 300,000 (males)
Menkes' disease	XLR	1: 35,000 (males)
Orofaciodigital syndrome	XLD	1: 50,000
Vitamin D–resistant rickets	XLD	1: 25,000

* AR: autosomal recessive; AD: autosomal dominant; XLR: sex-linked recessive; XLD: sex-linked dominant.

Source: Felissa Cohen, *Clinical Genetics in Nursing Practice* (Philadelphia: J. B. Lippincott Co., 1984).

Autosomal Dominant Disorders

With autosomal dominant disorders, if one of the parents carries the gene, on average, one-half of all their children will inherit the gene. Because the gene is dominant, the children who inherit the gene will eventually manifest the disorder. However, the severity of the disease can vary, and not all heterozygotes will exhibit the clinical symptoms of the disease.

Adult polycystic renal disease is one of the most frequently occurring autosomal dominant genetic disorders. The first symptoms usually appear in early middle age and are followed by progressive kidney failure. Treatment includes diet manage-

Figure 3

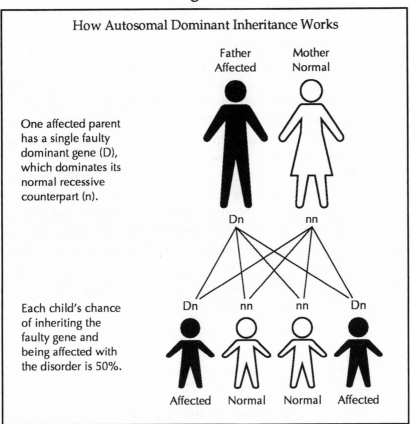

How Autosomal Dominant Inheritance Works

Father
Affected

Mother
Normal

One affected parent
has a single faulty
dominant gene (D),
which dominates its
normal recessive
counterpart (n).

Dn   nn

Each child's chance
of inheriting the
faulty gene and
being affected with
the disorder is 50%.

Dn   nn   nn   Dn

Affected   Normal   Normal   Affected

Adapted from the March of Dimes, *Genetic Counseling* (New York: March of Dimes Birth Defects Foundation, 1985), 13.

ment and, in advanced cases, dialysis treatment and kidney transplantation (Bergsma 1973, 667).

The most common autosomal dominant genetic disorder with devastating clinical consequences is Huntington disease, or Huntington chorea. This debilitating disease does not usually become apparent until age thirty to forty-five years, often after the afflicted person has already had children, as is also the case with adult polycystic renal disease. Onset of the symptoms is usually insidious and subtle in its early stages and may only be recognized in retrospect. These symptoms include progressive loss of motor coordination, as well as of emotional and intellectual functioning. Death results, on average, fifteen years after the onset of symptoms (Berini and Kahn 1987, 89). Sometimes the disorder does not express itself until the person is in his or her sixties or seventies (Volpe 1984, 102). One problem in diagnosing this disease on the basis of family history is that 10 percent of cases are the result of fresh mutations (Harris 1974, 55).

Table 7

Symptoms of Huntington Disease

Early symptoms
  Restlessness
  Poor motor coordination
  Lack of concentration
  Emotional instability
  Difficult or defective speech
  Mental impairment

Later symptoms
  Progressive deterioration of intellectual functions (dementia)
  Involuntary movements of the face, limbs, and trunk (chorea)

Sources: Ruth Berini and Eva Kahn, *Clinical Genetics Handbook* (Montvale, N.J.: Medical Economics Books, 1987), 88–89. Vincent Riccardi, *The Genetic Approach to Human Disease* (New York: Oxford University Press, 1977), 77.

Autosomal Recessive Disorders

Most metabolic diseases are caused by an abnormal recessive gene on an autosomal chromosome. If the deleterious gene is recessive, it will not manifest itself in the offspring unless both parents carry the recessive gene and pass it on to the child. The frequency of these genes varies from one population to another. When a genetic disorder is relatively common in a specific population, carrier screening—testing prospective parents to see whether they are carriers of a particular deleterious recessive gene—can sometimes be performed before prenatal diagnosis to determine whether the fetus is at risk for that particular disorder.

Prenatal testing for cystic fibrosis has only recently become available. Cystic fibrosis is the most common semilethal inherited metabolic disorder among people of northern European descent, occurring in about one of twenty of this population (Elias and Annas 1987, 104). It is hypothesized that the mutation responsible for cystic fibrosis is three thousand to six thousand years old (Serre et al. 1990).

Cystic fibrosis, which is a disorder of the exocrine glands (mucous, sweat, and salivary), is characterized by chronic and progressive obstructive respiratory disease and gastrointestinal insufficiency caused by blockage due to the buildup of mucous secretions. It can be detected by the presence of high concentrations of sodium, potassium, and chloride in the sweat. Infants with cystic fibrosis may fail to thrive and may also have intestinal problems, although symptoms may not occur until the child is older or even during adolescence or adulthood (Cohen 1984, 353). There is great variability in the prognosis, suggesting that the disorder probably involves several genes rather than a single gene.

Sickle cell anemia is found predominantly in people of African descent. More than three hundred variants of inherited hemoglobin disorders—disorders that affect the ability of the iron-containing pigment in the red blood cells to carry oxygen—have been identified (ibid., 87). Thalassemia, another common form of inherited anemia, mainly affects people of Mediterranean, Middle Eastern, southern Asian, and African ancestry. In sickle cell anemia, the red blood cells have a tendency to

Figure 4

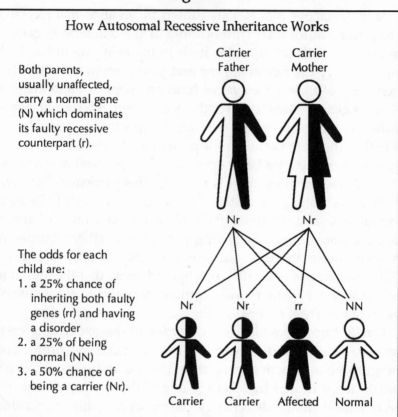

How Autosomal Recessive Inheritance Works

Both parents, usually unaffected, carry a normal gene (N) which dominates its faulty recessive counterpart (r).

Carrier Father   Carrier Mother

Nr   Nr

The odds for each child are:
1. a 25% chance of inheriting both faulty genes (rr) and having a disorder
2. a 25% of being normal (NN)
3. a 50% chance of being a carrier (Nr).

Nr   Nr   rr   NN

Carrier   Carrier   Affected   Normal

Adapted from March of Dimes, *Genetic Counseling* (New York: March of Dimes Birth Defects Foundation, 1985), 15.

become distorted, "sickle shaped," under certain conditions of low oxygen tension. This distortion results in increased viscosity of the blood, which in turn precipitates what is known as a "sickle cell crisis," which is characterized by severe pain. There is no successful cure for the disorder. Management includes avoiding or immediately treating the conditions, such as infections, that precipitate the crisis or, in the case of severe attacks, blood transfusions. There are reliable carrier tests and prenatal diagnostic tests for sickle cell anemia.

Tay-Sachs disease is one of the most devastating metabolic disorders caused by an autosomal recessive gene. This fatal disease is caused by a deficiency of the enzyme hexosaminidase A and the consequent accumulation of the lipid ganglioside GM2 in the nervous system. Tay-Sachs disease most commonly occurs among Jews of central and eastern European descent.

Table 8

Symptoms of Tay-Sachs Disease

Early symptoms
    Doll-like face, fine hair
    Cherry-red macula in retina
    Poor muscle tone (hypotonia)
    Exaggerated startle response
    Loss of ability to sit or hold up head

Later symptoms
    Psychomotor retardation
    Convulsions
    Blindness
    Macrocephaly (abnormal largeness of head)
    Loss of contact with the environment
    Paralysis

Sources: Ruth Berini and Eva Kahn, *Clinical Genetics Handbook* (Montvale: N.J., Medical Economics Books, 1987), 222–23. *Dictionary of Medical Syndromes*, 2nd ed. (Philadelphia: J. B. Lippincott 1981), 798.

About one of twenty-seven American Jews carries this gene. Onset of symptoms occurs between birth and ten months of age, usually by six months. Progressive deterioration, including psychomotor retardation, convulsions, blindness, and finally paralysis and what seems to be complete lack of contact with the environment follows. Death generally occurs by four years of age (*Dictionary of Medical Syndromes* 1981, 798).

Recently, an adult form of Tay-Sachs disease has been identified. All of the patients diagnosed with this disorder were found to be heterozygotes, with one gene for infantile Tay-Sachs and a mutation (Gly 269) on the allele (Maia et al. 1990).

X-Linked Genetic Disorders

X-linked abnormalities affect mainly males, as they do not have the extra X chromosome to offset the effect of the deleterious gene. In the vast majority of cases, X-linked abnormalities are inherited from the mother, who is usually a symptomless heterozygote. X-linked conditions include Lesch-Nyhan syndrome, Fabry disease, Duchenne muscular dystrophy, hemophilia, and color blindness. If the mother is a carrier of the deleterious gene, on average, half of her sons will have the disease and half of her daughters will be carriers. Probably the most common X-linked disorder is red/green color blindness, found in about one out of every twelve white men.

Lesch-Nyhan syndrome, which occurs in one of three hundred thousand newborn males, is characterized by mental retardation, aggressive behavior, self-mutilation, and jerky involuntary movements. Menkes' disease and Fabry disease, although relatively rare, affect a significantly greater number of males than does Lesch-Nyhan syndrome. Menkes' disease, which is a disorder of copper metabolism, is characterized by severe mental retardation, seizures, and abnormal hair, which is kinky, fragile, and sparse. Death usually occurs in the first two years (Bergsma 1973, 607).

The onset of symptoms of Fabry disease is during childhood or adolescence. The primary symptom is periodic episodes of

Figure 5

How X-Linked Recessive Inheritance Works

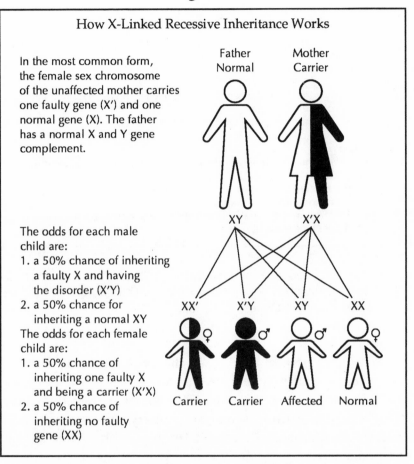

In the most common form, the female sex chromosome of the unaffected mother carries one faulty gene (X') and one normal gene (X). The father has a normal X and Y gene complement.

Father
Normal

Mother
Carrier

XY   X'X

The odds for each male child are:
1. a 50% chance of inheriting a faulty X and having the disorder (X'Y)
2. a 50% chance for inheriting a normal XY
The odds for each female child are:
1. a 50% chance of inheriting one faulty X and being a carrier (X'X)
2. a 50% chance of inheriting no faulty gene (XX)

XX'   X'Y   XY   XX

Carrier   Carrier   Affected   Normal

Adapted from March of Dimes, *Genetic Counseling* (New York: March of Dimes Birth Defects Foundation, 1985), 16.

Table 9

Signs and Symptoms of Duchenne Muscular Dystrophy

Early symptoms
Hypotonia and clumsiness
Delay in walking and an inability to run
Pseudohypertrophy of the calf muscles (increase in size accompanied
by decrease in function)
Mental retardation in less than half of those afflicted

Later symptoms
Muscle weakness beginning in the pelvic area and rapidly spreading
to other skeletal muscles
Lateral curvature of the spine (kyphoscoliosis)
Permanent contraction of some muscles
Atrophy of the muscles (patients lose the ability to walk between five
and fifteen years of age)

Sources: Ruth Berini and Eva Kahn, *Clinical Genetics Handbook* (Montvale, N.J.: Medical Economics Books, 1987), 103. Daniel Bergsma, ed., *Birth Defects Atlas and Compendium* (Baltimore: National Foundation–March of Dimes, 1973), 237.

excruciatingly painful tingling in the extremities, which may recur weekly and may last several hours or even one to two weeks in severe cases (Bergsma 1973, 400). Complications may include kidney, cardiovascular, pulmonary, and skeletal problems. Fabry disease is detectable through both carrier testing and prenatal testing.

One of the most widely publicized X-linked disorders with significant clinical effects is hemophilia, also known as the bleeders' or royal disease. Hemophilia is caused by a deficiency in one of the blood coagulation factors. The major problem faced by hemophiliacs is internal bleeding into the joints and muscles, which if not stopped can result in deformities and immobilization. Symptoms range from very mild to severe, depending on the level of the coagulant factor in the blood. The disease is usually diagnosed in infancy, when the infant develops bruises for no apparent reason. Sometimes the parents are accused of child abuse before the true cause of the bruising—internal bleeding—

is diagnosed. As with Duchenne muscular dystrophy, which affects about the same number of males, about one-third of the cases of hemophilia are the result of fresh mutations (Williamson and Murray 1988).

Duchenne muscular dystrophy sets in at three to five years of age, when the child develops difficulty with walking and other motor skills. Mental retardation is present in less than half of all the cases. The disorder is characterized by a progressive loss of strength in the muscles, with death usually resulting around the age of twenty years (Riccardi 1977, 82). Researchers, using recombinant DNA techniques, are presently attempting to pinpoint the gene or gene sequence responsible for Duchenne muscular dystrophy.

Multifactorial (Polygenic) Disorders

The third category of birth defects detectable by prenatal diagnosis is multifactorial or polygenic disorders. These disorders are apparently caused by an interplay between a number of factors both genetic and environmental. An estimated 1 to 2 per-

Table 10

Common Multifactorial Disorders

Name	Frequency in Liveborns	Sex Most Frequently Affected
Congenital heart defects	1 : 140	Equal
Anencephaly	1 : 1,000	Female
Spina bifida	1 : 1,000	Female
Cleft lip with or without cleft palate	1 : 1,000 (whites) 1 : 600 (Japanese) 1 : 1,400 (blacks)	Male
Cleft palate alone	1 : 2,000–1 : 2,500	Female
Congenital dislocation of the hip	1 : 1,000	Female
Clubfoot	1 : 1,000	Male

Source: Felissa Cohen, *Clinical Genetics in Nursing Practice* (Philadelphia: J. B. Lippincott Co., 1984), 101.

cent of newborns are born with a serious multifactorial disorder, such as anencephaly, spina bifida, malformation of the heart, congenital scoliosis, cleft lip and/or palate, and club foot (Harris 1974, 60). The causes of more than 60 percent of all congenital abnormalities are still obscure (Milunsky 1986, 2).

Neural Tube Defects (NTDs)

The most common type of serious multifactorial disorder is a neural tube defect (NTD). NTDs are caused by a failure of the neural tube—which will contain the spinal cord—to close during the third and fourth weeks of gestation. About six thousand infants per year in the United States, representing 0.31 percent of births, are born with NTDs (Elias and Annas 1987, 106). Ninety-five percent of all infants with this defect are born to parents with no previous family history of the disorder (Burton 1988, 294). However, after having one child with the disorder, the risk of having another child with an NTD is ten to fifteen times greater than that of the general population (ibid.).

The incidence of NTDs varies, for reasons yet unknown, with the sex of the child as well as between geographic locales and over time. For example, the rate in the British Isles is significantly higher than that in the United States. In the west of Scotland three out of every one thousand pregnancies are affected by an NTD (White-Van Mourik et al. 1990, 497). People from lower socioeconomic groups are at higher risk as well (Burton 1988, 294). However, spinal defects are more common among whites than Asians or blacks, regardless of geographic location. This difference indicates that there is a genetic as well as an environmental predisposition to having an NTD.

Anencephaly and spina bifida, which occur with about equal frequency, account for approximately 95 percent of all cases of NTDs (Nicolaides and Campbell 1986, 525). Anencephaly is a disorder in which the neural tube fails to close along its entire length, resulting in the absence of cerebral hemispheres. About 75 percent of anencephalic infants are stillborn (Brock 1982, 68). In the remainder of cases, the condition is fatal at or very shortly after birth.

Spina bifida, on the other hand, has a much more variable prognosis. There are two types of spina bifida: meningocele and myelomeningocele (or myelocele). Both involve an incomplete closure of the spinal canal, which causes the spinal cord and/or membrane of the cord (meninges) to push up (herniate) through the opening, forming a tumor known as a spina bifida. In meningoceles, the cord itself stays in its normal position in the spinal canal and only the meninges herniates. More than 90 percent of cases of spina bifida are of the more severe myelomeningocele type, in which the neural tissue itself herniates (ibid.). In open myelomeningocele, the neural tissue is exposed on the surface of the hernia. Because of the variability of the nature of the disorder, the prognosis for open spina bifida ranges from complete freedom from handicap in a small percentage of cases (Lorber 1973, 203) to early death and/or severe paralysis and mental retardation for over 85 percent of cases (Brock 1982, 71).

Table 11

Signs and Symptoms of Spina Bifida (Myelomeningocele)

A saclike structure protruding over the spine
Permanent neurological dysfunction with severity of dysfunction
  dependent on the location of the lesion
Bowel and bladder incontinence
Hydrocephaly (70 to 90 percent of the cases)
Curvature of the spine
Paralysis of legs in the most severe cases

Sources: *Diseases and Disorders Handbook* (Springhouse, Pa.: Springhouse Corp., 1988), 718–19. March of Dimes Birth Defects Foundations, Public Information Sheet on Spina Bifida (New York: March of Dimes, 1985).

Prenatal diagnosis was first used to detect NTDs in 1972 through the use of ultrasound (Campbell and Pearce 1983). With the exception of anencephaly, however, most NTDs are difficult to diagnose with ultrasound, especially in the first two trimesters (Romero et al. 1988). On the other hand, 80 to 85 percent of open NTDs can be detected by measuring the amount of alpha-fetoprotein (AFP), a protein manufactured in the liver of the fetus, in the amniotic fluid or maternal blood (Nicolaides and Campbell 1986).

Even when an NTD, such as spina bifida, is diagnosed, it is impossible to determine the severity of the disorder prenatally through either ultrasound (Romero et al. 1988) or AFP testing (Milunsky 1986). Studies are under way on the use of a test for the presence of acetylocholinesterase, which is of neural origin and can be used in conjunction with AFP testing and ultrasound to give a more accurate prenatal diagnosis of neural tube defects.

Conclusion

The term *genetic disorders* commonly refers to any genotype that is deemed "abnormal" or "undesirable" by society or the medical profession. A genetic disorder may involve an extra chromosome or only a single mutant gene or may result from a combination of genetic and environmental factors. With some disorders, the exact cause remains a mystery.

While some of the disorders discussed above are incompatible with postnatal life, others are so mild that they often go undetected. The range of the prognosis of a single disorder can also vary greatly. Because of the great variation among genetic disorders, there is no one method of prenatal diagnosis that can be used to detect all disorders.

2

Prenatal Diagnostic Procedures

Introduction

More than five thousand distinct genetic disorders have been identified to date. However, only four hundred of these—less than 10 percent—have been successfully diagnosed prenatally (Connor 1989). Prenatal diagnostic procedures vary greatly, ranging from relatively noninvasive, risk-free techniques that involve taking a sample of the mother's blood to highly invasive, high-risk techniques, such as fetoscopy and amniography. The diagnostic procedure used in a particular case depends primarily upon the type of disorder for which the fetus is most at risk.

Types of Prenatal Diagnosis

Amniocentesis

Amniocentesis is currently the most widely used method of prenatal diagnosis. While it has been used to detect both monogenetic disorders and NTDs, it is used more than 90 percent of the time for cytogenic (chromosomal) analysis (Simpson and Elias 1989).

In 1978, there were only 125 active prenatal diagnostic programs in the United States. Together, they performed about fifteen thousand amniocenteses. By 1982, the number of amniocenteses performed had doubled, and the number of programs had increased to 155 (Sachdev 1988, 481). In recent years, a growing number of private commercial laboratories have also been offering cytogenic analysis of amniotic fluid (Fuhrmann 1989, 380).

In the developed countries about 50 percent of all pregnant women over the age of thirty-five years undergo prenatal diagnosis (Fletcher and Wertz 1987a). This figure is somewhat lower in the United States, ranging from 16.8 percent in Ohio to 41 percent in New York City (Fuhrmann 1989, 380). Women who request amniocentesis tend to be more affluent and better educated than the average (Bannerman et al. 1977). Because the availability of insurance coverage for the procedure is the major predictor of acceptance, this may account for the disproportionate number of more affluent women seeking amniocentesis.

The Procedure

Amniocentesis is performed in an outpatient clinic, generally at about sixteen weeks' gestation, when there is the highest ratio of viable to nonviable cells in the amniotic fluid; also, sufficient amniotic fluid is present at this time (200 ml) to permit the removal of an adequate amount for testing. The procedure is usually preceded by ultrasound, which allows the physician to determine fetal position, number of fetuses, and placental placement. Most physicians also use ultrasound during amniocentesis so that the position of the needle can be monitored visually (Simpson and Elias 1989, 83).

After the woman's lower abdomen is cleaned and a local anesthetic is applied, a spinal needle is inserted through the abdominal wall into the amniotic cavity surrounding the fetus, and 20 to 30 ml of amniotic fluid is drawn out. In multiple pregnancies, a sample of amniotic fluid is taken from each sac. This multiple sampling is necessary because most twins, even monozygotic (identical) twins in the case of major structural birth abnormalities, are discordant for chromosomal and metabolic disorders. The amniotic fluid sample is sent to a laboratory

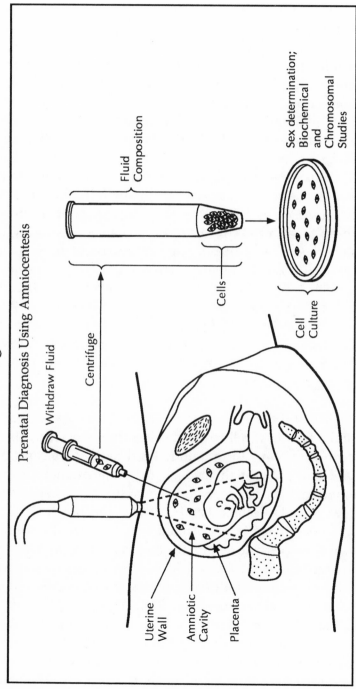

Figure 6

Prenatal Diagnosis Using Amniocentesis

Adapted from James D. Watson, John Touze, and David T. Kurtz, *Recombinant DNA: A Short Course* (New York: Scientific American Books, 1983), 213.

for cell culture and cytogenic analysis, which usually takes three to four weeks to complete.

Cell cultures are primarily used to determine chromosomal abnormalities and the sex of the fetus. This latter information is important when the mother is a sex-linked carrier; it is also used for sex selection. Although the use of amniocentesis for sex selection is still frowned upon by many physicians, the recent emphasis on a woman's reproductive freedom has made it more acceptable.

A cell culture can also be used to test for certain metabolic enzymes, to predict the presence of hemophilia A and some sickle cell diseases, and for DNA analysis. Metabolic disorders can take up to six weeks to diagnose. Reliable tests for cystic fibrosis (Dechecchi et al. 1989), Menkes' disease (Tonnesen and Horn 1989), and Lesch-Nyhan syndrome are being developed (Danks 1990, 1778). The amniotic fluid itself can be directly examined for certain enzyme defects as well as an elevated AFP level, which is indicative of a neural tube defect. One of the more recent developments in prenatal diagnosis involves DNA analysis for genetic defects, which will be discussed in greater detail later in this chapter.

Limitations and Risks

While the failure in cell cultures is less than 1 percent, about 13 percent of the taps for amniotic fluid have to be repeated because of poor cell growth, inadequate fluid, maternal contamination, mosaicism, or inconclusive results (Monteleone and Moraczewski 1981). Technical and culture failure are the highest when amniocentesis is performed before fourteen weeks. Because of these possible delays, the results may not be obtained until after the fetus is viable.

Less than 5 percent of all amniocenteses reveal some sort of serious fetal aberration (Milunsky 1986). Although its accuracy rate exceeds 99.5 percent when it is used in conjunction with ultrasound, amniocentesis is still not error free. The accuracy rate may be expected to drop as amniocentesis is used more and more for DNA analysis of genetic disorders. While all

Table 12

Current Genetic Indication for Amniocentesis

Indication	Primary Analysis Done
Pregnancy at risk for chromosomal aberration	
Maternal age thirty-five years and over	Chromosome
Previous child with chromosomal abnormality or instability	Chromosome
Chromosomal abnormality in parent	Chromosome
Previous stillbirth or perinatal death (cause unknown)	Chromosome
History of infertility in either parent	Chromosome
Habitual abortion history	Chromosome
Previous child with malformations (no chromosomes analyzed)	Chromosome
Low maternal serum alpha-fetoprotein (MSAFP) level	Chromosome
Pregnancy at risk for neural tube defect (NTD)	
High MSAFP level	AFP
Previous child with NTD	AFP
NTD in either parent or close relative	AFP
Pregnancy at risk for X-linked inherited disorders	
Mother a known carrier; close maternal male relative affected	Fetal sex determination, specific assay if possible; DNA analysis
Pregnancy at risk for detectable inherited biochemical disorder	
Parents known carriers	Specific biochemical assay; DNA analysis
Previous child or close family member with a known biochemical disorder	Specific biochemical assay; DNA analysis
Other	
High parental anxiety	Chromosome, AFP
Significant environmental exposure to radiation, chemicals, or drugs	Chromosome, ultrasound
Diabetes mellitus in mother	Ultrasound, AFP

Adapted from Felissa Cohen, *Clinical Genetics in Nursing Practice* (Philadelphia: J. B. Lippincott Co., 1984), 183.

chromosomal disorders are theoretically detectable by amniocentesis, the great majority of genetic disorders are not, or tests
that are available are not very reliable. Thus, it is important to
inform the parents that amniocentesis does not guarantee the
birth of a "normal" baby.

Amniocentesis is a relatively safe procedure for the mother. In
an international study of twenty thousand amniocenteses, only
one maternal death was reported as a result of the procedure
(Santurri 1985). Infection occurred in fewer than twenty cases.
Other problems, which are rarely serious, include spotting,
amniotic fluid leakage, and uterine cramping following the procedure (Elias and Simpson 1986, 44).

The risk to the fetus is somewhat higher—slightly more than
1 percent. In an extensive study of three thousand amniocenteses, the risk of spontaneous abortion after an amniocentesis was
found to be about 1.5 percent (Golbus et al. 1979). This is about
five times the normal rate of 0.3 percent (Finegan et al. 1987,
379). Few well-designed longitudinal studies, ones that follow
the child's progress over the years, have addressed the long-
term effects of amniocentesis. One study of six-month-old
infants whose mothers had had amniocentesis found that 5 percent had skin lesions caused by the amniocentesis needle
(Finegan et al. 1987). However, no other significant differences
were found in their mental and physical development. Another
study of newborns suggested a correlation between amniocentesis and unexplained severe respiratory difficulties in neonates
delivered between thirty-four and thirty-seven weeks' gestation
(Medical Research Council 1978).

Amniocentesis performed late in pregnancy has also been a
source of concern. Besides the slight risk of the procedure to the
fetus and mother, should the parents opt for selective abortion
the morbidity and mortality rates associated with second-
trimester abortions is higher than that of first-trimester abortion
(Turnbull and MacKenzie 1983, 312). While selective abortion
has been found to be more traumatic for parents than elective
abortion (Donnai et al. 1981, 621), an additional factor increasing
the trauma of selective abortions based on amniocentesis

findings is that they are often performed after the mother has felt the fetus move and has begun to bond with her infant.

Because the pregnancy itself was wanted and the fetus is already felt as a real presence, the majority of parents who have a late selective abortion suffer from adverse psychological consequences (Blumberg et al. 1975; Blumberg 1984; Donnai et al. 1981; Fletcher and Wertz 1987b). In a study of thirteen families that had selective abortions based on the results of amniocentesis, Bruce Blumberg and his colleagues (1975) found that 92 percent of the women and 82 percent of the men suffered from depression as a result of the experience (799). With new medical developments resulting in a lowering of the age of viability, more selective abortions based on the findings of amniocentesis are being performed after viability. *Roe v. Wade* (1973) set the date of viability as "28 weeks but [it] may occur earlier at 24 weeks." More recently, the World Health Organization set 22 weeks as the dividing line between spontaneous abortion and birth (Callahan 1986, 34). This ruling is especially disturbing to people who regard viability as the beginning of personhood.

For the 95 percent of cases in which no fetal defect is found, amniocentesis can still be a traumatic experience. These parents often suffer "significant anxiety and observed trauma," including disruption of healthy family functioning, during the three- to four-week wait for the results (Blumberg 1984, 207). Also, the procedure itself is invasive and a source of stress for many mothers.

Because of these and other problems, more attention is now being focused on a relatively new method of prenatal diagnosis—chorionic villus sampling, which, although still an invasive technique, can be performed during the first trimester of pregnancy.

Chorionic Villus Sampling (CVS)

Chorionic villus sampling (CVS) offers several advantages over amniocentesis. It can be performed as early as nine to eleven weeks' gestation. The results from cytogenic analysis are also available within several days rather than several weeks, as is the case with amniocentesis. The indications for CVS are the same as those for amniocentesis with the exception of testing for possible NTDs.

The chorionic villi, which are part of the material of the developing placenta, are the most accessible fetal tissue in the early stages of pregnancy. Because the chorionic tissue is derived from the fertilized ovum, it is assumed to be a fairly accurate reflection of the genetic makeup of the fetus.

The Procedure

The history of CVS dates back to 1968, when the use of a modified endoscope—"a device consisting of a tube and optical system for observing the inside of a hollow organ or cavity" (*Taber's Cyclopedic Medical Dictionary* 1989, 594)—was attempted for transcervical biopsy of the chorion for diagnostic purposes (Mohr 1968, 73). However, poor visualization prevented successful biopsies of the chorion in about half of the cases. Complications caused by puncturing the amniotic sac were also a common problem in early attempts to use CVS for prenatal diagnosis (Hahnemann 1974, 47). In 1975, a group of Chinese researchers reported a 94 percent success rate in the use of CVS for fetal sex determination (Department of Obstetrics and Gynecology, Tietung Hospital 1975, 117). The widespread use of CVS as an effective diagnostic tool has only become a real possibility since the improvement of ultrasound in the early 1980s (Kazy et al. 1982). By 1988, an estimated greater than thirty thousand CVS procedures had been performed worldwide (Maidman 1989, 17).

Like amniocentesis, CVS can be performed in an outpatient clinic. It is a relatively simple procedure for the mother. With the use of ultrasound for guidance, a catheter is inserted through the vagina and cervix, and a sample of the chorionic villi is removed by suction. An alternative approach, which was first developed in 1984, involves the use of a transabdominal spinal needle to acquire a sample. This method, which is the method of choice for many physicians, is especially useful when the mother has herpes or another vaginal or cervical infection.

Disorders That Can Be Diagnosed

Unlike amniotic fluid, which must be cultured for a long time, cytogenic analysis on the chorionic villus sample can be performed within twenty-four hours. If a greater number of metaphases are desired for biochemical or DNA analysis, the villi can be cultured instead. One disadvantage of CVS is that it cannot be used to diagnose NTDs.

Although CVS is still not available in most hospitals and clinics in this country, it may not be long before it replaces amniocentesis as the most popular type of prenatal diagnosis for chromosomal and genetic disorders.

The safety of CVS is still under investigation. The risk to the woman appears to be minimal. However, the procedure-related fetal loss (the spontaneous abortion rate above the normal rate for this time in gestation) is estimated to be about 3.2 percent (Bergman et al. 1991, 190). Another potential drawback to CVS may be a possible connection between it and malformations ranging from relatively minor ones such as strawberry hemangiomas (reddish discoloration of areas of the skin) to major malformations such as limb reduction (Medical Research Council Working Party on the Evaluation of Chorionic Villus Sampling 1991, 1497; Kaplan et al. 1990, 366).

Because CVS is being performed at an earlier time in pregnancy it is also being used more for nonmedical reasons, such as sex selection, than would be expected with amniocentesis (Rhoads et al. 1989, 613). Parents also appear to be more willing to choose abortion for relatively minor anomalies. Marion Verp and colleagues (1988), for example, found that 97.6 percent of women who had a positive result from CVS decided to terminate the pregnancy, while only 78.1 percent of women who had similar results from amniocentesis chose to do so (613).

The earlier stage at which CVS is performed greatly increases the chance of finding a fetal abnormality. The rate of spontaneous fetal loss after clinical diagnosis of pregnancy is 12 to 15 percent, resulting mainly from chromosomal and genetic abnormalities in the young fetus or embryo. After sixteen weeks, however, the rate of spontaneous loss is only 1 percent (Simpson

1990). A test performed at eight weeks' gestation, consequently, will detect more than five times as many chromosomal abnormalities as a test done at sixteen weeks (ibid.). This means that five times as many parents will have to suffer through the anguish and subsequent feelings of guilt involved in deciding whether to abort—actively bring about the death of—their fetus. Thus, the emotional costs of CVS must be weighed against the benefits of early diagnosis in light of the fact that the great majority of fetuses diagnosed with genetic disorders by CVS would have spontaneously miscarried in the next month or two anyway. While this is not to belittle the tragedy and grief associated with losing a child through spontaneous miscarriage or stillbirth, the psychological effects of a miscarriage on parents are not as severe or long-lasting as those of a selective abortion (Blumberg et al. 1975).

At present, the accuracy of CVS is lower than that of amniocentesis, although this may improve somewhat with increased experience in performing the procedure. One of the problems with CVS is that genetic disorders, usually in the form of mosaicism, may be present in the chorion that are not present in the fetus. In a study of 4,395 pregnancies, chromosomal mosaicism was found in 1.3 percent of the cytotrophoblasts but in none of the fetal tissue (Johnson et al. 1990). In a 1991 study on the effectiveness of CVS, the procedure needed to be repeated or followed up by amniocentesis in 13 percent of the cases because of sampling failure, mosaicism, or maternal cell contamination (Medical Research Council Working Party on the Evaluation of Chorionic Villus Sampling 1991, 1493).

One of the questions regarding the accuracy of CVS is whether the chorion is truly representative of the fetus's genetic code. In some cases, abnormal mosaic cells are found in the chorion but not in the amniotic fluid or in cells from the fetal skin or blood (Stetten and Meissner 1981, 719). This discrepancy could lead to a diagnosis of a genetically abnormal fetus when in fact the fetus is normal.

A Comparison of Amniocentesis and CVS

The risk of fetal loss and procedure failure is still higher for CVS than for amniocentesis. CVS requires more skill and more of a team approach than amniocentesis and is more limited in its application. For example, it cannot be used to diagnose NTDs. Because CVS does not deal directly with fetal tissue, it should be supplemented with amniocentesis if mosaicism or any other questionable result is found. The ability to perform CVS at an earlier stage of pregnancy and to generate results more quickly is offset somewhat by the higher number of fetal abnormalities that will be detected and the trauma to the parents in cases of induced abortion. While CVS cannot replace amniocentesis altogether, it is possible, in the not-too-distant future, that CVS may replace amniocentesis as the preferred method of prenatal diagnosis for chromosomal and genetic disorders.

Fetoscopy and Cordocentesis

Fetoscopy

Fetoscopy involves the use of an endoscope to either visualize or remove tissue from the fetus. Because fetoscopy, like amniocentesis, involves invasion of the abdominal cavity, it must be performed under sterile conditions. An intravenous sedative is given to the mother and fetus first, and then an incision is made in the abdominal wall for the insertion of the fetoscope. The procedure is usually accompanied by ultrasound visualization.

Fetoscopy can be used to detect minor external abnormalities that cannot be seen by ultrasound and to obtain fetal blood samples and skin tissues for analysis. The earliest stage of pregnancy at which it is safe to take a tissue sample is at seventeen weeks, which is well into the second trimester (Romero et al. 1986, 574).

Until recently, with the introduction of DNA analysis, fetoscopy was used primarily for fetal blood sampling and the diagnosis of sickle cell anemia, thalassemia, and hemophilia. The blood sample is taken from the umbilical cord or placenta. Fetal skin samples for biochemical analysis can also be taken from the fetal scalp, back, or extremities.

The greatest risk of fetoscopy is fetal death or premature birth. The reported incidence of spontaneous abortion following fetoscopy is 3 to 16 percent, depending on the nature of the procedure (Romero et al. 1986, 580; Elias and Annas 1987, 139). There is also a 10 percent incidence of preterm delivery (Benzie et al. 1980, 29). Because of the higher risk of fetal death associated with fetoscopy, it is usually not used unless ultrasound and amniocentesis cannot provide the desired information. Fetoscopy, however, is sometimes preferred over amniocentesis for rapid late-pregnancy karyotyping.

One of the advantages of fetoscopy is that it provides an opportunity for therapeutic intervention by administering drugs, blood products, and genetic material directly into the fetal circulatory system. In the future, its main use may well be therapeutic rather than diagnostic (Rodeck and Nicolaides 1983, 337).

Cordocentesis

Cordocentesis, which is very similar to fetoscopy, was first utilized in 1983 to obtain fetal blood samples. Under ultrasound guidance, a spinal needle is introduced into the abdominal cavity, and a sample of umbilical blood is withdrawn. The procedure requires neither sedation nor an overnight stay as fetoscopy does. Unlike amniocentesis, karyotyping can be completed within seventy-two hours (Boulot et al. 1990). Cordocentesis can also be used to detect congenital infections, to assess the fetal metabolic condition, and to provide direct medical therapy.

While cordocentesis is reported to be relatively safe for both the mother and fetus (Weiner 1988, 286), the fetal death rate in fact ranges from 7.6 percent for fetuses under 18 weeks to 0.7 percent for fetuses over 18 weeks (Levi-Setti et al. 1989).

Recombinant DNA Analysis

DNA analysis can be performed on tissue obtained by any of the methods discussed above. Despite the complexity of many genetic disorders, it has been predicted that, with the growth of molecular human genetics and the perfection of the different methods of DNA analysis, the prenatal diagnosis of all genetic diseases will soon be a reality (Elias and Annas 1987, 106).

The Procedure

Although the DNA coding for a defective gene is present in each cell, prenatal diagnosis of genetic disorders is much more difficult than the diagnosis of chromosomal disorders, because the individual nucleotides cannot be visualized. The limit of resolution for nucleotides is about 1 million nucleotides (Williamson and Murray 1988). Most of the advances in the pre-natal detection of genetic disorders have been very recent. Until now, the prenatal diagnosis of genetic disorders such as Tay-Sachs disease generally involved testing for the products or effects of the defective gene—enzymes or other proteins associated with the disorder—rather than the defective gene itself. Unfortunately, this is not a highly reliable method (Elias and Simpson 1986, 63).

Recombinant DNA analysis, a relatively new technique of prenatal diagnosis, involves isolating suspect DNA segments that have been obtained from the parent or fetus. This procedure was not possible until recently because there was no way to sep-arate the DNA at specific points so that the fragments containing the genes could be studied. The big breakthrough came in 1970 when a bacterium was discovered that could break down DNA (Smith and Wilcox 1970). Since this discovery, restrictive enzymes—enzymes that can recognize specific sequences of four to six nucleotides—have been isolated from over 230 bacterial strains (Watson et al. 1983, 59).

In 1976, direct DNA techniques were first used to prenatally diagnose a genetic disorder—alpha-thalassemia (Kan et al.

1976). The following year, fetal blood samples were successfully used to diagnose sickle cell anemia (Kan et al. 1977). Both of these disorders usually involve a single nucleotide. However, despite some notable successes, so far only a handful of the thousands of known genetic disorders can presently be detected directly. Other genetic disorders may involve many more nucleotides. For example, Duchenne muscular dystrophy involves a very complex gene with nearly two million nucleotides (Williamson and Murray 1988).

The sequences of nucleotides that are isolated by restrictive enzymes are called "restriction sites," and the molecules of DNA between the sites "restriction fragments." Restriction sites are relatively narrow and occur within or immediately adjacent to the diseased gene. There is a great deal of variation in the length of restriction sites. These variations are called restriction fragment length polymorphisms (RFLPs).

In some disorders, such as cystic fibrosis, Huntington disease, neurofibromatosis, and polycystic kidney disease, no abnormal biochemical cause has been found (Williamson and Murray 1988). While direct DNA analysis is preferable because it pinpoints the exact defective gene, in these cases indirect DNA analysis using linkage—that is, identifying RFLPs that are situated near the site of the defective gene(s)—can sometimes be used to diagnose the disorder.

The use of RFLPs to make genetic linkage maps for humans was first proposed in 1980 (Botstein et al. 1980). Genetic linkage maps show which distinct genes are located near each other on a chromosome. The maps tend to vary from family to family, so it is best to obtain RFLPs from family members for use in prenatal diagnosis as well as carrier screening. The use of linkage maps has been followed by rapid advances in this area of prenatal diagnosis. Some diagnostic centers in England are now forming consortiums in which DNA information from families is stored so it can be used by any other of the member clinics should a member of that extended family come for genetic testing (Brock 1990).

Disorders That Can Be Diagnosed

Despite its lower accuracy, indirect DNA analysis has been used to prenatally diagnose Duchenne muscular dystrophy, hemophilia A, cystic fibrosis, and Huntington disease (Elias and Annas 1987, 100; Spurdle et al. 1991, 177). The first reported successful use of prenatal diagnosis for Duchenne muscular dystrophy occurred in 1985 (Bakker et al. 1989). Recently, 50 percent of all cases of Duchenne muscular dystrophy have been traced to molecular deletions on the twenty-first chromosome (Koenig et al. 1987). Other deletions are currently being mapped, and studies are being conducted on similarities in deletions between unrelated patients with Duchenne muscular dystrophy (Wulff et al. 1989). The current reliability of prenatal diagnosis of Duchenne muscular dystrophy ranges from 63 percent (Sugino et al. 1989) to greater than 90 percent (Bakker et al. 1989)

Indirect DNA analysis can also be used in the prenatal diagnosis of cystic fibrosis (Serre et al. 1990). The mutated gene for cystic fibrosis, which is located on the long arm of the seventh chromosome, has recently been cloned (Lemna et al. 1990).

Limitations and Risks

While these achievements should greatly advance the reliability of prenatal diagnosis for cystic fibrosis and other genetic disorders, most at-risk parents are unaware of or do not fully understand the limitations of DNA analysis, especially indirect DNA analysis, for prenatal diagnosis, believing it to be far more accurate that it really is (Denayer et al. 1990). Also, the uncertainty of the diagnosis makes the choice of selective abortion much more difficult for parents because there is always the risk that they may be aborting a "normal," much-wanted child.

Alpha-fetoprotein Testing

Alpha-fetoprotein Testing and Neural Tube Defects

Alpha-fetoprotein (AFP) testing is used primarily to diagnose neural tube defects (NTDs). AFP was first discovered in the amniotic fluid in 1956, but the connection between the level of AFP and NTDs was not established until 1972 (Brock and Sutcliffe 1972, 197).

AFP is a member of a class of proteins that are found in fetal and embryonic tissues but disappear shortly after birth, except in the presence of certain tumors. It is manufactured in the fetal liver and is excreted into the amniotic fluid by the fetus. Some AFP also crosses the placenta into the mother's circulatory system. As a result, AFP testing can be done by either withdrawing amniotic fluid by amniocentesis or using a sample of maternal serum (blood). The concentration of AFP in the amniotic fluid (AFAFP) reaches its peak between the tenth and fourteenth weeks of gestation and then decreases steadily, while the concentration in the mother's blood (MSAFP) reaches its peak at thirty to thirty-two weeks' gestation (Burton 1988, 295).

When there is an open NTD, the AFP seeps through the open lesion into the surrounding amniotic fluid, causing an elevation in the AFP level. A high AFP level, therefore, for the time of gestation is an indication of a possible NTD in the fetus.

Disorders That Can Be Diagnosed

In reality, AFP testing is a screening tool rather than a diagnostic tool, because elevated AFP levels can also be caused by other factors, such as multiple gestation, fetal death, liver disease in the mother, or incorrect assessment of fetal age, or the cause may simply be unknown.

Despite its limitations, by the late 1970s AFAFP testing was being routinely offered to women known to be at risk for NTDs. MSAFP testing is a much less invasive procedure because it only involves taking a sample of the mother's blood, generally between fifteen and twenty-one weeks of gestation. MSAFP testing was, until recently, considered an experimental technique. In 1984, reagent kits for MSAFP testing were licensed by the U.S. Food and Drug Administration, and in 1985 the American College of Obstetricians and Gynecologists sent a notice to its

Table 13

Findings Associated with Elevated MSAFP

More advanced gestational age
Multiple gestation
Fetal demise
NTDs
Ventral wall defects
Congenital nephrosis
Other fetal malformations
Oligohydramnios (deficient amount of amniotic fluid)
Placental anomalies
Fetomaternal transfusion
Maternal liver disease or malignancy
Normal pregnancy

Source: Barbara Burton, "Elevated Maternal Serum Alpha-fetoprotein (MSAFP): Interpretation and Follow-up," *Clinical Obstetrics and Gynecology* 31 (June): 297

members advising them to make MSAFP screening part of their routine prenatal care (Burton 1988, 293).

The cutoff for a high MSAFP level, 55 percent above the normal level for a given gestational age, is set so that it will identify the majority of fetuses with open NTDs (ibid., 297). MSAFP testing has also been used to successfully detect anencephaly in twins (Cuckle et al. 1990); 86 percent of cases of anencephaly and 78 percent of cases of open spina bifida can be detected through MSAFP screening (Nicolaides and Campbell 1986). Unfortunately, the severity of the NTD cannot be determined by the level of AFP (Milunsky 1986, 465).

MSAFP testing can also be used to screen fetuses for Down syndrome and possibly other chromosomal abnormalities (Knight et al. 1988, 317). In 1984, it was discovered that MSAFP levels were approximately 25 percent lower in pregnancies in which the fetus had Down syndrome (Merkatz et al. 1984, 886). However, the correlation between AFP level and Down syndrome is not nearly as strong as that between AFP level and NTDs. MSAFP testing is also age sensitive and is not useful to predict the risk of Down syndrome in younger (under thirty-

Figure 7

Frequency of MSAFP Values, Expressed as Multiples of the Median, for Down Syndrome and Unaffected Pregnancies

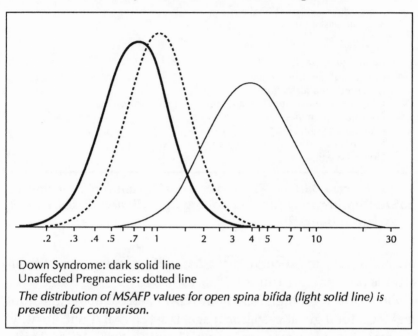

Down Syndrome: dark solid line
Unaffected Pregnancies: dotted line

The distribution of MSAFP values for open spina bifida (light solid line) is presented for comparison.

Source: George Knight, Glenn Palomaki, and James Haddow, "Use of Maternal Serum Alpha-fetoprotein Measurements to Screen for Down's Syndrome," *Clinical Obstetrics and Gynecology* 31 (June): 307.

five years) women. Despite the limited usefulness of MSAFP testing, an estimated one million pregnancies were screened for Down syndrome by this method in the United States by mid-1988 (Palomaki et al. 1990).

When the MSAFP level is low, amniocentesis is performed for cytogenic analysis for possible chromosomal defects. When the MSAFP level is high, a second AFP sample is usually taken to confirm the results. If the second result is also high, ultrasound is performed to eliminate other possible causes, such as multiple gestation, fetal death, or advanced fetal age, and to check for anencephaly. If there is no evidence of any reason for the high reading, amniocentesis can be performed to obtain an AFAFP sample. Of these samples, only about 22.4 percent will also yield a high AFAFP reading.

Acetylcholinesterase (AChE) Testing

About 4.6 percent of fetuses with serious congenital defects will have AFP levels within the normal range (Milunsky 1986, 479). The number of fetuses with serious congenital defects that are not detected by AFP has dropped considerably since AChE testing has been added as an adjunct to AFAFP testing. Testing for NTDs using AChE levels was first introduced in 1981 (Report of the Collaborative Acetylocholinesterase Study 1981, 312). Unlike AFP, AChE is of neural origin and is secreted directly into the cerebrospinal fluid. It is, therefore, far more accurate than AFP testing in diagnosing open NTDs. Also, AChE testing is not dependent on the age of the fetus. The detection rate of AChE testing in conjunction with amniocentesis and AFAFP testing is 98 percent for anencephaly and 99 percent for open spina bifida (Wald et al. 1989).

If both the AFAFP and the AChE levels are high, high-resolution ultrasound can be performed to locate the open lesion. The success rate of ultrasonically locating the lesion in spina bifida is between 80 and 94 percent, depending on the skill of the operator (Romero et al. 1988, 41).

While of limited usefulness in detecting chromosomal abnormalities, the joint use of AFP testing, AChE testing, and ultrasound is highly accurate in detecting NTDs. As a first step in screening for NTDs, MSAFP is both efficient and inexpensive. Because 90 to 95 percent of all women who give birth to infants with NTDs have not previously had children with NTDs and have no family history of the disorder (Milunsky 1986, 495), many physicians now recommend that MSAFP testing be offered to all pregnant women as a routine part of their prenatal care (Burton 1988, 204).

Figure 8

Flow Chart for Follow-up of MSAFP Elevations

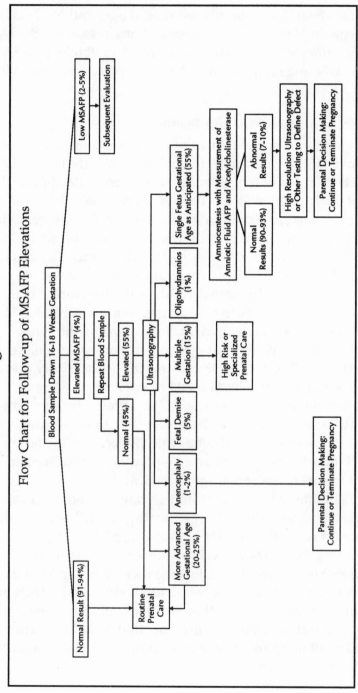

Source: Barbara Burton, "Elevated Maternal Serum Alpha-fetoprotein (MSAFP): Interpretation and Follow-up," *Clinical Obstetrics and Gynecology* 31 (June): 298.

Ultrasound

Ultrasound is a useful diagnostic tool alone or in conjunction with amniocentesis, CVS, fetoscopy, or AFP screening. More than 60 percent of mothers in Great Britain have an ultrasound examination during pregnancy (Nicolaides and Campbell 1986, 521). First-trimester ultrasound examinations are generally performed to determine the age of the fetus because correct fetal age is essential for an accurate AFP reading. Menstrual dates are unreliable in 25 to 45 percent of women (ibid., 551), whereas ultrasonic measurements of crown-rump length can reliably predict fetal age from as early six weeks (Brock 1982, 10). Ultrasound was first used to diagnose congenital heart disease in 1980 (Allan et al. 1980, 444).

The Procedure

As a diagnostic tool, ultrasound is now used primarily to detect gross congenital abnormalities, such as anencephaly or severe skeletal disorders.

Ultrasound, unlike amniocentesis and CVS, is a noninvasive procedure. There are two types of ultrasound scanners: "stills" and "real-time." Real-time ultrasound is especially useful as an adjunct to amniocentesis and CVS because it permits visualization of fetal movement. The ultrasound transducer is placed on the abdomen of the mother, and low-intensity sound waves are beamed into the uterus. These waves are reflected back from tissues of varying densities, creating an image of the fetus that can be visualized on a screen.

Disorders That Can Be Diagnosed

Until recently, the usefulness of ultrasound as a prenatal diagnostic tool was mostly limited to disorders that had major structural effects on the fetus. For instance, the diagnosis of anencephaly can be made as early as twelve weeks (Romero et al. 1988, 45). With a highly skilled operator, second-trimester ultrasound can also identify about 96 percent of cases of spina bifida (Nicolaides and Campbell 1986, 526).

With improvements in instrumentation, particularly the development of high-resolution real-time equipment, ultrasound can now be used to diagnose disorders such as congenital heart defects, tumors, and gastrointestinal, renal, and urinary abnormalities (Campbell and Pearce 1983, 322).

Bowel anomalies associated with cystic fibrosis are potentially detectable by ultrasound at sixteen to eighteen weeks of gestation in 75 percent of all cases (Muller et al. 1985, 109). Urinary tract anomalies, which occur in about 0.2 percent of all births, can be visualized as early as fourteen to fifteen weeks' gestation (Nicolaides and Campbell 1986, 537). Ultrasound has also been used to determine the sex of the fetus. The success rate in identifying the sex of the fetus is approximately 66 percent (Elejalde et al. 1985, 638).

Attempts are also being made to identify Down syndrome ultrasonically using fetal biometry—that is, by measuring the length of certain bones and comparing them to norms, in terms of absolute length and ratios between bones, for a given time in gestation. While some researchers predict that this method holds promise as a screening tool for Down syndrome (Dicke et al. 1989), others believe that the variation from the average is too insignificant for ultrasound to be useful (Shah et al. 1990).

Limitations and Risks

Ultrasound, though limited in its application as a prenatal diagnostic tool, is a safe and effective means of diagnosing NTDs and other visible disorders in the fetus. To date, there is no evidence that ultrasound has any adverse effects on the fetus or the mother (Berini and Kahn 1987, 32; Wilson et al. 1986, 353; Nicolaides and Campbell 1986, 522–23). One of the benefits of ultrasound is that it provides parents with the first "picture" of their child. Women who have an ultrasound between ten and fourteen weeks generally report the experience to be positive (Reading et al. 1988).

However, this "benefit" may make a decision to abort the fetus, should the fetus have a disorder, even more traumatic. There is evidence that women who have seen their fetus on

Table 14

Uses of Ultrasound in Prenatal Diagnosis

Before amniocentesis, fetoscopy, and chorionic villus sampling, to
  Locate the placenta
  Locate the fetus and assess position
  Detect multiple pregnancy
  Establish gestational age
  Detect uterine abnormalities
  Assess amniotic fluid volume

Confirm or identify nonviable pregnancies

Directly detect fetal abnormalities such as
  Neural tube defects
  Urinary system abnormalities
  Skeletal abnormalities
  Abdominal wall defects
  Cardiac anomalies
  Conjoined twins
  Abnormalities caused by maternal diabetes mellitus
  Abnormalities caused by exposure to drugs or X-rays in early pregnancy

Assess gestational age in order to
  Determine accurate expected date of delivery
  Detect intrauterine growth retardation or other growth alterations
  Determine optimal time for amniocentesis or AFP determinations

Aid in the correct interpretation of AFP values in order to
  Assess gestational age
  Detect multiple pregnancy
  Determine fetal viability
  Detect fetal anomaly

Evaluate oligohydramnios or polyhydramnios in order to
  Detect fetal abnormalities
  Ascertain fetal viability
  Detect multiple pregnancy

Adapted from Felissa Cohen, *Clinical Genetics in Nursing Practice* (Philadelphia: J. B. Lippincott Co., 1984), 190.

ultrasound can become bonded very early in pregnancy as a result of this experience (Fletcher and Evans 1983, 392). For those who support the morality of the pro–abortion rights position by minimizing the human traits of the developing fetus, "sonographic visualization has the power of making those characteristics of relatively well-developed fetuses compellingly vivid" (Callahan 1986, 35).

Other Methods of Prenatal Diagnosis

Radiography

Research is presently being conducted to develop new and better methods of visualizing the fetus. Radiography, which uses X-rays to visualize the skeletal structure of the fetus, is used only when there is a high likelihood of severe abnormalities, such as anencephaly or hydrocephaly, because of the possible danger to the fetus from the radiation.

Amniography and Fetography

Amniography and fetography, two other methods of visualization, both involve injecting a radiopaque medium containing iodide into the amniotic sac. Because of the high false-negative rate and the high risk to the fetus, these two procedures are not often used for prenatal diagnosis (Cohen 1984, 192).

Magnetic Resonance (MR) Imaging

Magnetic resonance (MR) imaging has been successfully used to accurately define maternal and fetal soft tissue and has been particularly useful in studying the fetal brain. It can also be used in conjunction with ultrasound or a computed tomographic scan to diagnosis spina bifida. Despite the usefulness of MR imaging as a prenatal diagnostic tool, its safety has yet to be ascertained (Mattison and Angtuaco 1988, 304–5).

Future Directions in Prenatal Diagnosis

The present emphasis in research is on finding earlier and less invasive methods of prenatal diagnosis. The use of fetal lymphocytes from maternal blood for cytogenic analysis is currently in the experimental stages. This method is both inexpensive and noninvasive. If a reliable method of culturing these fetal cells could be developed, the taking of blood samples from all pregnant women could someday become a routine part of prenatal care (Verp and Simpson 1985, 40). Embryoscopic visualization of the fetus in the first trimester may become sophisticated enough some day to allow accurate diagnosis of some disorders (Grannum and Copel 1990). Studies are also being conducted in Europe to determine the relationship between fetal development and disorders, as well as the size of the yolk sac, which can be observed by vaginal sonogram between the fourth and fifth weeks of pregnancy (Bonilla et al. 1990).

Other researchers are working to develop tests that can be performed before implantation. While this research is an advance if one believes that the value of an unborn human's life is a factor of age or stage of development, such testing might amplify the problem associated with other early prenatal diagnostic tests, because it will detect an abnormality rate far in excess of that present even at eight to nine weeks, when CVS is performed.

Conclusion

Prenatal diagnosis focuses only on the short-term prevention of the birth of children with genetic disorders and has no long-term effects on decreasing the rate of genetic disorders (Kevles 1985). The greater availability of prenatal diagnosis, especially less invasive methods that can be performed earlier in the pregnancy, even though they are not completely reliable, has contributed to a trend for parents who are at risk for being carriers of disorders such as Tay-Sachs disease to delay testing until pregnancy rather than being tested themselves to see whether they are carriers (Ambani et al. 1989). A Dutch study found that 70 percent of women, within twelve months of having a selective abortion following CVS, request CVS for a subsequent pregnancy (Jahoda et al. 1989, 621).

The psychosocial issues that might arise from prenatal diagnosis have not yet been systematically studied. Among those that should be investigated are possible acceptance of increasingly greater procedural risks to the fetus and tolerance of false-positive results (incorrect diagnosis of the presence of a disorder) at the expense of missing any fetuses with defects. The relationship between prenatal diagnosis and the increase in favorable attitudes toward selective abortion, especially for sex and minor disorders, the psychological effects on the families using prenatal diagnosis, and the effects on our attitudes toward people who are disabled also require more thorough investigation.

3

Justifications of Prenatal Diagnosis

Because the goals of prenatal diagnosis are not strictly therapeutic, prenatal diagnosis has generated controversy and demanded justification in ways that other forms of medical diagnosis have not.

The technology involved in prenatal diagnosis has developed much more rapidly than an understanding of its impact. Because of the predominant belief that prenatal diagnosis is a private matter, few systematic studies have been conducted to date to determine the effects—the harms and benefits—of prenatal diagnosis on those involved.

Fetal Therapy

One of the primary justifications given for the use of prenatal diagnosis is that it facilitates the development of new methods of fetal therapy. Fetal therapy, although still uncommon, is not a new field. In the early 1960s, the first successful intrauterine blood transfusion was achieved in a fetus with a hemolytic (blood) disease.

The development of in utero fetal therapy was hampered for many years by the inability to access or accurately visualize the fetus. The practice of fetal externalization (partially removing the fetus from the womb for surgery), has been associated with a high infection rate and is rarely used today.

Present Use

With the improvement of high-resolution, real-time ultrasound, these problems have, to some degree, been overcome. With the use of ultrasound and a 22-gauge needle, rather than a fetoscope, the survival rate in fetuses undergoing intravascular transfusions is now between 85 and 95 percent (Grannum and Copel 1990, 219).

Surgical intervention, with the aid of ultrasound, has been used to relieve hydrocephaly (Grannum and Copel 1990) and to prevent external genital masculinization in certain female fetuses. Catheters have been surgically implanted between the affected fetal organ and the amniotic fluid to relieve obstruction of the fetal urinary (Mandell et al. 1990) and gastrointestinal (Langer et al. 1989) tracts. In the area of organ transplantation, bone marrow transplants have been attempted for genetic disorders such as thalassemia and sickle cell anemia (Johnson and Elkins 1988).

Limitations and Risks

These procedures are not without significant risk to both mother and fetus. Indeed, the long-term value of these procedures has recently come under scrutiny. For example, the risk of fetal death following implantation of a catheter is as high as 40 percent (Grannum and Copel 1990, 222). The International Fetal Registry reports that the results of fetal shunt placement are not significantly better than those of untreated fetuses. Most hospitals have stopped performing shunt procedures for hydrocephaly for this reason (ibid., 223).

The great majority of work in fetal therapy is still in the experimental phase. While surgical correction of cranial and facial anomalies, such as cleft palate and cleft lip, have been successfully performed on animal fetuses, they have not yet been attempted on human fetuses (Strauss and Davis 1990).

Future Directions in Fetal Therapy

Future therapeutic intervention using cordocentesis may include supplying deficient metabolites for disorders in which there is an inborn error of metabolism and supplying needed proteins, such as clotting factor VIII in classic hemophilia (Watson et al. 1983, 212). Research is also being done on developing a technique for using crushed bone particles for patching open spina bifida lesions (Elias and Annas 1987, 249).

With the great advances that have been made in recent years in recombinant DNA technology, genetic therapy might someday be available for almost all inborn metabolic errors, possibly even at the preimplantation embryonic level. The new DNA technology has the potential to supply physicians with pure cloned genes in unlimited numbers. These genes could be introduced, using recombinant retroviruses, into the embryo or fetus either in the specifically affected somatic cells (somatic cell therapy) or directly into the germ cell (germ cell therapy). The latter method would actually change the genotype of the recipient, whereas somatic cell therapy would only change the phenotype (Johnson and Elkins 1988).

Moral Issues: The Fetus as Patient

With new developments in the field of fetal therapy, the concept of the fetus as patient could bring about a whole new set of ethical dilemmas. For example, what happens when there is a clash between the therapeutic needs of the fetus and the rights of the mother? Would it be morally acceptable to allow a child to be born with a disorder that could have been treated in utero? Peter Volpe, in his book *Patient in the Womb* (1984), points out that before the advent of fetal therapy, there were only two options—abortion or the birth of a defective child. Would fetal therapy, he asks, "put a lid on these two options" (134)? John Fletcher (1981c) also questions the apparent inconsistency of encouraging fetal therapy at the same time that we are supporting maternal autonomy regarding abortion.

The use of germ cell therapy raises additional ethical issues. Is it right to tamper with the genes of another human being? If so, who is to determine which genes are the most desirable? Indeed, could genetic therapy pose a threat to our very concept of humanness as an intrinsically valuable entity? On the positive side, fetal therapy and a regard for the fetus as patient could enhance our respect for the moral status of the fetus and result in a decline in the number of abortions.

The rationale given for fetal therapy is that it can be used to prevent deterioration of a fetal condition to a point where the damage is beyond repair. This rationale seems to be in line with the purpose of medicine, which is to heal or at least offer comfort and aid to the incurable. There is little doubt that fetal therapy has the potential to bring about a significant reduction in the suffering of both children with severe disorders and their families.

Unfortunately, despite a few noteworthy successes in the field of fetal therapy, the vast majority of genetic disorders remain untreatable both before and after birth. If physicians accept the care of the fetus as a child and patient as their guiding principle for prenatal diagnosis, then it should be used only for serious or life-threatening disorders that can be treated in utero (Johnson and Elkins 1988, 409). In fact, use of this principle could raise the question of whether prenatal testing for such disorders should be mandatory.

Selective Abortion as Therapy

Whatever the potential of and problems with fetal therapy, the reality is that at present prenatal diagnosis is rarely performed with a therapeutic goal in mind. Because in utero treatment is rarely an option, some people argue that prenatal diagnosis followed by selective abortion is justified as an interim solution while techniques are being developed to treat the disorders (e.g., McCormick 1974, 299; Littlefield 1969, 723). One of the assumptions that seems to underlie this position is that because we have the technology to prenatally diagnose certain disorders, we have to put it to use somehow. Since the advances in prenatal diagnosis of abnormalities have not been matched by progress in treatment of these disorders, selective abortion remains the only "therapy" or "form of management" (Seller 1976, 140) presently available in most cases.

"Prenatal genetic disorder," writes John Littlefield (1969), "will constitute a major medical advance only if therapy can be given once a diagnosis has been made. . . . But society and the professionals must appreciate and accept that the proper therapy now is for the family and at times that means abortion" (723).

However, this is clearly a very odd use of the term *therapy*. Paul Ramsey (1972) maintains that the use of the words *therapy* and *treatment* in reference to selective abortion are a kind of "logical and moral contradiction" or what he dubs "medical doublethinking" (161–62).

The accepted medical definition of the word *therapy* is "any specific procedure used for the cure or the amelioration of a disease or pathological condition" (*Taber's Cyclopedic Medical Dictionary* 1989, 1897). But it is the fetus, rather than the family, who has the disease or pathological condition. While selective abortion is often referred to as "therapeutic abortion," in fact it is not "therapeutic," in the strict medical sense of the term, for either the mother or the fetus.

The purpose of prenatal diagnosis is, in almost all cases, the opposite of that of other types of medical diagnosis. In conventional medicine, the purpose of diagnosis is to allow for more effective treatment of the patient, or, if no cure is available, to at least offer the patient palliative treatment in the form of comfort and pain relief. The primary objective of prenatal diagnosis, on the other hand, seems to be to find out whether the fetus has a defined abnormality and if so, to abort rather than treat the fetus. While the parents have the option not to abort their fetus, abortion is chosen in the great majority of cases. Geneticist Aubrey Milunsky (1986) writes: "sadly the ideal goal of prevention or treatment rather than abortion following prenatal detection of a fetal defect is only rarely achieved" (2).

Several professionals in the medical field (e.g., Beck et al. 1983; Faden et al. 1987; Lejeune 1970) have expressed fears that the availability of selective abortion may actually cause physicians to "lose their commitment to true therapeutics in the face of the technically easier practice of preventive diagnosis and selective abortion" (Beck et al. 1983, 303).

Research on cures for genetic disorders, whether in utero or after birth, may also be put aside in favor of selective abortion. During the 1960s, for example, there were two to three times as many people working on a cure for Tay-Sachs disease than at present. The emphasis now is on genetic screening programs rather than therapy (Rothman 1986, 230). Similarly, as soon as a test became available in the early 1980s to prenatally diagnose Huntington disease, "funds began to disappear for research to find a cure" (Hubbard 1985, 575). The development of methods of actually preventing genetic disorders, such as germ cell therapy, may also be postponed for economic reasons because, as one geneticist puts it, "the goal of germline therapy could almost always be accomplished more simply and safely by prenatal diagnosis and selective abortion" (Davis 1990, 87).

Time to Prepare

Another argument used to support prenatal diagnosis is that even though fetal therapy may not be an alternative in the case of a positive diagnosis, the information from prenatal diagnosis provides time for the family to prepare, both psychologically and in terms of having proper medical resources available, for the arrival of a child with a serious birth defect.

Therapeutic Intervention at Birth

At present, the effectiveness of immediate therapeutic intervention at birth, beyond that which is already available in most hospitals with obstetric facilities, is very limited. In a study of the treatability of about 350 randomly selected monogenic disorders, prospects of effective treatment were found to be bleak in most cases. Present methods of postnatal treatment were found to be effective in prolonging life in only 25 percent of cases. Productive capacity could be increased in another 11 percent, and in only 6 percent was there improvement in social adaptiveness (Motulsky 1989, 873).

Facilitating Parental Adjustment before the Child's Birth

Upon learning of their child's disability, parents typically go through a period of mourning the loss of the perfect, expected child before coming to accept their actual child. It has been suggested that prenatal diagnosis may benefit parents in terms of allowing them to begin the process of mourning before the actual arrival of the child with the disorder. This claim, however, has yet to be substantiated. In a recent article on the role played by prenatal screening, Neil Holtzman (1990) concluded that "there is no data to show that advance knowledge of an affected fetus will lead to a better outcome" (S44).

There is compelling evidence that the fetus is sensitive to the psychological state of his or her mother (Rossi et al. 1989; Verny 1981, 83). The possible benefits to parents of information from prenatal diagnosis, therefore, have to be weighed against the possible harm to the fetus of maternal anxiety and feelings of rejection that accompany the mourning process. Also, many of the processes that facilitate adjustment cannot begin until the child's actual birth. Several investigators have found that a mother's actual contact with her disabled child is a major factor in reducing her anxiety and promoting bonding (Drotar et al. 1975; Klaus and Kennell 1976).

One of the strongest arguments against this justification of prenatal diagnosis is the uncertainty of the prognosis. While the prognosis for disorders such as Tay-Sachs disease and anencephaly is relatively predictable, this is not the case for the great majority of genetic disorders. Also, the false-positive rate is relatively high for some monogenic disorders, such as Duchenne muscular dystrophy. In cases of other sex-linked disorders, where there is no test for the disorder itself and the fetus is diagnosed 46, XY, the family is left hanging—not knowing whether their son is affected or not. Thus, a parent whose fetus has been diagnosed as being at risk for having one of these conditions is faced with what psychiatrist Deborah Zuskar (1987) describes as "the untenable task of adjusting to the unknown" (95).

Without actual visual contact with their child, the parental anticipation of impairment may not be related to objective reality.

Table 15

Selective Abortion Based on Abnormal Alpha-fetoprotein Levels
Rhode Island Hospital: Fall 1983–Spring 1989

Disorder	Number Diagnosed	Continued Pregnancy	Abortion
Anencephaly	27	27	0
Spina bifida	20	18	2
Down syndrome	9	8	1
Trisomy 18	3	2	1
X	3	0	3
XXX	1	0	1
XYY	1	1	0
Unbalanced translocation	1	1	0
Total	65	57	8

Many people, when faced with the unknown, imagine the worst. Thus, rather than clarifying the situation for the parents, "the fact that parents are often reacting to poorly-defined, anticipated circumstances rather than existing ones would complicate the situation even further" (Zuskar 1987, 100–101).

Carrying a Fetus to Term after a Positive Diagnosis

The reality of the present situation is that relatively few couples choose to continue the pregnancy following a positive result from prenatal diagnosis (Blumberg 1984, 210). For example, when a chromosomal abnormality is diagnosed through amniocentesis, 95 percent of parents choose to have the fetus aborted (Edwards et al. 1989, 21). Even in cases in which effective treatment is available, such as for phenylketonuria, families will often prefer to abort the fetus rather than adhere to a rigid dietary treatment (Motulsky 1989, 873).

Reassurance

Many people justify prenatal diagnosis not in terms of its potential benefit to families who receive a positive diagnosis but as a means of reassuring anxious parents that their fetus is normal. For example, physician A. V. Campbell (1984) argues that the "primary purpose of prenatal diagnosis is the continuation of normal and wanted pregnancies in which the welfare of both mother and fetus is the prime consideration" (1634). Selective abortion of the handicapped fetus, he claims, is only a "modulation of this dominant theme" (ibid.).

Reassurance as Motive for Seeking Prenatal Diagnosis

Many physicians are reluctant to perform amniocentesis for the purpose of reassurance. A recent international survey of physicians found that only 75 percent of those who performed the procedure would do so solely to reduce maternal anxiety (Wertz et al. 1990, 1200). While reassurance may be effective as a means of marketing prenatal diagnosis, it does not, according to professor of epidemiology and biostatistics Abby Lippman (1991), take into account why reassurance is sought, how risk groups are generated, and how eligibility for obtaining this kind of "reassurance" is determined. Whatever else, prenatal diagnosis is a means of separating fetuses we wish to develop from those we wish to discontinue. Prenatal diagnosis approaches children as consumer objects subject to quality control. This attitude is implicit in the assumption that induced abortion will follow the diagnosis of fetal abnormality. (23)

It is indisputable that part of the fear of pregnancy is that of giving birth to a baby with disorders who will be a burden to the family and possibly to himself or herself. A recent Swedish study found that 20 percent of younger women seeking prenatal diagnosis did so for "psychological reasons"—that is, their decision was influenced by their "private interpretation of risk" rather than the statistical risk of having a child with a genetic disorder (Sjogren and Uddenberg 1987, 111). The fact that 95 percent of fetuses are found to be normal does not mean that the primary purpose of the diagnosis was to reassure the parents of this so that they could continue the pregnancy. In the majority of cases, there is no intention before prenatal diagnosis of not continuing the pregnancy. Instead, a decision to change the course of the pregnancy only comes into play when there is a positive diagnosis.

Benefits to Parents Who Receive a Negative Diagnosis

Advocates of prenatal diagnosis might still argue that because only a small percentage of women seeking prenatal diagnosis actually end up having a selective abortion, the benefits in terms of reassurance to the more than 95 percent who receive a negative diagnosis make it well worth continuing the present programs of prenatal diagnosis. It is difficult to morally justify interfering with someone else's behavior and autonomy when the risk is informed, is freely undertaken, and does not jeopardize anyone. On the other hand, one is generally expected to provide a moral justification for risk-taking behavior that might cause harm to an innocent bystander, especially if that innocent bystander is one's child. Recent studies, though inconclusive and few, suggest that the prenatal diagnostic procedure itself may be harmful not only to the mothers, but also to those fetuses without disorders who are not selectively aborted (Medical Research Council Working Party on the Evaluation of Chorionic Villus Sampling 1991; Kaplan et al. 1990).

Lippman (1991) points out that the type of reassurances pregnant women really want are not those derived from prenatal diagnosis, but low technology programs that provide essential nutrition, and other perinatal support services to women and children (25).

Prenatal Diagnosis as a Cause of Anxiety

With prenatal diagnosis, the stages of pregnancy, which used to correspond roughly to the three trimesters, are now experienced more in relation to the steps involved in prenatal diagnosis. The parental anxiety characteristic of the third trimester that was related to the anticipation of labor and delivery and the sex and condition of the newborn is "now felt and relieved earlier, during the decision to undergo genetic tests and in the weeks until the results are learned" (Beeson et al. 1983,

234). However, while older women who have amniocentesis for Down syndrome report lower anxiety levels in the third trimester than women who declined the procedure (Marteau et al. 1989), this gain has to be weighed against the stress caused by the procedure itself. For example, the anxiety scores (using the State-Trait Anxiety Inventory) of women awaiting amniocentesis is significantly higher than that of women who are not undergoing amniocentesis (Rossi et al. 1989).

This anxiety continues during the waiting period between amniocentesis and test results, which could last up to six weeks (Rothman 1986). In a recent study, maternal anxiety in women undergoing amniocentesis was linked to physiological changes in the fetus, which, the research suggested, could adversely affect their subsequent psychological and physical development (Rossi et al. 1989). Bruce Blumberg (1984), one of the forerunners in the study of the psychological effects of amniocentesis, also reports significant anxiety and family disruption during the waiting period (207).

In another study, mental and psychosomatic symptoms were found to be common in women who had fetoscopy performed for hemophilia. These effects were especially severe when the diagnosis was followed by an abortion or miscarriage. Of the women in the study who continued the pregnancy with a healthy fetus, eight of the twenty-two experienced the period up to delivery as trying and felt that this "adversely influenced their daily life" (Tedgard et al. 1989, 692).

The increased use of MSAFP screening routinely early in pregnancy for Down syndrome and NTDs cannot help but further increase the so-called genetic anxiety. While the rate of NTDs is about one in one thousand births, about 5 percent of women tested will have a positive result on the first test. Of every one hundred women who receive a positive result, ninety-eight of them will be false-positive results. The false-positive rate is even higher for Down syndrome. Thus, tens of thousands of women each year undergo the stress of worrying about the very real possibility of having a child with a serious disorder. Many of these women will have to wait until the second trimester to undergo amniocentesis and then another month for the results. Of those 2 percent whose initial positive diagnosis of an NTD is finally confirmed, there is no test to tell them how severe the defect will be (Hubbard 1985, 574).

Consistent with these findings, several writers have refuted the argument that the need for reassurance led to the development of prenatal testing, suggesting instead that it is the availability of prenatal testing that has created the need for reassurance.

Kass (1985) writes that although

> relief of anxiety, if tests are negative is, of course, a remedy for the apprehensive parents-to-be . . . it must be said that the availability of genetic counseling is itself probably responsible for much of our increased anxiety about genetic disease, especially where there has been no previous family history (81).

In a study of amniocentesis and the social construction of pregnancy, Aliza Kolker and Meredith Burke (1987) cautiously conclude that "amniocentesis sometimes generates an anxiety of its own" (95). With the availability of prenatal diagnosis, parents can now be held responsible for the birth of a child with a disorder, whereas previously it was out of their control. In the United States especially, where the major responsibility for reproductive choices are placed on the woman, it is often assumed that the woman will do everything possible to assure the birth of a healthy, wanted child. "To the extent that she is expected generally to do everything possible for the fetus/child," physician Neil Holtzman (1991) maintains, "a woman may come to 'need' prenatal diagnosis, and take testing for granted" (28). Indeed, it is possible that the women in a 1989 study (Marteau et al. 1989) who declined amniocentesis may not have experienced the higher levels of anxiety in the third trimester had amniocentesis not been an option in the first place.

According to Barbara Rothman (1986), the medical profession itself has created a need for prenatal diagnosis by creating genetic anxiety and, therefore, capitalizing on women's normal fear of having an abnormal, socially unacceptable child—just as deodorant manufacturers first had to create anxiety about socially unacceptable body odor, by capitalizing on everyone's normal fear about being socially unacceptable, before they could market their product (109).

Lippman (1991) also points out that "women only come to 'need' prenatal diagnosis after the test for some disorder has been developed. Moreover, the disorders to be sought are chosen exclusively by geneticists" (27). In the monologue *Calming or Harming? A Critical Review of Psychological Effects of Fetal Diagnosis on Pregnant Women*, J. Green (1990) introduces the notion of "iatrogenic anxiety," which is substantial among women being tested. This anxiety is precipitated by laboratory results that indicate chromosomal abnormalities that have never been reported before and whose significance is yet unknown.

One cannot help but wonder whether the battery of tests pregnant women are encouraged to submit to for their own peace of mind are not done more to reassure the physicians that they will not be held legally liable should a fetus with disorders go undetected. W. Fuhrmann (1989), of the Institute of Human Genetics at the University of Giessen in Germany, writes that

> the largest impact of prenatal diagnosis may not be in the field of genetics or eugenics, or even avoidance of the birth of affected individuals, but in a changing attitude towards pregnancy with a possible affected fetus. In the early years amniocentesis and, if necessary, abortion were realized to be the ultimate means in an unbearable situation. . . . [However] failure to offer amniocentesis to a 35-year-old woman in Germany may now lead to physician liability and malpractice suits. This is true in spite of the fact that abortion is still prohibited by law . . . [with few exceptions] . . . one of which is a high probability of a severely affected fetus (383).

In the United States, given the much higher public approval of abortion coupled with the rise in the number of lawsuits, especially in the field of obstetrics, one can hardly blame physicians for being cautious. Also, as physicians become more fearful of lawsuits, they may become more tempted to put detection of genetic disorders above concerns for autonomy and confidentiality. In a recent survey of geneticists in eighteen nations, a slight majority of those surveyed reported that they would reveal a diagnosis of Huntington disease or hemophilia A to relatives at risk, against the wishes of their patients (Wertz et al. 1990).

Maternal-Fetal Bonding

Another possible harmful effect of amniocentesis is the postponement of normal earlier maternal-fetal bonding. The period of waiting after amniocentesis for the results of the test is "characterized by a 'suspension of commitment to the pregnancy'" (Beeson et al. 1983, 234). Parents who are awaiting the results of amniocentesis often deny emotional attachment to their fetus until after the results are in and do not usually tell others, except family, that they are pregnant.

Thus, prenatal diagnosis and the possibility of selective abortion create what Rothman (1986) terms a "tentative pregnancy." Not only are women poorly informed of this added anxiety when seeking amniocentesis, but physicians themselves, because they usually only see the woman briefly, are often unaware of it. Susan Hodge (1989), a member of the faculty of a medical school who had taught about amniocentesis in her classes, wrote a letter to the editor of the *New England Journal of Medicine* about her experience awaiting the results of her own amniocentesis:

> I was unprepared for two phenomena. One was just how difficult the wait is. . . . The other more disturbing phenomenon is how the waiting period has affected my attitude toward the pregnancy. At many levels I deny that I really am pregnant until after we get the results. I ignore the flutterings and kicks I feel. I talk of 'if' rather than 'when' the baby comes. I dream frequently and grimly about second-trimester abortions. In sense I am holding back on 'bonding' with this child-to-be (63).

Hodge's experience is not unique. Another woman who also underwent amniocentesis reported:

> Those of my friends who have had amniocentesis report terrible fantasies, dreams, and crying fits, and I was no exception. I dreamed in lurid detail of my return to the lab of awful damage. I woke up frantic, sobbing, to face the nagging fear that is focused in the waiting period after amniocentesis (Rapp 1984, 97).

Rothman (1986) found that one of the most dramatic differences between women who chose amniocentesis and those who refused the procedure was when they first felt fetal movement. Most women first feel fetal movement at about sixteen to eighteen weeks. By twenty weeks, fetal movement can be seen by an external observer. While all the women in her study who refused amniocentesis remembered when they had first felt fetal movement, those women who opted for amniocentesis could not. The women who refused amniocentesis also generally experienced fetal movement much earlier. Rothman's findings are confirmed by a later study in which women having amniocentesis "experienced fewer feelings of attachment before the procedure and before the results were known" (Heidrich and Cranley-Mecca 1989, 81). A Swedish study likewise found that 73 percent of the 211 women they surveyed who underwent amniocentesis or chorionic villus sampling (CVS) reported that they "withdrew their feelings for the child-to-be to some extent, probably preparing themselves for a fancied loss of the fetus" (Sjogren and Uddenberg 1988, 73). These feelings of withdrawal, they report, seemed to be temporary. However, there was no follow-up study of the mother-child relationship after birth to substantiate this conclusion.

While working at an abortion hospital, Magda Denes (1976) noticed that women who had had amniocentesis and were awaiting saline abortions often claimed that they did not feel any fetal movement until after twenty-four weeks. She believed that this stemmed from an unconscious denial of the fetus's real living presence until it could be medically confirmed to be "normal" or "socially acceptable" (158–59).

Because CVS is performed earlier in pregnancy and has a much shorter wait for results, it eliminates many of the problems of amniocentesis. However, as mentioned earlier, one of the main drawbacks of CVS is that the number of fetal abnormalities detected is five to six times higher, thus compelling five to six times as many women to make the agonizing choice between induced abortion and continuing the pregnancy, which in all likelihood would have ended in spontaneous miscarriage during the following month or two.

The "Medicalization" of Pregnancy

Ultrasound, because it is noninvasive and gives parents immediate feedback, is often accepted by women who otherwise refuse prenatal diagnosis. While a normal ultrasound does have a reassuring effect on parents (Langer et al. 1988), it has also contributed to the "medicalization" of pregnancy and the externalization of the fetus.

The widespread use of prenatal diagnosis ostensibly for reassurance has contributed to a growing tendency of women to rely on medicine for feedback about their pregnancy and their fetus. Unlike the women in Rothman's (1986) study who did not choose amniocentesis, almost all of the women who underwent prenatal diagnosis reported that they felt no reassurance from fetal movement (108). Feeling fetal movement within her body no longer reassured the mother of her child's presence or of the developing mother-fetus bond. Instead, reassurance is sought from medical technology—an external authority.

Just as many men see having a baby, or becoming a person, in terms of birth, when the fetus/baby first comes into contact with the external world, Rothman (1986) suggests that because of prenatal diagnosis, women are also beginning to "externalize" the fetus more and more. The fetus is something that can be seen on the ultrasound screen—this is what reassures the mother and confirms his or her existence as a baby rather than the intimate physical relationship with the mother (115). Thus, while most women manage to cope with the anxiety entailed in prenatal diagnosis, they do so at a cost. "The cost," Rothman maintains, "is the developing relationship with the fetus" (102).

Justifying the Risk to the Fetus of Prenatal Diagnosis

Both the reassurance and the time-to-prepare justifications are further weakened by the fact that amniocentesis and other forms of invasive prenatal diagnosis pose a risk, albeit low, to the fetus. One must question the morality of subjecting twenty women and twenty fetuses to the risks of amniocentesis simply to identify one fetus with a genetic disorder. Hilgers and his colleagues (1981) calculated that the amount of screening by amniocentesis needed to abort 523 anencephalic fetuses and 555 fetuses with spina bifida would result in 63 spontaneous abortions and 57 other fetuses suffering damage from the procedure (55). It is difficult, given these figures, to justify the risk of spontaneous abortion following the procedure in terms of an extra few months of reassurance in the case of a negative diagnosis or in terms of time to prepare in the case of a positive diagnosis. Even if a woman is at high risk for having a child with a certain di; order, reassurance that her child is normal, or the few extra months of preparation time should the child have the disorder, can hardly justify the potential threat of the diagnostic procedure to the life of the fetus, especially given that the great majority of disorders that can be diagnosed prenatally cannot be treated even at birth.

It was precisely because of the risks to the fetus that many physicians and clinics in the 1970s would only perform an amniocentesis if the parents agreed beforehand to abort the fetus should the diagnosis be positive (Gentile and Schwarz 1986, 723; Dougherty 1985, 89). "Only parents who are definitely at risk for genetically defective children," John Fletcher reflected in 1972, "should be admitted to amniocentesis. . . . Prevention [i.e., abortion] of known and verifiable risk of serious genetic disease may be, in particular families, an acceptable protection of the family" (480).

The ethical guidelines for the British Medical Association like-wise suggest that prenatal diagnosis not be recommended to Catholic women because they would not accept abortion should the diagnosis be positive (Marsh 1982, 747). Because of the ele-ment of coercion involved in withholding the procedure and the increasing emphasis on maternal autonomy, about 95 percent of physicians will still perform prenatal diagnosis even when par-ents have refused the option of abortion (Fletcher and Wertz 1987a). Nevertheless, there is still a strong tendency to discour-age amniocentesis, unless the family intends to take "pre-ventive" action in the case of a positive diagnosis. Even where a prior agreement to abort a fetus with a defect is not a policy, the great majority of women who have a positive diagnosis will choose to abort the fetus. Holtzman (1990) also points out that because of the "cost-savings" that result from the abortion of fetuses with expensive disabilities, if abortion were not the pri-mary goal of prenatal diagnosis, "there would be little interest in screening and the programs would flounder" (S44). It is also unlikely that third-party payers would be willing to pay for the procedure, as they now do, if it were not cost-effective.

Thus, it is evident that the dominant theme of prenatal diag-nosis, in the vast majority of cases, is not the protection of and concern over the welfare of normal fetuses, but the abortion of fetuses with disorders.

Conclusion

Prenatal diagnosis is not a morally neutral procedure, as is usually supposed. Adopting a somewhat utilitarian stance, Patricia Monteleone and Albert Moraczewski (1981) argue that prenatal diagnosis is justifiable only if "the procedure will markedly assist the well-being of the fetus without dispropor-tional harm to the mother" (56). However, given our present state of medical technology, "with regard to most malformations . . . prenatal diagnosis is virtually by definition a rational activ-ity only if abortion is seen as an acceptable alternative" (Carmenisch 1976, 38).

It seems highly likely that the proportion of these cases will increase in the future with new advances in prenatal therapy and the development of safer and earlier prenatal diagnostic techniques. However, the present state of technology regarding fetal therapy, the lack of information regarding harms and benefits to parents of knowing their child's condition in advance, and the current widespread use of selective abortion as the primary method of managing a pregnancy in which the fetus has a genetic disorder make it clear that justification of prenatal diagnosis, as it is presently used, must also include a justification of selective abortion.

4

Selective Abortion

The current use of prenatal diagnosis is justified only if one accepts selective abortion as a moral alternative. With advances in prenatal diagnosis, as well as the development of safer methods of abortion, the number of selective abortions performed can be expected to increase significantly in the future.

The Incidence of Selective Abortion

The number of abortions performed annually in the United States has remained relatively stable since 1980, at just over 1.5 million (Sachdev 1988, 484). Close to 90 percent of all abortions are performed in the first trimester, 9 to 10 percent are performed between thirteen and twenty weeks' gestation, and about 1 percent are performed after twenty-one weeks' gestation (Tietz and Henshaw 1986).

Amniocentesis, the most widely used form of prenatal diagnosis, cannot be performed until fifteen to sixteen weeks' gestation and is followed by a three- to four-week waiting period for results. Therefore, the great majority of selective abortions are performed between eighteen and twenty weeks' gestation, although some occur after twenty weeks. Of all abortions performed after twenty weeks, 63 percent are at twenty-one weeks' gestation, while only 0.11 percent are performed after twenty-four weeks (Henshaw et al. 1985, 91).

Most hospitals will not perform abortions after the twentieth week. This means that a woman who does not have the results of her amniocentesis until after this time may have a difficult time finding a hospital that will perform an abortion. One of the main reasons for this policy is the possibility of live birth resulting from a late abortion and "the psychological stress for all concerned" when this happens, as well as the legal and ethical problems that arise (Tietz and Henshaw 1986, 724).

It is difficult to establish an exact figure regarding the number of selective abortions performed annually in the United States, because women are no longer required to give a reason for requesting an abortion. The 1988 *Handbook on the Reporting of Induced Termination of Pregnancy* issued by the U.S. Department of Health and Human Services does not include a space in the report for the indication of reason for the abortion. Consequently, less than 10 percent of the reports of abortion received by the Centers for Disease Control include this information (Hollerbach 1979, 198).

In 1971, only 0.8 percent of abortions reported to the Centers for Disease Control stated "risk of fetal abnormalities" as the reason for the abortion (ibid.). This figure is surprisingly low, considering that elective abortion was illegal in 1971. At the same time, prenatal diagnosis was a relatively new field in 1971, and very few women had access to it.

A demographic study of worldwide abortion rates in the early 1980s reported an even lower rate of 0.1 to 0.3 percent of abortions performed because of risk of fetal abnormalities. However, the overall reported abortion rate was much higher at that time, so this is not at all indicative of a decrease in the total number of selective abortions being performed. In other countries, such as Sweden and Scotland, where the overall abortion rate is only about one-half that of the United States, the figures are significantly higher but still less than 4 percent (ibid.).

More recently, David Reardon, author of *Aborted Women: Silent No More* (1987), estimated the proportion of abortions performed in the United States for genetic reasons to be somewhere between 0.4 and 1.6 percent. This percentage range translates into approximately six thousand to twenty-five thousand selective abortions performed annually in the United States alone.

In a review of abortions performed in the West Midlands of England because of the risk of Duchenne muscular dystrophy, it was found that the number of abortions had increased significantly between the second half of the 1970s and the first five years of the 1980s (Bundy and Boughton 1989, 795). This change was attributed in part to the increasing social acceptability of abortion for genetic reasons.

With the availability of prenatal diagnosis for a growing number of disorders, especially monogenic disorders, followed by abortion of the affected fetuses, more high-risk couples are now attempting pregnancy, whereas in the past they would have opted to avoid having a child with a genetic disorder by limiting their family size. In addition, the increased accessibility and reliability of prenatal diagnosis (especially in the first-trimester), the leveling off of the overall abortion rate, and the development of safer, more effective methods of mid- and late-term abortions can all be expected to contribute to a future increase in the proportion as well as the overall number of selective abortions performed.

Abortion: The Medical Procedure

Two main types of techniques are used for abortion. The first, surgical removal of the fetus from the uterus, can be further subdivided into instrumental evacuation and surgical removal. Instrumental evacuation can be performed by means of vacuum aspiration (suction curettage) or dilation and curettage (also known as D&C or sharp curettage). Surgical removal includes hysterotomies and hysterectomies. The second type of abortion technique involves the medical induction of uterine contractions by means of intrauterine instillation of hypertonic saline solution or prostaglandins.

Table 16

Number and Percentage Distribution of Abortions by Type of Procedure, According to Weeks Since LMP (Last Menstrual Period), 1981

Procedure	Number of Abortions	Weeks Since LMP						
		8	9–10	11–12	13–15	16–20	21	Total
Suction curettage	1,347,820	85.4	93.8	94.2	92.3	–	–	–
Sharp curettage (dilation and curettage)	79,950	5.1	5.7	5.2	6.0	–	–	–
Dilation and evacuation	90,280	5.7	–	–	–	86.4	44.5	20.0
Hysterotomy/hysterectomy	1,140	0.1	0.1	0.0	0.0	0.1	0.3	0.7
Intrauterine saline instillation	35,040	2.2	0.1	0.3	0.8	6.9	35.1	64.5
Intrauterine prostaglandin instillation	9,650	0.6	0.0	0.1	0.3	2.5	11.3	6.9
Other	13,460	0.9	0.3	0.2	0.6	4.1	8.8	7.9
Total	1,577,340	100.0	100.0	100.0	100.0	100.0	100.0	100.0

Reproduced with the permission of The Alan Guttmacher Institute from Stanley K. Henshaw, Nancy J. Binkin, Ellen Blaine, and Jack C. Smith, "A Portrait of American Women Who Obtain Abortions," *Family Planning Perspectives* 17 (2): 93.

Instrumental Evacuation

With the predicted increase in chorionic villus sampling as a prenatal diagnostic tool, first-trimester selective abortion may become an option for more women. The most frequently used means of first-trimester abortion is vacuum aspiration, also known as suction curettage.

About 85 percent of all abortions performed in the United States and Canada are by instrumental evacuation (Henshaw et al. 1985, 90). This method, using syringe suction, was first used in 1960 to "induce menstruation" (Tietz and Henshaw 1986, 85). Vacuum aspiration, which takes only about five minutes to perform, is usually done on an outpatient basis with a local anesthetic. The cervix is first dilated enough so that a flexible cannula (tube), which is connected by another tube to an electric suction machine, can be inserted through the woman's vagina and into her uterus. The parts of the fetus and other fetal tissue, such as the placenta, are then suctioned into a jar. Some physicians scrape the uterus afterward as a precaution to ensure that none of the fetal tissue remains behind. Medical complications, most of which are minor, from this procedure occur in less than 1 percent of the cases (Allgeier and Allgeier 1988, 372).

D&C can also be used during the first trimester. Before the late 1970s, when vacuum aspiration became the method of choice for most physicians, D&C was the most common method of abortion (Tietz and Henshaw 1986, 85). It has since fallen out of favor, as it carries with it a significantly increased risk of premature birth in subsequent pregnancies because of damage to the cervix from forced dilation (Allgeier and Allgeier 1988, 373). D&C is similar to suction curettage, except that the fetal tissue is scraped rather than suctioned out of the uterus.

Each year about 150,000 women have an abortion during the second trimester. The mortality rate for second-trimester abortions is much higher than that for first-trimester abortions, with the risk increasing about 50 percent for every week into the second trimester (Tyler 1981, 463). Suction curettage is not practical after twelve weeks' gestation because of the size of the fetus. For early second-trimester abortions, dilation and evacuation (D&E) is the safest and easiest method.

D&E is used in almost 90 percent of all abortions performed between thirteen and fifteen weeks' gestation (Henshaw et al. 1985, 90).

While the woman is under general or local anesthesia, her cervix is dilated, and a forceps is inserted into the uterus to crush the body of the fetus so that the parts can be removed. After all the parts of the fetus have been identified and the physician is sure that none remain entrapped in the uterus, the uterus is suctioned with a large vacuum curette.

The rate of major complications of D&E is 0.69 percent, with infection being one of the most frequently reported (Tyler 1981, 466–67). Nevertheless, the mortality rate for an abortion performed before sixteen weeks' gestation is still lower than that for delivery of a term pregnancy (ibid., 463). After sixteen weeks, the rate of maternal death is about twenty in every one hundred thousand abortions performed (Fletcher 1983c, 227).

Surgical Removal of the Fetus

At one time, hysterotomy—cesarean section or the surgical removal of the fetus through an incision in the uterus—was the primary method of midtrimester abortion. However, the mortality rate of this procedure is 0.045 to 0.271 percent with a reported rate of medical complications for the mother ranging from 23 to 51 percent (Allgeier and Allgeier 1988, 375). Another problem with hysterotomy is the significant number of fetuses that survive the procedure. Because of these complications, the current use of hysterotomy has been limited to emergencies, except in India, where both hysterotomy and hysterectomy are still widely practiced methods of abortion (Tietz and Henshaw 1986, 4).

Hysterectomy, which involves removal of the entire uterus, is a safer surgical method and can be used if the woman wants an abortion and sterilization at the same time. About 1.4 percent of women request sterilization at the time of an abortion. This figure is probably considerably higher for women seeking a selective abortion because of "genetic impairments" (Tietz and Henshaw 1986, 93). With improvements in the methods and accuracy of prenatal diagnosis, however, one could expect fewer women at high risk for having a fetus with a genetic disorder to seek sterilization.

Medical Induction of Uterine Contractions

As yet, there is no satisfactory method of midterm or late abortion—the time when most selective abortions are performed. Because the results of amniocentesis are not available until after the sixteenth week, D&E is not usually practical. Intrauterine instillation of a solution to induce uterine contractions is considered to be the safest method of abortion after week fifteen (Tyler 1981, 465). The purpose of intrauterine instillation is to induce labor and to kill the fetus.

The injection of a prostaglandin or hypotonic saline solution, the two most commonly used solutions, into the amniotic sac is most successful—in terms of inducing an abortion—between sixteen and twenty weeks' gestation (Gentile and Schwarz 1986, 727). With a saline abortion, about 200 ml of amniotic fluid is withdrawn from the amniotic sac and replaced with a similar amount of saline solution. The fetus's heartbeat usually stops within one to one and one-half hours after the injection (Tietz and Henshaw 1986, 87). Labor contractions begin within a few minutes to a few hours after the injection, and the fetus is expelled from the uterus within seventy-two hours, with the average time being about thirty-six hours (Tietz and Henshaw 1986, 87). The procedure can be quite painful and distressing for the woman (Shapiro 1977, 167).

The success rate of abortion using intra-amniotic injection ranges from 76 to 100 percent (Gentile and Schwarz 1986, 729). The risk of complications is about 1.78 percent—2.5 times higher than the risk associated with D&E (Tyler 1981, 466). Maternal complications include vomiting, infection, fever, convulsions, bleeding, rupture of the uterus, and trauma to the cervix because it is not yet prepared for delivery this early in the pregnancy. While complication rates tend to be higher with saline than with prostaglandins (Gentile and Schwarz 1986, 728–30), prostaglandins are potent substances that can even cause cardiorespiratory collapse in some women (Wein et al. 1989). Rupture of the uterus, although rare, can also result from over-stimulation when the prostaglandin or saline solution is used in combination with oxytonic drugs, which stimulate uterine contractions (Hagay et al. 1989). Uterine rupture may lead to sterility as well as to shock and death in extreme cases.

Although the solutions injected are intended to kill the fetus as well as induce labor, this method of abortion sometimes results in a live birth. Each year, about four hundred to five hundred live births occur during abortions in the United States (Reardon 1987, 99). The rate of live births with intrauterine instillation ranges from one to seventy per one thousand procedures, depending on the type of solution used (Tietz and Henshaw 1986, 88). Beyond twenty weeks' gestation, live births are five to forty times more common with saline solution than with prostaglandins (Grimes et al. 1980, 198). Some physicians use urea or a combination of urea and a prostaglandin to increase the probability of fetal death (Gentile and Schwarz 1986, 732).

Because of the greater risks accompanying surgical removal of the fetus and medical induction of uterine contractions, there has been a gradual shift away from the use of these two techniques to the use of instrumental evacuation. In 1983, 96.8 percent of all abortions were by instrumental evacuation compared with 89.7 percent in 1973. Likewise, the use of medical induction of contractions declined from 9.7 percent in 1973 to 3.1 percent in 1983, and the use of uterine surgery declined from 0.6 to 0.1 percent (Sachdev 1988, 494).

Selective Feticide

In cases of multiple gestation in which only one fetus has a disorder, the parents may want to abort only the affected fetus. Theoretically, selective feticide, although it is sometimes called selective abortion, is not an abortion because the pregnancy is not terminated. Instead, the affected fetus, after his or her death, is carried to term along with the unaffected sibling(s).

The first successful selective feticide was performed in 1978. Under ultrasonic guidance, the heart of the affected fetus was punctured and enough blood was removed (exsanguinated) to bring about the death of the fetus (Aberg et al. 1978, 990). One of the more successful current methods of selective feticide—in terms of bringing about the death of the affected fetus—is intravascular air embolism (Romero et al. 1986, 595).

Selective feticide carries more risks than a normal abortion. Unless there is a gross physical abnormality, it can be difficult, in the absence of a persistent marker or distinguishing trait, to identify the affected fetus. There is also a risk of injuring or causing the spontaneous abortion of the unaffected fetus(es). Although some physicians express great enthusiasm about the use of selective feticide (Kerenyi and Chitkara 1981, 1527), it should be regarded, at best, as an experimental technique.

Because of the risk of selective feticide to the healthy fetus(es), some physicians suggest that it not be offered as an option unless two provisos are met: the physician must be comfortable with the medical procedure and must be willing to abort both fetuses should the attempt at selective feticide fail and the woman must be fully informed of the risks involved and the possibility that both or all fetuses may have to be aborted (Elias and Annas 1987, 129).

Selective feticide tends to be frowned upon more than selective abortion. Margaret Somerville (1981), for example, argues that because the purpose of selective feticide is the killing of the fetus, rather than the "evacuation of the uterus" and termination of the pregnancy, it cannot be justified in terms of protecting the mother's health or privacy, as can a normal abortion (1218).

While selective feticide raises several interesting ethical issues, it will not be discussed in the remaining chapters of this book because it is not an abortion procedure.

5

Personhood and the Fetus:
A Historical Perspective

The personhood of the fetus is regarded by most philosophers and theologians as the single most important issue in the abortion debate. Much of the current debate over the nature of personhood has originated in the past few decades in the context of the abortion controversy. The current definitions of personhood, therefore, have tended to include a hidden agenda aimed at advancing a particular position on the morality of abortion.

Western Philosophy

There is no single accepted definition of the term *person* either in common usage or in philosophy (Edwards 1967, 110). As used in the abortion debate, *personhood* generally refers to the moral status of beings, and *humanhood* to their biological status. Supporters of selective abortion have generally taken one of two possible approaches regarding the personhood issue.

The first approach, which is the one adopted by most pro–abortion rights advocates, claims that the fetus, especially the young fetus and/or the fetus with a disorder, is not fully human or a person with moral rights. In this argument, a distinction is sometimes drawn between "human being" and

"human life," in which the fetus is relegated to the latter category along with sperm, spleens, and sometimes even cancer
cells, as well as other types of living human tissue.

The second approach claims that, although the fetus may be a
person, there is some characteristic of the fetus or the nature of
the fetus's relationship (or potential relationship) with the family or society in general that overrides the normal prohibition
against killing a person. For example, philosopher Judith Jarvis
Thomson, in her renowned article "A Defense of Abortion"
(1971), argues that it is not the personhood of the fetus but the
involuntary and hence "coercive" relationship of the fetus to the
mother that is the key issue in the abortion debate. To clarify her
argument, she draws an analogy between pregnancy and a person being kidnapped and unwillingly hooked up to a famous
violinist who would surely die unless the person agreed to act
as the violinist's life-support system for the next several months.
Under these circumstances, Thomson argued, the woman has a
right to unhook the violinist, even though her action may cause
the violinist's death. However, her violinist-fetus analogy holds
only in cases in which the pregnancy was forced upon the
woman against her will, such as rape and incest involving
minors. Thus, this version of the argument does not apply to the
issue of selective abortion in cases in which the pregnancy, at
least prior to prenatal diagnostic results, is wanted.

Aristotle, in his search for the distinguishing characteristic of
human beings, settled upon rationality as the trait that distinguishes us from other creatures. Degree of rationality also
distinguished men, whom Aristotle considered superior, from
women. In the thirteenth century, Thomas Aquinas, in his
Summa Theologica, revived this philosophy, weaving it into his
natural law theory and Catholic theology. Aristotle's definition
of personhood has since been accepted, almost uncritically, by
both Western philosophers and the church.

Immanuel Kant, who has had perhaps the greatest influence
on modern thinking about personhood as a moral category
(Beauchamp and Walters 1982, 88), defined "persons" as rational,

autonomous beings capable of imposing moral laws upon themselves. Because of this, they are of infinite worth as ends in themselves. Beings who are ends in themselves have, as termed by philosophers, intrinsic worth. That is, they are valuable in and of themselves regardless of their usefulness to or desirability in the eyes of others. Because of their intrinsic worth, there is a duty to respect persons and never use them merely as a means.

"Things," on the other hand, lack intrinsic moral worth and, therefore, may be used as a means only. The reference to the fetus or the young child as "it," rather than "he" or "she," even though the fetus or child is male or female, is perhaps a reflection of this thing/person dichotomy found in Western philosophy. In this sense, the fetus is tacitly denied personhood or moral status by our very use of this pronoun.

It is not clear, however, whether Kant and other philosophers, such as Descartes and Locke, who were also interested in the issue of personhood, had a theory or definition of personhood other than the common usage in which a person is "any human being in a general way" as opposed to a "thing" (Edwards 1967, 110). Their intent seems to have been not to separate humans into persons and nonpersons, but rather to come to a deeper understanding of our human nature and our relationship to one another as moral beings.

Depersonalization and Anthropocentricism in Western History

The fundamental anthropocentric assumption that rational humans are superior to nonhumans, and that the moral "superiority" of their humanness justifies their using, dominating, and even killing nonhumans as they wish, is fundamental to Western philosophical and religious thought (Bok 1981, 54).

Consistent with the anthropocentric assumption, one popular method of depersonalizing different groups of humans (denying them intrinsic personal moral worth) has been to compare them to animals, other so called lower forms of life, vegetables, or subhuman things. For example, in a 1942 pamphlet issued by the German Race and Settlement Main Office, the Jews were declared to be "only a rough copy of a human being, with human-like facial traits but nonetheless morally and mentally lower than any animal . . . subhuman, otherwise nothing, for all that bear a human face are not equal" (as quoted by Brennan 1983, 96). Jews were described by German propaganda as "an arrested development in evolution, a fossil that lacked the strength or roots to nourish itself" (Mosse 1964, 143).

People of African descent have also been subjected to depersonalization. Throughout history, they have been compared to apes and dismissed by the Boers in South Africa as "just another form of animal life" (Arendt 1951, 194). The 1857 U.S. Supreme Court *Dred Scott v. Sanford* ruling stated that blacks were not persons but "property [things] in the strictest sense of the word." The Tasmanian aborigines of Australia were likewise denied full human status by the European settlers, who regarded them as simply another game animal and hunted them for sport almost to the point of extinction.

Fetal development has been described, incorrectly, in terms of an evolutionary recapitulation in which the fetus goes through vegetative and animal phases before reaching the human phase at some time late in pregnancy or at birth. The fetus's brain, in particular, has been compared to that of a lower animal, thus leading to the unfounded assumption that their behavior is likewise purely reflexive (Touwen 1984, 121). Philosopher Mary Anne Warren, for example, refers to fetuses as "nonhuman animals" and the five- to six-month-old fetus as perhaps having less capacity for sensation and pain than "a fish or an insect" (1978, 23–24).

Handicapped fetuses, like handicapped adults, are especially subject to depersonalization. In fact, some physicians still refer to people with Down syndrome as "vegetables" (Buresh 1981, 63).

Judeo-Christian Perspectives

Old Testament and Jewish Traditions

The Bible gives little direct guidance regarding the personhood of the fetus. According to Genesis, human beings were created in the image of God and given dominion over all of the other animals on earth (Genesis 1:26–31). They were not to shed the blood of other human beings because "God made man in his image" (Genesis 9:6). Human beings are regarded as God's supreme achievement here on earth, and it is through them that God "manifests his rule on Earth" (Commentary on Genesis 1:26–31, *The New Oxford Annotated Bible* 1977, 2).

As in the Western philosophical tradition, there does not seem to be any clear distinction drawn in the Bible between being a human and being a person. However, many liberal and reform Jews, as well as some Protestants, interpret Genesis 2:7 as meaning that Adam did not become a living being or fully human until God breathed the breath of life into him (Williams 1970a, 19). Likewise, it has been concluded, the infant does not become fully human, a being created in the image of God, until he or she takes the first breath of air. "Only the fetus that had come out 'into the air of the world' could be considered a 'nephesh,' a person with a soul" (ibid.). The traditional Jewish belief that the fetus is not a separate person was confirmed by a statement issued by the Central Conference of American Rabbis in 1958. In a ruling on a so-called therapeutic abortion involving a pregnant mother who had rubella, the conference ruled:

> an unborn fetus is actually not a nephesh [soul-person] at all and has no independent life. It is part of its mother, and just as a person may sacrifice a limb to be cured of a worse sickness, so may this fetus be destroyed for its mother's benefit. . . . One may not destroy anything without purpose. But if there is a worthwhile purpose, it may be done (122).

The belief that the taking of the first breath of air at birth signals the beginning of personhood has been popular among Westerners. However, basing this belief on an analogy with Genesis 2:7 proves troublesome in several respects. Adam did not begin his physical life as a zygote or even a neonate but apparently as a full-grown human without having gone through any of the previous stages of physical human development. If the analogy is taken literally, this passage could be used to eliminate not only fetuses but all humans, except grown men, from personhood, as Eve, according to Genesis 2:21–23, was apparently created from Adam's rib without the assisting breath of God. In fact, this passage has been used not only to deny personhood to the fetus but also to deny full personhood to women—a conclusion most Jews and Christians now find unacceptable.

Biblical support for abortion and the lesser moral status of the fetus have also been claimed by reference to Exodus 21:22–24. This passage discusses the penalty incurred by someone who accidentally hurts a woman and causes a miscarriage. Unfortunately, the language in this passage is somewhat ambiguous, lending itself to use by both pro-life (Gorman 1982) and pro-abortion rights (Gregory 1983) advocates in support of their positions.

The Orthodox Jews place greater emphasis on the passages in the Torah, such as those in Genesis, which teach that human life is inviolable and sacred. According to the *Jerome Biblical Commentary* (1968), "after Jeremiah, it became an accepted idea, that God himself forms the young child in its mother's womb; the significance is that God knows man and stands as his unique master from the very first moment of his existence" (vol. 1, 304). The Orthodox Jews still accept this view. The Mishnah, a Jewish book of rabbinical law, makes it clear that, while the life of the mother takes precedence over that of her fetus, the fetus is still endowed with a right to life (Oholot 7:6; Bleich 1979, 135). Orthodox Jews are, therefore, opposed to abortion, except to save the health or life of the mother (Bleich 1979, 135–36). The present Orthodox Jewish position prohibits selective abortion in all but exceptional cases, which are decided through individual consultation with a rabbinical authority (personal conversation, Rabbi Shmuel Singer, Temple Beth Shalom, Providence, R.I., June 23, 1989).

The New Testament and the Early Christian Church

The infancy narratives in the gospels of Matthew and Luke (Matthew 1:18–25 and Luke 1:15), the calling of the prophets Jeremiah (Jeremiah 1:5) and Isaiah (Isaiah 49:1) and the apostle St. Paul (Galatians 1:15) before their births, the struggle between Esau and Jacob while still in Rebekah's womb (Genesis 25:22–23), and Psalm 22:10 and Psalm 131:13 have all been used by Christians to support the belief that fetal life had a special moral value (Gorman 1982). Even in the womb, the "previable" fetus John the Baptist was "filled with the Holy Spirit" and leapt for joy at the approach of the embryonic Christ who resided in the womb of Mary (Luke 1:15).

The early Christian church took a position regarding the moral status of the fetus similar to that currently held by Orthodox Jews. The command to love one another was understood to extend to unborn infants as well as born humans. The "Epistle of Barnabas" in the *Didache*, which was written no later than A.D. 100, contains a prohibition against abortion, calling those who procure abortions "destroyers of God's image" (1948, 157). Tertullian (1950), one of the earliest Christian writers, wrote in about A.D. 197: "With us, murder is forbidden once for all. We are not permitted to destroy even the fetus in the womb, as long as blood is still being drawn from a human being" (32). The only exception to the early Christian prohibition against abortion was when it was necessary to save the life of the mother.

Tertullian regarded the embryo to be a human simply because it had the physical form of a human. He did not distinguish between the physical human and the person. Among modern Christian theologians, this position, known as traducianism, is defended by John Noonan (1970), who argues that "at conception the new being receives the genetic code . . . a being with a human genetic code is a man" (57).

A more dualistic concept of the person, and one that persists today, appeared in the church around the fourth century. Known as creationism, it was based on the presupposition that the so-called rational soul is created *ex nihilo* and fused into the embryo or fetus not at conception but at some later stage in development (Williams 1970b). According to this doctrine, the human body does not become a person until the moment of ensoulment. Before ensoulment, the fetus was held to be "unformed," or a nonperson. Thus, only the destruction of the "formed" fetus was murder.

The main drawback with this and other dualistic theories lies in pinpointing the exact moment of ensoulment. The notion of a formed fetus for centuries was loosely linked to the point of quickening, which usually occurs between sixteen to twenty weeks' gestation, when the mother first feels fetal movement. In the United States, the English common law tradition, which held that abortion was not a crime until the fetus quickened, prevailed well into the nineteenth century (Tietz and Henshaw 1986, 15).

Roman Catholic Tradition

Unfortunately, because the fetus could not be seen, one could not be certain that there was no movement or animation before the time of quickening. Faced with this difficulty, Augustine (1955) chose to value all fetal life rather than take a chance on erring in the wrong direction. "I do not know," he wrote in the *Enchiridion*, "whether it is in man's power to resolve at what time the infant (homo) begins to live in the womb: whether life exists in a latent form before it manifests itself in the motion (motibus) of a human being" (65–66).

By the time Thomas Aquinas began writing in the thirteenth century, the Tertullianian doctrine of traducianism had long since been abandoned in favor of the dualistic creationist theory, and the distinction between a formed and an unformed fetus was firmly accepted. Throwing Augustine's caution to the wind, Thomas set the time of ensoulment, or being formed, at forty days for males and eighty days for females (Thomas, *Summa Theologica*, I, q. 118, a. 2). Based on this distinction, for centuries the Church regarded late abortions as more sinful than early abortions (Williams 1970a, 31).

The Roman Catholic Church has since reaffirmed its earlier stand against abortion and in favor of the personhood of the fetus from the moment of conception. In the 1968 encyclical *Humanae Vitae*, which forbade both abortion and artificial birth control, Pope Paul VI (1968) wrote: "Human life is sacred. From its very inception it reveals the creating hand of God" (294).

The Protestant Tradition

Unlike their Roman Catholic contemporaries, both Calvin and Luther were emphatic in their opposition to abortion, believing that one is fully human from the moment of conception. Calvin argued: "the fetus carried in the mother's womb is already a man and it is quite unnatural that a life be destroyed of he who has not yet seen its enjoyment" (Opera 24, Braunschwieg, 1883. As quoted by George Huntston Williams 1970a, 37). By the nineteenth century, the Catholic Church had again revised its position and adopted the Protestant principle of ensoulment from the moment of conception.

Ironically, the Calvinist belief that the individual's destiny and salvation were already determined before conception and the prevailing Protestant view, that we are justified through faith, both led to a neglect of fetal welfare, in the first instance because the fetus's salvation was already a settled issue and in the second instance because fetuses and infants were too young to attempt to convert.

By the mid-nineteenth century, abortion was a highly visible and common method of family limitation in the United States, even among devout Christians (Mohr 1978, 46). Those few officials of the church who continued to oppose abortion generally did so not because it was the taking of the life of a person but because abortion was often associated with adultery and, hence, sin. In the 1860s and 1870s, when physicians were working toward having abortion outlawed, "the major organs of the various Protestant churches in the United States simply did not discuss the issue; and neither, for that matter, did the Catholic press" (ibid., 182).

The reaction of modern Protestants to the issue has been more varied. Taking a position similar to that of many Catholics and evangelical Protestants, Protestant theologian Paul Ramsey (1978) grounds his belief in the personhood of the fetus and sanctity of all human life on these and other passages in the Bible that seem to demonstrate God's love for all humans. Regarding the biblical notion of personhood, Ramsey argues that "God never looked for indicators of personhood but loved us even in the womb" (205). The fetus, the newborn, and the adult human are all on a par morally because they all derive their dignity from God. God "makes his rain to fall upon all people" and even shows a special concern for the weak and vulnerable (207). "He [God] cares for us," Ramsey continues, "according to need, not capacity or merit" (205). This position is in sharp contrast to those that hold that it is precisely our capacity and merit that define our personhood.

Most of the mainstream Protestant churches in the United States, however, accept the position of *Roe v. Wade*, which denies the fetus protection before viability. The support for selective abortion is even higher, with 84 percent of Protestants in 1975 approving of selective abortion (Hollerbach 1979, 202).

The evangelical churches and the predominantly African-American churches, for the most part, oppose abortion. The Church of Christ, the Assemblies of God Church, and the Church of the Latter Day Saints oppose abortion, except to save the life of the mother and in some cases of incest and rape. The Eastern Orthodox churches and the American Muslims allow abortion only to save the life of the mother; they do not make an exception for selective abortion.

Of those churches that oppose abortion on demand, the Southern Baptist Convention, the Southern Presbyterian Church, and the American Baptist Church all allow abortion in cases of fetal deformity. The American Lutheran Church, which also takes a moderate position on abortion, does not allow it for eugenic purposes, citing Hitler's destruction of the deformed as a reason for its opposition (Nathanson and Ostling 1979, 294–303).

Historical, philosophical, and theological perspectives on personhood no longer offer the guidance many feel they need to come to a decision about the personhood of the fetus. Instead, most people, religious and nonreligious alike, look to sectarian definitions of personhood in formulating their views on the morality of abortion.

6

Personhood: Biological, Psychological, and Social Definitions

There are two extremes regarding the definition of criteria of personhood. At one end are those who think biological evidence is sufficient and that we can discover personhood. At the other end are those who think personhood is purely prescriptive or a value judgment. Both types of arguments have been used to exclude the fetus from, as well as to include the fetus in, personhood.

Medical and Biological Definitions

Physical Appearance

Pictures and descriptions of the fetus's development have frequently been used to support the position that the fetus is indeed a person. The heart begins beating at twenty-two days (Moore 1983, 2). By eight weeks, "everything is present that will be found in the full-term baby" (ibid., 4). The eight-week-old fetus, an illustrated pamphlet entitled *Life or Death* tells its reader, "will grab an instrument placed in his palm and hold on; an electrocardiogram can be done; [and] he swims freely in the amniotic fluid with a natural swimmer's stroke" (Wilke and Wilke 1981). Fetal advocates also point out the importance of early fetal-maternal bonding as an indication that the young fetus is a being who exists in an interactive relationship, rather than just an inanimate thing (Bluglass 1984, 57).

Besides affirming the personhood of the fetus, developmental approaches have promoted a sliding scale of personhood in which the embryo and young fetus are eliminated from personhood on the basis of appearance, with the young unborn human becoming more of a person the closer the physical and behavioral resemblance to a born human without defects.

One of the problems with the study of the fetus, before the advent of ultrasound, was inaccessiblity. While the small size of the fetus before eight weeks makes a detailed analysis of their movements difficult (de Vries, et al. 1984, 49), studies of the fetus after seven or eight weeks have revealed surprising results.

Brain Activity

Until recently, most people thought of the brain of the fetus as, at best, an undeveloped adult brain. The fetal brain was described in terms such as "primitive," "archaic," and "primary" (Touwen 1984, 120). It was consequently assumed that the movements of the young fetus were purely reflexive. Refuting this notion, neurologists Johanna de Vries and her colleagues (1984) found that "spontaneous fetal motility emerges and has already become differentiated by a very early age" (61). From their studies of fetal movement, they concluded that there is good evidence that, ontologically, reflexive movement does not precede spontaneous movement or vice versa. In support of their position, they note that in the first trimester the movement patterns of an anencephalic infant, whose cerebral hemispheres fail to develop, are clearly distinguishable from those of the normal fetus. "Observing these anencephalic [fetuses], one is doubly impressed," they write, "by the fluent, coordinated patterns seen in the normal fetus" (63). Thus, the once commonly held assumption that early fetal movements are purely reflexive and stem from the spinal cord rather than the brain are unfounded.

Bert Touwen (1984) also questions the adequacy of terms such as *primitive* to describe the fetal brain (120). The functioning of the fetal brain has even been compared, incorrectly, he points out, to the brain of an adult with senile dementia (121). Comparisons have also been made to a comatose person, the assumption being that because the latter appears to be unconscious and functions only reflexively, the same must be true of the fetus. Touwen argues that this analogy between the fetal brain and that of a brain-damaged adult is simply inadequate. "The adult brain," Touwen writes, "is morphologically different from the brain of an infant, so it functions differently"(ibid.). The brains of fetuses are not "primitive, archaic or primary; rather, they are an age-specific display adapted to the infant's needs" (120).

Nobuo Okado and Tobuzo Kojima (1984) report that the differentiation of the human central nervous system occurs at an early age. "Neurons and synaptic density, as well as transmitters, in the cervical spinal-cord are sufficiently developed by seven to eight weeks postmenstrual age [five to six weeks' gestational age] to produce spontaneous movement patterns" (42). Besides noting a "high degree of organization" in these "early motor patterns," they also found that there are transient sensory neurons in human embryos that disappear at later stages of gestation (40).

Ability to Feel Pain

Some contemporary philosophers maintain that all that is necessary for personhood, besides being alive, is the ability to feel pain. For example, Peter Singer (1988) argues that "The limit of sentience . . . is the only defensible boundary of the concern for others" (322). This is because the capacity for suffering and enjoyment is a prerequisite for having any interests at all. Without this capacity, there is nothing to take into account.

Our present knowledge of how the fetal brain works is inadequate to answer the question of whether the fetus or the older embryo feels pain (Grobstein 1988, 54). "Whether and to what extent a fetus can consciously experience pain—as distinguished

Figure 9

Human Embryonic and Fetal Development

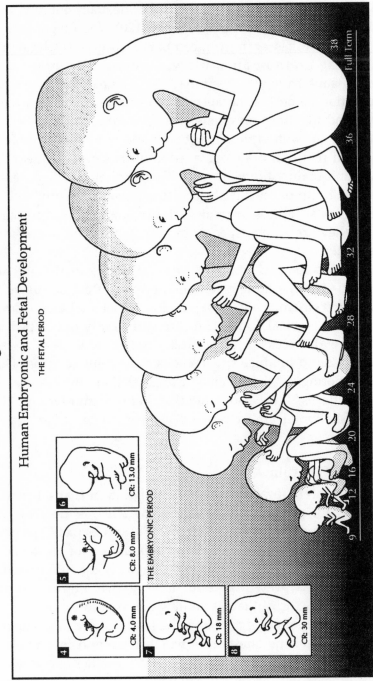

The numbers beside each figure indicate the gestational age in weeks. CR: crown-rump length. Adapted from Keith Moore, *Before We Are Born*, 3rd ed. (Philadelphia: W. B. Saunders and Co., 1989), 3–5.

from reflexively responding to external stimuli," medical ethicist Daniel Callahan (1986) writes, "is scientifically uncertain and probably undecidable by any empirical tests" (35). Pro-abortion rights philosopher H. Tristam Engelhardt (1986), who is probably one of the most prolific writers on the subject of personhood, responds that even if fetuses are able to feel pain, their "underdeveloped and underconnected frontal lobes" make it unlikely that they are able to experience suffering (218).

This response, however, merely further muddies the waters, because the concept of suffering, and particularly the measurement of another's suffering, is even more elusive and subjective than that of pain. For example, psychologist Thomas Verny (1981) believes that the young fetus not only feels pain but can experience psychological suffering (54–72).

Even if one does not believe that sentience alone is sufficient to establish personhood, given the probability that the fetus—especially the midterm fetus in the case of most selective abortions—is able to feel pain should cause one to give more thought to the abortion techniques presently used, which do not take into consideration the possible pain suffered by the fetus. It is generally considered immoral to cause unnecessary suffering to living animals, even if they are thought to be nonpersons.

Normal Genotype

Developmental criteria of personhood have also been used to specifically justify selective abortion of fetuses with gross physical disorders, such as anencephaly or severe skeletal disorders, on the grounds that they lack sufficient physical resemblance to other humans. The criterion of normal genotype has also been used after birth. Some people (for example, Lebacqz 1973; Kett 1984; Kass 1985) maintain that infanticide of so-called defective newborns is merely an extension of selective abortion.

Historically, the courts have long drawn a distinction between "infants born with various malformations and 'monsters'" (Kett 1984, 34). The former had human heads, while the latter had heads that "were so deformed that they appeared to be brutes" and thus were denied full human status (ibid.). "Since the monsters were not human, their destruction was not viewed as murder. . . . The idea died slowly that at least some of those whom we would consider impaired newborns were non-human" (ibid., 34–35). Indeed, we might ask if this prejudice is not still alive and well (see especially Duff and Campbell 1973; Engelhardt 1975, John Fletcher 1983c; Joseph Fletcher 1979; Kohl 1978; and Margolis 1978).

Ethicists Karen Lebacqz (1973) and Leon Kass (1985) both caution that selective abortion establishes a distinction between "normal" and "defective," thus assigning moral value to humans based on their genetic characteristics. Kass (1985) refers to this as the "normal standard" view, in which personhood is dependent upon "living up to a certain standard of normalcy" (97). This view brings up the question of what level of normalcy is necessary for a fetus to be placed in the "category of fetuses that are destructible" (Lebacqz 1973, 122). John Fletcher (1983a) points out that the unjustness and unfairness of setting apart of certain genotypes as deserving of abortion is one of the major criticisms of selective abortion (145). He suggests instead that we look for other morally relevant differences between the person and the nonperson.

Developmental Milestones

The age of the fetus in terms of its stage of development, rather than simply physical humanhood or genetic normalcy, is the most commonly used factor to assign the fetus moral status (Johnson and Elkins 1988, 411). Lejeune (1970), who refers to this as the "practical approach to personhood," points out that according to this approach to personhood "there is no 'humanity' there, just human cells" and that different landmarks must be used to decide when "'humanity' has been acquired by the 'thing'" (128). This approach is reflected in the use of "it," rather than "he" or "she," for the fetus. The developmental milestones of quickening or, more commonly, viability—either at birth or at the point when the fetus is potentially able to survive after birth—are most often chosen as marking the moment when the fetus rises above status as a thing and becomes initiated into personhood.

Quickening

Quickening is problematic as a criterion of personhood in that it merely signals the point when the mother perceives the movement of the fetus, not when the fetus actually begins moving independently. In fact, the very techniques used in prenatal diagnosis are actually changing this perception. Blumberg (1984) writes in this regard:

> While earliest pregnancy is characterized by a narcissistic concern with prominent physiological and anatomical alterations, later pregnancy additionally involves a growing awareness of the fetus as an independent entity. Although this incipient 'infant'-mother relationship develops gradually, quickening . . . must be viewed as a milestone in this process. Current techniques, allowing initial auscultation of fetal heart sound by 11–13 menstrual weeks present the woman with undeniable evidence of fetal life at an earlier stage. . . . The visualization of fetal form and movement by sonography or the identification of fetal sex by sonography or amniocentesis can be expected to accelerate even further the process of fetal personification. (202)

Viability

Viability, which was used by the U.S. Supreme Court in their *Roe v. Wade* decision, has replaced quickening as the most commonly used indicator of fetal personhood. The term *viability* literally means "the ability to live, grow and develop" (*Taber's Cyclopedic Medical Dictionary* 1989, 1992). Under this definition, all living embryos and fetuses are viable. In fact, they are growing and developing at a rate faster than they ever will after birth.

In the abortion debate, the concept of viability has been narrowed to refer "only to capability to survive disconnection from the placenta" (Grobstein 1988, 109). This redefinition of viability in relation to the fetus, however, is more troublesome than might first appear when it comes to deciding which fetuses are persons and which are not. Under this definition, fetal viability

> does not imply complete independence which is not, of course, achieved until many years after birth. Moreover, the exact time and degree of viability after disconnection from the placenta is heavily influenced by the amount and nature of available supportive care, whether from the parents, a surrogate, or a specially equipped technological nursery (ibid.).

Therefore, fetal viability—except in the case of the anencephalic fetus, who is never viable under this definition—is an elusive measurement of personhood.

In 1950, fetal viability occurred at about thirty weeks' gestation. When the *Roe v. Wade* decision was handed down, viability had changed to twenty-four weeks. Now, with improved technology, there are cases of even younger newborns surviving (Callahan 1986, 34). The World Health Organization has recently set the dividing line between spontaneous abortion and birth at twenty-two weeks (ibid.). Because the age of viability is slowly being pushed backward, it simply is "not a very stable principle on which to base decisions" about a "fetus's moral worth" (Johnson and Elkins 1988, 411).

The difference in the time of viability is primarily related to the fetus's environment rather than any feature of the fetus. The fetus is usually viable at all stages, unless removed from the natural uterine environment, just as a born person is viable unless removed from the natural extrauterine environment. With modern technology, zygotes, unlike young fetuses, can live independently of their mother and are therefore viable, or persons, unlike their more highly developed counterparts (Callahan 1986, 35). Thus, viability is not an inherent condition in the fetus or zygote but is dependent on the current state of technology.

If an artificial womb is created or a means for the young fetus to breathe and survive outside the womb, fetal viability, according to the narrow definition, could occur much earlier. Presumably a fetus/neonate in an artificial womb would be considered viable and, therefore, a person with a right to continued existence, just as an adult whose life is utterly dependent on a pacemaker or a respirator is viable, as complete dependence on technology, so the argument generally goes, does not compromise our moral worth, while complete dependence on the womb of our mother does.

Nonviability in terms of physical dependence on another person is also troublesome in that it is the very helplessness and dependence of very young children and sick people on their adult caretakers that has usually been regarded as a reason for granting them *greater* protection by the moral community, while at the same time dependence in the fetus is used as a reason to deny the same protection. If one carries this reasoning to its logical conclusion, it could even be argued that "the previable fetus should have a greater claim on the woman because its life depends on her, whereas a viable fetus can be removed and still survive" (Rhoden 1989, 34).

The viability argument, therefore, can become very odd, if one examines its implications. Indeed, in light of the above inconsistencies, one might suspect that the narrow definition of viability, in terms of ability to survive detachment from the placenta, was evolved after the fact simply to eliminate the fetus from personhood rather than established beforehand as a universal criterion for determining personhood. Consequently, one might argue, this definition of viability is by its very nature discriminatory.

If viability is consistently defined in reference to being able to live independently of other human beings, then, strictly speaking, no human being is viable. Albert Einstein (1949) once wrote:

When we survey our lives and endeavors, we soon observe that almost the whole of our existence and desires is bound up with the existence of other human beings. We see that our whole nature resembles that of social animals. We eat food others have grown, wear clothes that others have made, live in houses that others have built. The greater part of our knowledge and beliefs has been communicated through the medium of language which others have created (8).

While the use of the term *viability* in *Roe v. Wade* as the point at which the state begins to take a compelling interest in the welfare of the fetus may have had a liberalizing effect on elective abortion, it has had the opposite effect on selective abortion. With the lowering of the age of viability, unless earlier methods of prenatal diagnosis, such as CVS, come to replace amniocentesis, most selective abortions will soon occur at or after the point of viability (Rush 1983, 125). A number of states that allowed third-trimester selective abortion before *Roe v. Wade* no longer do so (Dougherty 1985, 105). Ironically, the *Roe v. Wade* decision may soon become a right-to-life decision, especially for fetuses with disorders diagnosed after the time of viability and perhaps, in the near future, for all fetuses (ibid., 116).

John Fletcher (1983a) argues that the physical separateness of the newborn compared to the midterm fetus, rather than viability, is morally significant when it comes to placing the former under the protection of personhood, although he agrees that this concept of separateness "loses some of its logical and moral clarity in an era when advancing technology saves extremely small premature infants, and the embryo is separate for a time following external fertilization" (146). Because of this loss, he suggests that "fresh approaches to the concepts of viability and treatability will probably be a better way to distinguish morally relevant differences between the fetus and the newborn" (ibid.).

Engelhardt (1983) likewise admits that viability is more useful as a medical generalization than as a moral generalization about personhood (195). Nevertheless, speaking pragmatically, he believes that "viability functions as a useful criterion as long as it is late enough in pregnancy to allow the use of prenatal diagnosis and to allow women time to reflect on whether they would like to be a mother" (194–95). For this reason, he suggests that we retain the 1973 *Roe v. Wade* criterion for viability, even though infants may now be able to survive at a younger age.

Like Engelhardt, Thomson (1971) argues that the issue of non-viability, in terms of the absolute dependence of the fetus on another person's body, is more relevant to the question of maternal autonomy than to the personhood of the fetus. Personhood is not destroyed by dependence; but the caretaker's autonomy can be severely compromised, especially in the case of an unwanted pregnancy, where only that specific person can function as the caretaker.

Lebacqz (1973) challenges Thomson's argument on the grounds that a severely disabled child compromises his or her parents' autonomy far more than does a healthy child, although in most instances the parents can walk away from the child without directly causing his or her death. Using the example of a young child who needs medication every few hours to survive, Lebacqz asks, given that there is no one else available to care for the child, "is not that child's mother morally (and perhaps) legally culpable if she 'removes' herself from the child and it dies?" (120). She goes on to suggest that arguments like Thomson's, despite claims to the contrary, do not take the personhood of the fetus seriously. Otherwise, the argument would entail the right of "any human being to remove himself from one who is dependent on him" (ibid.)—be it a sick child, an elderly parent, or a Siamese twin. If we are not willing to accept these conclusions, she argues, we must reject the premise that autonomy gives one the right to withdraw assistance from a dependent person, even at the cost of that person's life.

The Harvard Criteria

Some people reject viability as the key determinant of personhood and instead argue that the same criteria that are used to determine when personhood ends should be resolute, if we are to be consistent, in the decision as to when personhood begins. These criteria, which are similar to those accepted by most physicians and courts (Beauchamp and Walters 1982, 272), are usually referred to as the Harvard Criteria. According to the Harvard Criteria, all four of the following conditions must be met before a patient is declared dead or a "nonperson: (1) no response to external stimuli, (2) no deep reflexes, (3) no spontaneous movements or respiratory efforts, and (4) no brain activity" (Verny 1981, 196).

Focusing mainly on the last condition, advocates of this view of personhood note that the brain waves of the fetus can be measured by the end of the sixth week. The other criteria are also met by the six-week-old fetus, who has not only a functioning heart but also a functioning respiratory system (Brody 1982, 245). Even the very young fetus responds to external stimuli and exhibits deep reflexes, although the mother may not be aware of the movement of the fetus. According to the Harvard Criteria, then, the fetus "surely is not a human being at the moment of conception and it surely is one by the end of the third month" (ibid., 246).

Others take this argument even further and suggest that mere physical continuity, from conception to death, with persons is sufficient to establish personhood. Lejeune (1970), who is an outspoken opponent of selective abortion, stresses the continuum of human qualities and existence from the moment of conception.

Engelhardt (1986), on the other hand, questions the assumption that there should be symmetry in definitions of personhood at the beginning and end of life. While the signs of life listed by the Harvard Criteria may be a necessary condition for personhood, they are not enough. The significance of the measurement of brain waves at the end of life, Engelhardt claims, is to measure, as best we can, when consciousness (and hence moral agency) ceases. However, the mere "presence of neocortical activity is not sufficient for the presence of a moral agent" (217).

Michael Tooley (1973), another ethicist who has written extensively on the issue of personhood and abortion, likewise criticizes the above positions as equating a physical function with personhood. If one were to be consistent in the application of these definitions based on physical functioning, then any animal with a brain that functions at the level of a young fetus, he argues, should be treated as a person (149). Thus, if we are to accept Brody's (1982) argument, then we must also embrace vegetarianism. Brody's response that God gave humans permission to kill and dominate other animals, while he did not give us permission to do so to other humans (602), removes the argument from the realm of philosophy or medicine, into the realm of religion. In fact, some philosophers, such as Albert Schweitzer (1987) and Peter Singer (1988), do consider embracing vegetarianism a necessary consequence of this position.

The position that personhood is more than just a matter of scientific discovery is amply illustrated by the number of physicians and scientists who are unable to come to a consensus on the issue of personhood of the fetus. For example, Verny (1981) argues that even the very young fetus is much more capable and similar to the newborn than we previously believed. Yet, he accepts a pro–abortion rights position regarding abortion (197). "Fetology," he contends, "cannot prove either side of the fetus/person debate" (195).

While new medical and scientific evidence may not be conclusive, it is not irrelevant to the fetus/person debate. In a 1985 *Newsweek* poll, 18 percent of the people questioned said that they are now less in favor of abortion because of "new scientific evidence" (Callahan 1986, 39). One of the problems, however, is that certain qualities, such as consciousness and pain, which on first glance appear to be biologically measurable are not (in either an adult human or a fetus). What other considerations, then, besides purely physical traits, might be used to determine whether the fetus is a person?

Psychological Criteria for Personhood

The basic presumption of these definitions of personhood is the traditional Thomistic/Aristotelian distinction between biological and human (personal) life. Purely descriptive (medical/biological) criteria are rejected as involving the reduction of persons to "brute biological criteria" (Harrison 1983, 221). Even though fetuses have individuated human bodies, they are not considered persons because they lack certain psychological and/or social qualities.

Membership in the biological species *Homo sapiens* is morally significant not in itself but only by "virtue of its relation to other properties that are morally significant in themselves" (Tooley 1973, 77). Human rights exist, not in natural processes but in self-conscious participation in a community. A life must "gain entitlement to the range of rights," anthropologist and psychiatrist Virginia Abernathy (1984) likewise argues. "It is the community [that] grants or withdraws personhood" (132). Personhood must be earned. It is not a free gift from God, as Ramsey (1978) maintains. Thus, it is possession of certain qualifications, and not species membership per se, "that gives something a right to continued existence" (Tooley 1973, 95).

Lists of Criteria

Regarding these qualifications, Tooley (1973), like Engelhardt (1986), suggests that self-consciousness is a necessary condition of personhood, although both recognize that there are problems in the interpretation of what is meant by "self-consciousness" (Tooley 1973, 144). Nevertheless, Tooley maintains that "an individual cannot have a right to continued existence unless there is a least one time at which it possesses the concept of a continuing self or mental substance" (ibid., 121). Because the fetus and the young child lack self-consciousness they do not qualify as persons. Unfortunately, Tooley does not state at what age the child does become self-conscious or how self-consciousness might be measured.

Adopting a position similar to that of Tooley and Engelhardt, Mary Anne Warren (1973) presents a more detailed list of social and psychological traits that she thinks are central to personhood: (1) consciousness (of objects and events external and/or internal) and the capacity to feel pain; (2) reasoning (the developed capacity to solve new and relatively complex problems); (3) self-motivated activity (activity that is relatively independent of either genetic or external control); (4) the capacity to communicate, by whatever means, messages of an indefinite variety of types, that is, not just with an indefinite number of possible contents, but on indefinitely many possible topics; and (5) the presence of self-concepts, and self-awareness, either individual or racial or both. (54)

Joseph Fletcher (1972), who has written extensively on the subject of personhood, abortion, and infanticide, compiled an even more comprehensive list of twenty indicators of personhood, adding to Warren's list of qualifications, such as "minimum intelligence of 40 IQ," a "sense of futurity," a "sense of the past," "concern for others," "curiosity," "change and changeability," "balance of rationality and feeling," and "idiosyncrasy" (1–4).

Philosopher Jane English (1975), while accepting personhood as a psychological/social concept, believes that the "concept of person cannot be captured in a strait jacket of necessary and/or sufficient conditions" (234). Instead, she argues, a person is a cluster of features of which rationality, self-consciousness, and legal status are only a part. However, as Tooley (1973) points out, English's "solution" doesn't really get us any closer to deciding who is and who isn't a person (93). One still has to decide how many of the "cluster of features" a human must have before he or she can be called a person. Would infants who are mentally handicapped, infants with Down syndrome, for example, fall lower on the cluster count because they will never exhibit the type of rationality found in "normal" humans?

The criteria used in these lists are problematic to most people in that they eliminate not only the fetus and newborn but also young children and others who are handicapped. Rather than attempting to increase our knowledge of human nature, as did Kant, Locke, and Descartes, modern "definitions of humanity," philosopher Sissela Bok (1981) maintains, "have been sought in order to try to set limits to the protection of life" (53).

Another problem with the list-of-criteria approach is that even normal humans do not acquire all of these abilities at the same time or to the same extent. Should we make distinctions of moral worth dependent on the degree to which a human fulfills the various criteria of personhood? Just as young children are regarded as property of their parents under these definitions of personhood, one might legitimately inquire, does it mean that the more intelligent, rational human can treat an "inferior" as property or a slave (Singer 1988, 320)? Thomas Jefferson emphatically rejected the qualification approach to personhood. "Sir Isaac Newton," Jefferson wrote in a letter to Henri Gregoire, "was superior to others in understanding, [yet], he was not therefore lord of the property or person of others" (Letter to Henri Gregoire, February 25, 1809; as quoted by Peter Singer 1988, 321).

Definitions that include lists of social and personal criteria of personhood, Philip Heymann and Sara Holtz (1975) cautioned physicians attending a spina bifida study group, "would surely suffer from the difficulties of inconsistent application and lack of security against drift" (412). If the value of the young, and presumably irrational, child comes only from its attractiveness to its parents, then retarded humans are also candidates for treatment as mere means by the intellectual/rational elite. Regarding treatment of mentally handicapped people, it is a well-documented phenomenon that the stigmatization of handicapped people in our society by their nonhandicapped counterparts involves "a process of attaching visible signs of moral inferiority" (Darling 1979, 31).

This stigmatization has also involved the belief among certain people that intellectually and socially "inferior" people can be used as a means for the more "noble" ends of the intelligentsia. In the 1960s, geriatric patients at the Jewish Hospital and Medical Center of Brooklyn were used, without their informed consent, for a study on the immunological effects of the injection of live cancer cells. A similar study at Willowbrook, New York, involved the deliberate exposure of severely retarded children to a hepatitis virus (Barber 1976, 26). In the 1930s and 1940s, when one's skin color was still considered a relevant indicator of personhood, the U.S. Public Health Service conducted a longitudinal study on the effects of untreated syphilis in 399 "male Negroes" living in Macon County, Georgia (Tuskegee Syphilis Study 1973). The study was conducted without their consent even after penicillin had been discovered as a cure for syphilis.

Not only has the assumption that moral worth is based on the possession of a Kantian type rationality and moral agency led to discrimination against the mentally handicapped and ageism, in terms of denying moral status to the fetus and newborn, but it also has been used to support cultural imperialism and sexism. This Western concept of rationality has been used to legitimate the depersonalization of "primitive" peoples and those from other cultures who do not reason the way we do. Lack of rationality, as defined by the particular culture, has also long been used to justify the depersonalization of women. Aristotle, in his book *On the Generation of Animals,* compared women to lower forms of animal life on the grounds that the "rational part of the soul, which distinguishes men from the lower animals, is inoperative in women." Carol Gilligan (1982), in her book *In a Different Voice: Psychological Theory and Women's Development,* challenges as sexist the Western notion of moral development and reasoning, which emphasizes a more male-type reasoning based on abstract rules and places autonomously recognized universal principles at the pinnacle of moral reasoning (see Kohlberg 1981), rather than a "care perspective," which is more common in women.

Singer (1988) laments that the hierarchy based on sex or race has simply been replaced by one that is based on intelligence and rationality (320). This argument is sometimes backed up by a religious argument that claims that the Bible's statement that we are made in the "image of God" mean that the morally significant feature of God's image is *His* rationality and autonomy. Children have long been regarded as incomplete adults in the Western world. Using rationality as the defining characteristic of humanhood, St. Thomas divided humans into two types: perfect and imperfect. Man is perfect whereas boy is imperfect (*Summa Theologica* Q 90, 5th article). Obviously, the younger the child, the more "imperfect" he or she is.

But why choose adult rationality as the defining characteristic? Why not love and compassion? Why not interdependence? After all, humans have the most prolonged childhood of any species. The Bible also stresses our utter dependence on God, our "Father"—much as the fetus is utterly dependent on his or her mother. One might question here who was made in whose image—we in God's image or God in the image of our patriarchal culture. To make the Western adult male-type reasoning the measure of moral worth is simply to replace one sort of "ism" with another.

Also troublesome is the notion of self-consciousness as a presumably measurable quantity. Although these arguments reject the reduction of person to "brute biological criteria" (Harrison 1983, 221), implicit in them is the presumption that self-consciousness is directly related, in humans at least, to the linear development of the brain. The brain of the fetus and infant, especially the mentally handicapped fetus, is, therefore, assumed to be operating on a "primitive" level of consciousness. This assumption has not yet been proven (see especially Touwen 1984; and de Vries et al. 1984).

This Western concept of the fetus as a nonsentient entity is not shared by all cultures. For example, anthropologist Clifford Geertz (1960) reports that in Java it is believed that the "fetus doesn't eat or sleep, [instead the fetus] just meditates and learns about spiritual things. Later when the child is instructed in spiritual things he is reminded of this . . . that is why . . . a person can never talk back to his mother . . . because he meditated in her" (44). Verny (1981) points out that in our own culture

> a decade or two ago, the notion that a six-month-old fetus possessed consciousness would have been laughed at. Today, many consider it an accepted fact. A decade from now, as our techniques grow more sophisticated, that line could conceivably start at three, perhaps even two months. (195)

While "psychic individuality" requires, according to Grobstein (1988), "minimally adequate neural substrate," this minimum has not yet been defined, therefore leaving "a considerable zone of uncertainty as to the precise time of onset of psychic individuality during the developmental course" (35). In fact, we know very little about the psychological life of the unborn, let alone the psychology of the handicapped fetus. Psychiatrists and psychologists who have regressed their patients through hypnosis to birth and prebirth experience report hearing accounts such as the following, which are not uncommon and which seem to be recollections of early prenatal experience: "I am a sphere, a ball, a balloon, I am hollow, I have no arms, no legs, no teeth. . . . I float, I fly, I spin. Sensations come from everywhere. It is as though I am a spherical eye" (Verny 1981, 190).

Moral Agency

While both Tooley and Engelhardt acknowledge that there are different relevant senses of the term *personhood*, in the end they equate personhood with the ability to act as "moral agent," that is, to have the ability to make and be held responsible for moral decisions in one's life. Self-consciousness alone is not enough. Drawing heavily on the Kantian definition of persons as rational, self-conscious moral agents, the claim is made that self-consciousness and rationality are necessary conditions for personhood because only self-conscious, rational beings can act as moral agents (Tooley 1973, 86). Persons, therefore, may be defined as "moral agents, rational, able to choose freely according to a rational plan of life, and are possessed of a notion of blameworthiness and praiseworthiness" (Engelhardt, 1986, 145). Given this definition, moral treatment, as well as moral worth, "comes to depend, not implausibly, on moral agency" (Engelhardt 1982c, 96).

Strictly speaking, only persons are "protected by the moralities of mutual respect and beneficence" (Engelhardt 1986, 145). In other words, our obligation to treat others with respect depends on *their* ability to make moral judgments and to be held morally responsible for their actions. According to these criteria, then, the actions of the physicians at the Jewish Hospital and Medical Center of Brooklyn and at the Willowbrook home for severely retarded children were justified because, being unable to make reasoned moral decisions, these people had no claim to respectful treatment from their moral "superiors."

In an attempt to get around this somewhat morally repugnant conclusion, Engelhardt (1986) adds that although fetuses and young children (and other "mentally incompetent" humans) clearly are not persons "while adults exist in and for themselves as self-directive and self-conscious beings, young children, especially newborn infants, exist for their families and those who love them" (112). Therefore, we should treat young children with respect, just as we treat the property of other persons with respect, not because they have value in themselves but because they have value for their parents who are persons. Thus, while a wanted fetus should be treated with respect by others (such as the physician), a fetus or young child that is not valued by his or her parent(s) because of a genetic disorder no longer has to be treated with respect and ceases to have any right to a continued existence. If this is the case, then how does one explain the moral horror most people feel at hearing about the events at Willowbrook? After all, the parents (owners) gave their permission for their mentally retarded children to be used in these experiments.

Richard Sherlock (1987) strongly disagrees with the line of reasoning used by philosophers such Tooley and Engelhardt

> Though this distinction between 'human being' and 'person' forms no part of common law, it has a certain attractiveness of its own. Nevertheless, it is both deeply flawed. . . . The most crucial flaw in the strongest version of this maneuver is that confusion between the preconditions for moral agency and the preconditions for being a bearer of any rights at all (144).

The claim that moral treatment is conditional on one's ability to be a moral agent is contrary to the belief that certain humans, such as young children and very sick people and others who are rendered powerless due to their circumstances, can still be the bearers of rights, without at the same time being held morally responsible for their actions. In fact, as has already been pointed out, it is often their very helplessness and lack of moral agency that is cited as the reason for their deserving special moral treatment.

Social Definitions of Personhood

Participation in the Social Community

Pro-choice feminist and ethicist Beverly Harrison (1983) rejects the criteria-list approach because it eliminates too many humans from the protection of the moral community. These lists, such as Warren's, she claims, are "far too rationalistic" and focused "too exclusively on intellectual qualities" (219–20). Instead, the human becomes a person at the moment of birth, when he or she officially "joins society" (220). It is the quality of our social relationships with others, Harrison argues, that creates personal existence. Unlike the fetus, who merely exists in a biological relationship with his or her mother, the newborn is born into a "covenant of caring," a "love-relationship which is inherently personal" (223). "'Person,'" she writes, "is a moral category implying participation in a 'moral community.' . . . Morality presupposes social relations between centered beings. This is why birth is a critical juncture" (220).

Acceptance by the social community—being in a "covenantal relationship" with the community—is an important aspect of personhood since without it, an individual lacks a social role as well as the protection and support of the community. Human relationships, duties, and obligations toward others exist, Harrison maintains, within a social setting. Therefore, even though an individual woman may believe that her fetus is a person, it is difficult for her to act on this belief when there are no social institutions in place to support this relationship.

Harrison's definition of person is similar to Thomas's notion of ensoulment, whereby it is an external agent that bestows personhood on a human. However, it is no longer God but the human society that ensouls us and gives us worth in the eyes of our fellow humans. Our relationship with God is no longer the crucial relationship; instead, we acquire a social soul at birth.

The Nature of the Mother-Fetus Relationship

Traditionally, the mother and the fetus have been treated by the medical profession as one unit. It was only after birth that the physician, as well as other members of society, were confronted with two relationships. This expedient approach of treating the two as one unit, however, does not mean that in fact they are. Physically, mother and fetus are independent beings with separate brains, nervous systems, and circulatory systems. The advent of fetal therapy and the concept of the fetus as patient, as well as the use of ultrasound, which allows people to visualize the young fetus, are making people more aware of the separate identity of the fetus.

The notion of the mother and fetus as one unit also downplays the pregnant woman's ability to be in a relationship with her fetus and vice versa. If the separate identity of the fetus and the personhood of the fetus are to be socially recognized, then society has an obligation to protect and support that fetus and the maternal-fetal relationship.

Harrison (1983) replies by saying that it is only after birth that the survival of the infant depends on being in a social relationship. The very survival of the infant, unlike that of the fetus, she maintains

> depends upon the maintaining of the 'love-relationship' into which he/she is born. He depends for his existence, that is to say, upon intelligent understanding, upon rational foresight . . . the infant has a need which is not simply biological but personal, a need to be in touch with the mother and in conscious perceptual relation with her (223).

This claim that a personal need to be in a relationship does not exist before birth has not gone unchallenged. Bonding after birth, it is pointed out, is only a continuation of the bonding that started months before (Verny 1981, 74). Emotional patterns that exist after birth are an outgrowth of the prenatal relationship that is established long before birth. Verny (1981), for example, believes that the fetus communicates behaviorally with the mother as well as other people. Loud sounds, including angry voices, as well as maternal emotions, can provoke kicking on the part of the fetus (83). In support of his position, Verny notes that infants of women who emotionally rejected their fetus are crankier and more anxious (80). He cites cases such as that of a healthy newborn who refused to nurse from her mother and hypothesizes that the child's rejection of her mother stemmed from the mother's desire to abort the child (77–78).

More recently, it has been found that the fetus is sensitive to maternal anxiety surrounding the amniocentesis procedure, so much so that the anxiety, it is suggested, might actually have a detrimental effect on the psychological and physical development of the child (Rossi et al. 1989).

If, in fact, the fetus and mother are in a social relationship, and there seems to be good evidence that this is the case, then withholding personhood from the fetus privatizes what is essentially a social relationship. To deny the fetus personhood not only deprives the fetus of societal protection but also legitimates withholding from the pregnant woman the protection and support the social community gives to other participants in social and familial relationships.

Potential Personhood

A similar approach, which seems to overcome some of the problems of the earlier approaches, is that based on the notion of potential personhood.

> In order to attribute interests to a fetus that will most likely become an infant at a later stage of development . . . it is not necessary to ascribe to it the status of personhood. Nor is it necessary to assign rights to a fetus, while still a fetus, in order to recognize that the likelihood of its becoming an infant places it in need of certain protections while still in utero (Macklin 1984, 102).

Thus, the fetus is granted a sort of provisional personhood based on the fact that he or she will someday develop into a full member of human society. Applying this argument to prenatal care, Susan Johnson and Thomas Elkins (1988) counsel physicians that the intention of the mother is important in that if she plans to abort the fetus, that fetus no longer has potential to become a child and need not be treated with the same moral respect as a wanted fetus (412).

However, even a wanted fetus may fail to qualify for potential personhood status. A normal fetus (at least one who is wanted by his or her mother) has moral value, while one who, because of a severe genetic disorder lacks the potential to develop the characteristics of a person thus defined might not. In putting forth criteria for third-trimester abortions, Frank Chervenak and his colleagues (1984) argue that the anencephalic fetus can never have independent moral status and, therefore, can be aborted at any time during pregnancy. Obviously, given our emphasis on autonomy and the right to one's body, this conclusion does not entail mandatory abortion of fetuses with anencephaly. However, the reasons not to perform abortion stem from respect for the mother, not for the fetus.

Others take the potential-personhood argument even further and claim that the fetus with Tay-Sachs disease also lacks the potential to develop into a person, according to the criteria for personhood developed by philosophers Mary Anne Warren and Joseph Fletcher. One of the problems with this argument is that, like the viability argument, its definition of personhood is dependent on the current state of medical technology. If a treatment for Tay-Sachs disease is found in the next few months, then the same fetuses and infants with Tay-Sachs disease who were denied moral status before the discovery now have moral status.

The use of this argument as a means to eliminate fetuses with severe genetic disorders from the protection of the moral community is not always obvious at first glance. For example, Richard McCormick (1981), who at first glance appears to adopt a sanctity-of-life approach when he declares that "every human being, regardless of age or condition, is of incalculable worth" (166) or value, nevertheless, then turns around and qualifies this incalculable worthiness by asking "whether this undoubted value has any potential at all, in continuing physical survival, for attaining a share, even if reduced, in the 'higher,' more important good [which] . . . manifests itself in potential for developing human relationships" (ibid.). Applying this double standard of worthiness to infants with genetic disorders, he concludes that the anencephalic infant falls short of the criteria for even minimal participation in this "higher good" while "the same cannot be said of the mongoloid infant. . . . The task ahead is to attach relational potential to presumptive biological symptoms for the gray area between such extremes" (ibid.).

One problem with the application of the potential-personhood argument to fetuses with genetic disorders, such as spina bifida or Down syndrome, is that, because of the uncertainty of the prognosis before birth, their potential for personhood can only be assessed after birth (Lorber 1973; Duff and Campbell 1973). Thus, the potential-personhood argument is, in the case of the majority of genetic disorders, much more applicable to selective infanticide rather than selective abortion.

Most philosophers reject the concept of potential for personhood as a basis for granting a right to continued existence. If we found a vaccine that could potentially make dandelions rational and self-conscious, Engelhardt (1986) asks, would that entail treating all unvaccinated dandelions as persons because they now had the potential to become persons? Similarly, the fact that fetuses have the potential to become persons does not make them so. The notion of potential is confusing at best. Instead, he suggests, it is better to speak of the probability of X turning into Y. It is only when a fetus or young child actualizes his or her potential that he or she earns the right to be treated as a person.

Others also reject the notion of a potential person, but for different reasons. We are all, from the time of conception to the moment of our death, Ramsey (1970a) points out, in the "process of becoming" (11) or in the process of "self-actualization." Thus, the division between potential and actual persons is artificial.

Rejecting both the potential-personhood argument and the social definition of personhood, Theodora Ooms (1984), director of the National Center for Family Studies at the Catholic University of America, maintains that any definition of personhood in terms of one's social relationships is contrary to the tradition of American democracy, which "holds that liberty and the happiness of individuals are the supreme values and says very little about individuals' relationships with other persons or groups that may shape and qualify the nature of their autonomy" (86). Should our moral worth be dependent, she asks, on how much someone in power over us wants or values us or is willing to enter into a social covenant with us? The danger of making personhood dependent on community recognition is that whole groups of people, such as women, people of color, and Jews, have, in the past, been systematically depersonalized simply by being denied social recognition or opportunities for fulfillment as persons.

In fact, many women are still struggling to overcome the long-held belief that their worth as humans depends on their being wanted by a man. It was primarily for this reason that the early feminists opposed abortion. "When we consider that women are treated as property," Elizabeth Cady Stanton wrote in a letter to Julia Ward Howe, "it is degrading to women that we should treat our [unborn] children as property to be disposed of as we see fit" (October 16, 1878).

Also, God's special concern in the Bible for the outcast and the dispossessed should at least make Christians and Jews a little uneasy about making social acceptability and our potential to participate in the mainstream of society a criterion of personhood.

Regarding the process of denying a human personhood on the basis of lack of social potential, Lebacqz (1973) asks: "Should all persons who do not meet the 'standard of emotional involvement' be considered less than fully human—such as convicted criminals and any outcast group?" (118). The handicapped are especially, at present, denied opportunities for "emotional involvement" with the community. She points out that selective abortion of handicapped fetuses, because it involves the "assignment of relative rather than absolute value to human life on the basis of social criterion . . . violates fundamental principles of justice as we have understood these principles in Western society" (126).

Liberal Democracy and Equality of All Humans

The foundation of liberal democracy involves elimination of the notion that there are qualities that make some humans more morally valuable than others. Equality in a liberal democracy is not a statement of fact, as it is not true that all humans are equal in physical development, intelligence, ability to communicate effectively, or their experience of pleasure and pain. The equal worth of every human being is not a description but a moral ideal—"a prescription of how we ought to treat humans" (Singer 1988, 320). To be a bearer of the right to life entails only that one be in possession of the "great good," which is simply being alive.

Western Political Ideology

Modern libertarian democracy evolved as a reaction to social structures that claimed that certain humans, because of wealth or social position, religion, or nationality, were morally superior to others. The great Western philosophers Hobbes, Locke, Kant, and Rousseau all rejected the classical belief that natural rights were based on human excellence or achievement and, instead, affirmed the equal rights of all human beings as the fundamental moral principle upon which to found a political society (see Sherlock 1987, 41–43). Drawing upon this philosophical tradition, the U.S. Declaration of Independence begins with these words: "We hold these truths to be self-evident, that all men are created equal, that they are endowed by their Creator with certain unalienable Rights, that among these are Life, Liberty, and the pursuit of Happiness." These rights "are said to belong to us by nature, by mere membership in the human species, without qualification according to differences in intelligence, virtue, wisdom, beauty, strength, health, or genetic endowment" (Kass 1973, 84).

The belief in the equality of all humans is considered by many to be a fundamental tenet of the Judeo-Christian tradition as well as liberal democracy. However, the equality principle is not always consistently applied to all classes of humans. John Fletcher (1975), who is probably the most prolific writer on the subject of the morality of selective abortion, accepts the equality principle in regard to the care of newborns with birth defects:

> If we choose to be shaped by Judeo-Christian visions of the 'createdness' of life within which every creature bears the image of God, we ought to care for the 'defective newborn' as if our relation with the creator depended on the outcome. If we choose to be shaped by visions of the inherent dignity of each member of the human family, no matter what his or her predicament, we ought to care for this defenseless person as if the basis of our own dignity depended on the outcome. Care cannot fall short of this universal equality (78).

At the same time, Fletcher (1981a) adopts quite a different, less liberal, view of personhood when it comes to the fetus. No longer are "universal equality" and "inherent dignity of each member of the human family" decisive when it comes to our treatment of the fetus. Instead it is only when the fetus, through birth, "actualizes" its potential that it becomes a person (124). Thus, no longer is personhood inherent in humanness, at least when it comes to the fetus; instead, it is an achievement and must be earned.

While the idea of human equality has never been fully realized, it has been the motivating force behind much of the social criticism and progressive legislation throughout the world in the last two centuries. The preamble of the Charter of the United Nations, an organization representing more than 98 percent of the world population, begins by stressing the equality of all people and nations.

In the United States, the equality principle was the motivation behind the abolition movement. Only in the case of slavery and the current ruling on abortion, Sherlock (1987) points out, has there ever been in this country a separation between a human being and a constitutionally recognized person (203). Indeed, the current abortion issue, like slavery, he contends, has generated so much strife and division precisely because it is once again a test of our collective belief in the basic principle of equality (ibid., 266).

Medicine and Human Equality

Prenatal diagnosis followed by selective abortion, warns Lebacqz (1973), involves the "deliberate institution of medical programs designed to foster selective treatment of human life" and, because of this, "violates the fundamental principles of justice" (110). While paying lip service to the principle of democracy and equality of all people, genotype is used as an excuse to deny equal rights. With the institutionalization of prenatal diagnosis and selective abortion, we are moving in the direction of Orwell's *Animal Farm*, in which "all animals are equal, but some animals are more equal than others" (see Kass 1985).

Traditionally medicine has regarded all people as equals when it comes to treatment. British geneticist J. F. Brock (1976) writes that "the historic 'dogma' of the infinite value of the individual is the highest expression of our civilization and our medical idealism . . . [and it] must be reaffirmed again and again by the medical profession and supported by the community" (1333).

The Declaration of Geneva, adopted by the World Medical Association in 1948, grew out of a concern for the German medical profession's neglect of this principle and their complicity in the depersonalization of a specific group of humans—the Jews. The Declaration states:

> I will not permit considerations of religion, nationality, race, party politics or social standing to intervene between my duty and my patient.
>
> I will maintain the utmost respect for human life, from the time of conception; even under threat, I will not use my medical knowledge contrary to the laws of humanity (World Medical Association 1949, 109).

"One might even wonder," Kass ponders, "whether the development of amniocentesis and prenatal diagnosis may represent a backlash against these same humanitarian and egalitarian tendencies in the practice of medicine" (Kass 1985, 85).

Bok (1981) also warns of the dangers of adopting a qualification approach to personhood. She suggests that we abandon efforts, like that of Joseph Fletcher, to define personhood. The misuse of the concept of humanity, she contends, has led to

> so many practices of discrimination and atrocity throughout history. . . . To question someone's humanity or personhood is a first step to mistreatment and killing. . . . Slavery, witch-hunts and wars have been justified by their perpetuators on the grounds that they have held their victim to be less than fully human. . . . I submit that in the many borderline cases where humanity is questioned by some—the so-called 'vegetables,' the severely retarded, or the embryo—even the seemingly universal yardsticks of 'humanity' or rationality are dangerous (54–55).

Conclusion

Personhood is an elusive concept. Because most of the current definitions of personhood have evolved within the context of the abortion controversy to support a particular position, one must be especially cautious. In the past, definitions of personhood have too often been tailored to affirm the biases and conveniences of those in power.

> Precisely how individuals and societies come to have dispositions to see beings one way or another is a complex question of moral psychology, but in general terms, these perspectives must derive from social experience. Many civilizations, otherwise advanced and sophisticated, have denied the status of person to beings we clearly see as persons. This was the case of our own national history with respect to nonwhites and women . . . surely this moral blindness was interwoven with fixed patterns of social interaction that tended to obscure human similarities and highlight differences. . . . Part of the explanation for the Being

[nonperson] view [of the fetus] probably lies here. First, the fetus cannot literally be seen under ordinary circumstances and, therefore, there has traditionally been very little opportunity for interaction with it (Dougherty 1985, 113).

The majority of us are quite convinced that, had we lived "back then," we would have realized that people of color, Jews, and women were clearly persons. But would we have? Is being able to draw in air through one's lung (rather than taking oxygen in through an umbilical cord) any more rational a criterion for personhood than being able to urinate through a penis? Is one's age or size a more rational criterion than the color of one's skin? Is the level of development of one's culture any more relevant for eliminating a whole race of people from personhood than the level of development of one's body? Is the lack of physical viability any more relevant in granting "ownerhood" to those who are being depended upon, than is lack of economic viability? Are the criteria we are presently using to define the status of the fetus perhaps just as arbitrary and culturally determined as those used in the past? Are we willing to take a chance on being wrong again?

In a U.S. court of law, because of the tragedy that would result from the wrongful imprisonment or execution of a person and because of the greater power of the state, a person is presumed innocent until proven guilty. In the same manner, we are more likely to avoid moral tragedy if we also give the fetus the benefit of the doubt until we can prove beyond a reasonable doubt that he or she is not a person.

Giving the fetus the benefit of the doubt would also be consistent with the medical profession's presumption that someone is alive until it can be proven, beyond a reasonable doubt, that he or she is dead. In a similar vein, the burden should be upon those who deny that the fetus is a person with a right to continued existence to prove their position—which none of the above arguments on personhood has accomplished.

Following this line of reasoning, autonomy alone cannot be used to justify selective abortion. While autonomy or the "right to be left alone" (Elias and Annas 1987, xiii) may be "an essential feature of a pluralistic society" (Fletcher and Wertz 1987a, 306), it is not the foundational principle of a liberal democracy. Rather, it is limited by the principle of human equality and the right of all humans, no matter what their station in life, to enjoy a similar freedom. "Liberal democratic regimes begin with the belief in the equal worth of every human being, from whence they derive a commitment to individual liberty" (Sherlock 1987, 38). When other persons are involved, autonomy is not an absolute right. The vulnerability or helplessness of another human is not usually considered a legitimate reason for the stronger party's assertion of rights. In line with this belief, it is generally agreed that the rights of "weaker" humans, such as women, African-Americans, children, the elderly, and those who are seriously handicapped, should be protected by law and not rely on the goodwill of those individuals who wield power over them.

Professor of health law George Annas (1988a) writes: "If one really believes that embryos are persons from the moment of conception, their lives can hardly be left in the hands of a majority of state legislatures" (179). However, instead of concluding that we need federal laws to protect the fetus as we have to protect other persons, he concludes that decisions regarding the life of the fetus should therefore be left in the hands of individual pregnant women.

Surely, one of the primary purposes of law in a liberal democracy is to provide legislation that protects the weak from the strong. There is little doubt that women and African-Americans would not even have the rights they have today if their personhood and their right to life had been kept out of the hands of legislators and had remained a private decision to be made by those individual white men who had power over them.

Autonomy, in a liberal democracy, does not mean the right to do whatever one wants to other humans. The mother's autonomy can only be used to justify abortion on request if we first deny the fetus equal personhood, just as slavery could not be justified without first denying African-Americans equal personhood. One consequence of legally denying the fetus moral equality with other humans, as the U.S. Supreme Court did in 1973, is to weaken the very foundations of both liberal democracy and the medical profession's belief in human equality, and to instead condone a hierarchical social structure that assigns personal value on the basis of one's physical, intellectual, and/or social qualities.

If the "right to be left alone" is the "primary human value," as Elias and Annas (1987, xiii) claim, then this right has to be extended to the fetus as well. If the fetus is a person, abortion is no longer a private decision that affects only the mother but is a decision that affects at least two persons. Thus, autonomy alone is not a sufficient justification for selective abortion. Personhood entails the duty to respect other persons, a duty that often means having to share power with those in positions of lesser power.

Regarding the present trend toward the increased use of prenatal diagnosis and selective abortion in medical practice, John Fletcher and Dorothy Wertz (1987b) caution that we must be more critical of the "prevailing morality" of medical geneticists. "The major shortcoming," they maintain, "of the prevailing morality in prenatal diagnosis . . . which is strongly biased for the autonomy principle . . . is its neglect of the demands of justice and fairness" (306).

One obvious strength of the position that denies the fetus personhood is its sensitivity to the hard-won rights of women. "Given the long social history of our own cultural blindness to women's standing as persons, recognition of fetal rights appears to threaten a reversal of recent moral achievement in gender equality" (Dougherty 1985, 114). Some feminists even believe that there is "an inherent conflict between the woman's personhood and the fetus as a person with rights. If the fetus is regarded as a person," the argument goes, "then the woman is reduced to little more than a maternal environment" (Callahan 1986, 40).

At the same time, to empower women by denying an even more disenfranchised group of humans personhood only perpetuates injustice and moves the problem of discrimination to another class of humans rather than addressing the more global issue of equal rights for all humans. What needs to be explored instead are ways in which the rights of the fetus can be protected, while justice and freedom for women are maximized.

In conclusion, the various arguments presented to justify abortion by denying the fetus personhood fail to provide sufficient grounds for selective abortion. In determining whether and when selective abortion might be justified, therefore, we need to ask what kinds of justifications might override the obligation of the women, the family, and society to protect the life of the fetus. These justifications should provide clear guidelines in distinguishing acceptable and unacceptable kinds of selective abortion and between selective abortion and selective infanticide. Lastly, the justifications should be universal, covering all persons in identical circumstances (Kass 1985, 91).

7

Biomedical Justification for Selective Abortion

The eugenic argument and the fetal-wastage argument are two of the most straightforward justifications for selective abortion. The term *eugenic abortion* is sometimes used in reference to the abortion of a fetus at risk for a genetic disorder. The use of this terminology reflects the belief, at least of the great majority of nongeneticists, that prenatal diagnosis and the abortion of affected fetuses is a means to eliminate, or at least significantly reduce, genetic disease.

The fetal-wastage argument, on the other hand, points out that the great majority of embryos and fetuses with genetic disorders are lost in spontaneous miscarriages during early pregnancy. Induced selective abortion, therefore, is simply a continuation of this natural process of selection.

The Eugenic Argument

The goal of eugenics is to improve the physical and mental qualities of future generations by controlling mating and reproduction. An underlying assumption of eugenics is that there is something bad or undesirable about certain conditions, which are consequently classified as genetic diseases, and that, therefore, their elimination represents progress toward a desirable goal (Kenyon 1986, 122).

Deterioration of the Gene Pool

One claim that is sometimes used to add a sense of urgency to the eugenic justification is that the human genetic pool is deteriorating and that we must do something to halt this deterioration if we are to avoid a genetic "apocalypse." For example, Joseph Fletcher (1971) maintains that the "present increasing pollution of the human gene pool through uncontrolled sexual reproduction . . . [and] the spread of genetic disease" (779) justifies the use of compulsory genetic controls and eugenic abortion.

Geneticist Marc Lappé (1972) disagrees. Lappé presents evidence that suggests that the belief in the progressive genetic deterioration of the human race is unfounded and that we are not on the brink of a genetic apocalypse. The human "'gene pool' is, in fact, undergoing a period of stabilization, not change" (419).

While this is indeed good news, Fletcher (1971) could reply that we still have a moral obligation to do what we can to improve the human genetic pool and to reduce the number of people born with genetic disorders. "To be men," Fletcher asserts, "we must be in control. That is the first and last ethical word" (782). According to Fletcher we must actively control our genetic future instead of passively relying on the "invisible hand" of natural chance in nature.

With the increasing emphasis on autonomy and privacy in the United States, the primary agency of eugenic control has shifted from society, as was the case in Nazi Germany, to the individual (Rush 1983, 114). Most Americans, while nominally sympathetic to the eugenic goal in terms of reducing the number of serious genetic "diseases," would vehemently reject any such suggestion of state control over their reproductive lives.

The present programs of voluntary prenatal diagnosis and selective abortion, however, are not facilitating the goal of reducing genetic "disease." While the immediate effect of these programs may be a reduction in the number of newborns with genetic disorders, it is unlikely that there will be any significant reduction in deleterious genes in the gene pool as a result of these voluntary programs (Neel 1971, 222). In fact, the recent rapidly expanding use of these programs will more likely result in an overall increase in the number of deleterious genes in the population (as will be explained later in the chapter), thus working contrary to, rather than enhancing, the eugenics goal in the case of many genetic disorders.

Chromosomal Disorders

Unlike monogenic disorders, with chromosomal disorders, neither compulsory nor voluntary selective abortion of affected fetuses will significantly affect the gene pool, because chromosomal disorders are not usually inherited but are the result of errors arising during the development of gametes (ova and sperm), particularly in older women. Those children who are born with autosomal chromosomal disorders such as Down syndrome, should they live to adulthood, are usually infertile. "If all pregnant women over the age of 35 were compelled to undergo amniocentesis, 35% of all mongols [people with Down syndrome] might be eliminated by testing 8% of the total pregnancies" (Harris 1974, 59). Selective abortion of affected fetuses, however, will have little effect on the frequency of chromosomal disorders in future generations. In fact, although the actual birth rate has been decreased to 10.8 per 10,000 births through selective abortion, a recent study of the natural birth prevalence of Down syndrome in England and Wales found that this figure had actually increased slightly between 1974 and 1987 from 12.2 to 13.2 per 10,000 births (Cuckle et al. 1991).

While the small overall decline in the incidence of Down syndrome in newborns has been attributed by some to amniocentesis, in fact it is more likely due not to the greater availability of amniocentesis but to fertility reduction in older women following the legalization of hormonal contraception and unrestricted abortion (Mikkelsen et al. 1983).

Persons with the less severe sex-linked genetic disorders, such as Turner syndrome and Klinefelter syndrome, while they generally live to adulthood and may marry, are, with very few exceptions, infertile (Bergsma 1973, 555, 870). In the case of males with XYY syndrome, fertility is generally unimpaired, but, for reasons yet unknown, the syndrome is not passed on to their male offspring (Rogers and Shapiro 1986, 347).

Consequently, if the goal of eugenics is to "prevent the spread of genetic disease" (Fletcher 1979, 106), then the appropriate means for reducing chromosomal disorders in future fetuses is not selective abortion but childbearing restrictions on older women because it is mostly they, rather than the individuals affected with chromosomal disorders, who "spread the disease."

Multifactorial Disorders

The effect of prenatal diagnosis and selective abortion on the incidence of multifactorial disorders, such as anencephaly and spina bifida, is more difficult to assess because factors other than inheritance apparently are at work. The selective abortion of all fetuses with anencephaly will not reduce the rate of anencephaly in future generations because none of the infants with anencephaly ever survives to childbearing age. The same is true for children with the most severe forms of spina bifida. The risk of recurrence for a neural tube defect in the offspring of a person with a meningocele (the milder form of spina bifida), on the other hand, remains unsettled (Milunsky 1986, 497).

As with chromosomal disorders, the present programs of voluntary prenatal diagnosis and selective abortion have little or no known effect on the incidence of these disorders in future generations of fetuses. The process of prenatal diagnosis and selective abortion must be repeated each generation to prevent the birth of affected individuals.

Monogenic Disorders and Reproductive Compensation

In the case of monogenic disorders, particularly disorders carried on a recessive gene (which make up the great majority of serious genetic disorders), the long-term effect of voluntary programs of prenatal diagnosis and selective abortion may be an actual increase in the number of "defective" genes in the gene pool. Before the advent of prenatal diagnosis, parents who gave birth to a child with a serious disorder tended to refrain from having any more children (Neel 1971, 222). An estimated 10 to

25 percent of parents who have had a child with a serious disorder will refrain from having more children unless prenatal diagnosis is available (Milunsky 1986, 2). For couples with a 25 to 50 percent risk of having a child with a monogenic disorder because one or both of the parents are known to be carriers, this figure increases to 50 to 90 percent (Cohen 1984). There seems to be a consensus that the availability of prenatal diagnosis and selective abortion encourages couples to take risks that they would not have previously taken (Berg 1983, 265; Fletcher 1986, 848). Today, many parents use amniocentesis, rather than limiting their family size, to avoid the birth of a child with a genetic disorder (Blumberg et al. 1975, 205).

When women have another child to replace a fetus lost through selective abortion, it is known as "reproductive compensation" (Kevles 1985, 286). Many physicians argue that the loss through selective abortion of a small number of fetuses with serious disorders is outweighed by the higher number of normal children who will be born as a result of prenatal diagnosis and selective abortion because high-risk couples no longer have to forego more children (Milunsky 1986, 2). It is also pointed out that the availability of amniocentesis could be said to be responsible for preserving and promoting life by reducing the number of needless abortions based solely on the probability that a fetus might have a particular disorder (Berg 1983; Rush 1983). Therefore selective abortion, the argument concludes, actually has a "pro-life" effect for many couples (Rowley 1984, 140).

On the other hand, many of these children without disorders, who would not have been born if prenatal diagnosis and selective abortion had not been available, will be carriers of inherited, deleterious recessive genes and will likely pass these genes on to future generations. Given the nature of most recessive genetic disorders, which are targeted for selective abortion, it is unlikely that the deleterious gene will be passed on by an individual actually affected by the disorder.

Most recessive disorders severe enough to warrant abortion, such as Tay-Sachs disease, lead to death long before the affected person reaches reproductive age. The majority of people with cystic fibrosis, the most common serious recessive disorder among people of northern European descent, do not marry and have children. Of those who do marry, 98 percent of the males are infertile (Jones 1982).

If a recessive disorder is mild enough not to interfere with childbearing, then the ethical question is raised about whether the disorder is serious enough to justify selective abortion in the first place. Also, even with certain milder disorders, such as sickle cell anemia, the disorder is being genetically transmitted primarily through the carriers, who outnumber the affected individuals and are often unaware that they are carriers of the recessive gene.

With an autosomal recessive genetic disorder when both parents are carriers, one-half of the children, on average, will also be carriers and only one-fourth will be affected. However, if reproductive compensation is practiced and each affected fetus "replaced" with a nonaffected fetus, there would be a two-in-three chance, rather than a one-in-two chance, that these nonaffected children will be carriers who could pass on the recessive gene to the next generation (Kevles 1985, 286). Therefore, the proportion of carrier children in a family that practices "replacement compensation" will be higher by at least 50 percent than that in a family that has the same number of children and does not seek prenatal diagnosis and selective abortion or that limits the size of their family to avoid having children with a specific disorder.

With X-linked recessive disorders, such as Duchenne muscular dystrophy, the rate of increase of an abnormal gene in the gene pool may be even higher if selective abortion is used as a means to avoid the birth of a child with the disorder. Given the still imprecise nature of most indirect DNA testing for monogenic disorders, the mother, if she knows she is a carrier, may use amniocentesis to determine the sex of the fetus and then abort any male fetus based on the 50 percent chance that he may have inherited the deleterious gene. Without prenatal diagnosis and selective abortion, only one-fourth of the children, on average, would be afflicted and one-fourth would be carriers. With prenatal diagnosis and the abortion of all male fetuses one-half, on average, rather than one-fourth, of the children (daughters) born will be carriers who can pass on the gene to future generations. Thus, prenatal diagnosis and the abortion of male fetuses will not cut down on the frequency of the deleterious gene but will at least double the number in the gene pool each generation (Lebacqz 1973, 124).

Part of this trend toward reproductive compensation could be due, in part, to a lack of knowledge in the general population about genetics, especially about what it means to be a carrier. In a 1987 study in Belgium of 105 families that had children with cystic fibrosis, 87 percent of the families were aware of the 25 percent risk of having a child with the disorder in subsequent pregnancies, while all were unaware of the probability that their own healthy children could be carriers (Denayer et al. 1990).

The inheritance of dominant genetic disorders works somewhat differently in that the disorder is transmitted, except in the case of fresh mutations, by a person with the disorder rather than by a carrier. Huntington disease, which is carried on an autosomal dominant gene, is unusual because it does not generally manifest itself until after the person with the disorder has already had children. Thus, the abortion of fetuses with this genetic disorder would have the effect of diminishing the frequency of the gene in the gene pool. However, the abortion of fetuses with Huntington disease raises ethical issues of its own because, for the greater part of the affected people's lives they live a normal, pain-free, productive life. In a few cases, they may live their entire life symptom free. Woodie Guthrie is a good example of a person with Huntington disease who made great contributions to society and his family before succumbing to the disease in his later years.

Consequently, with the exception of some dominant disorders that do not interfere with childbearing, the carriers of these genes are at greater danger from a eugenics point of view than are those who are actually afflicted with the disorder. Thus, it is the so-called replacement children, whose numbers are growing as a direct result of voluntary programs of prenatal diagnosis

and selective abortion, and not their afflicted siblings, who are—
to use Joseph Fletcher's term—"Typhoid Mary's" spreading
their disease to future generations.

**The Eugenic Goal and Mandatory v. Voluntary Prenatal
Diagnosis and Selective Abortion**

The present program of voluntary prenatal diagnosis and
selective abortion is directly contrary to the eugenic goal and, in
fact, has the effect of "polluting" the gene pool rather than
improving it. The only way, therefore, to support the eugenics
justification of prenatal diagnosis and selective abortion is to
subordinate parental autonomy to the goal of eugenics and to
introduce compulsory prenatal testing and selective abortion. If
such a program is to be successful from a eugenics point of view,
it should be targeting for abortion the phenotypically normal
carriers, rather than only those affected with a genetic disorder.

The implementation of a eugenically sound program, therefore, would involve careful prenatal monitoring of all at-risk
women and mandatory selective abortion of any fetus who carries a deleterious gene or sterilization of all carriers before they
reach childbearing age. In addition to satisfying the eugenics
goal, compulsory testing would also ensure "higher compliancy
rates, lower unit costs, timely execution and facilitation of
recordkeeping of incidence and outcome" (Rowley 1984, 141).

Despite their professed interest in reducing the incidence of
genetic disorders and the economic savings that is involved,
few Americans would be willing to go along with such a program. Indeed, it is ironic, Ramsey (1970a) points out, that "some
geneticists who are most pessimistic about the rapid deterioration of the genetic pool under the conditions of modern life,
are also the most insistent upon the use of voluntary means
only" (16).

It is unlikely that the abortion of carriers, or even all affected
fetuses, will be carried out by most parents voluntarily. Because
prenatal diagnosis is readily available, many prospective parents
who might be at high risk refuse to undergo voluntary carrier
screening before pregnancy (Ambani et al. 1989). A study of

ninety-one people at risk for Huntington disease revealed that only 74 percent of these people would voluntarily take a test to see whether they had the deleterious gene (Lappé 1987, 7). Similar tests reported a 56 to 84 percent compliance rate (ibid.).

Much of the reluctance to participate in compulsory genetic screening is due to problems relating to privacy and confidentiality (Annas and Coyne 1975, 488), as well as the lifelong stigma of being a carrier, a stigma that cannot be erased as can a poor credit rating (Lappé 1987, 7).

Defining Eugenic Normalcy

McGill University professor of epidemiology and biostatistics Abby Hoffman (1991) believes that the dominant means of defining differences between individuals today is by reference to their DNA codes. She refers to this as "geneticization" (19). The establishment of programs of compulsory genetic screening and prenatal diagnosis would necessarily involve the establishment of legal standards of genetic normalcy and legal pressure on women to abort their fetuses should they fall outside this norm. One problem with this, however, is that normalcy is often defined in terms that serve the interests of those in power.

In the early 1970s state-run screening programs were established for sickle cell anemia in blacks. Similar programs were also established for Tay-Sachs disease, although they were carried out primarily by synagogues and other private organizations. In what has been called a "new sickle cell crisis" (Powledge 1974, 37), mandatory sickle cell testing programs, which were often politically motivated, were set up with concerns for confidentiality secondary. Those states that passed laws requiring sickle cell testing for blacks were "met with charges by blacks of attempted genocide" (ibid., 141). Individuals with positive results often suffered from a deterioration in their self-image and found themselves discriminated against for purposes of marriage, employment, and insurance (Rowley 1984, 141).

Because virtually everyone carries a small number of deleterious recessive genes (Lappé et al. 1972, 1130) everyone should be tested, if programs are to be nondiscriminatory as well as

eugenically effective. In addition to the "load of genetic deficiency" we inherited (usually unknown to us) from previous
generations, "one out of every five persons now living bears a
deleterious mutation that has arisen with him and which he will
pass on to or through any offspring he may have" (Ramsey
1970a, 3). In fact, fresh mutations may account for as many as
one-third of the cases of Duchenne muscular dystrophy and as
many as one-half of other recessive disorders (Harris 1974, 23).
In other words, we are all, as Ramsey (1970a) puts it, "fellow
mutants" (9). Each of us is eugenically suspect and a candidate
for prenatal diagnosis. Consequently, singling out only certain
so-called high-risk groups for compulsory testing raises the issue
of discrimination and a violation of equal rights for these groups.

Even if all of us "fellow mutants" were required to undergo
genetic screening and prenatal diagnosis, one would still have
to justify the coercion involved and the disregard of individual
autonomy, as well as the discrimination against those fetuses
who fall outside the norms. "Enforced cleaning of the gene
pool—by means of compulsory abortion of defective fetuses,
mandatory sterilization of carriers of hazardous genes, a refusal
to treat or care for victims of genetic disease," bioethicist Daniel
Callahan (1973) writes, ". . . would go a long way toward doing
away with liberal individualism" (18).

There seems to be, it has been suggested, an uncomfortably
strong parallel between the Nazi programs of eugenic abortion
and the present use of selective abortion to "weed out inferior
humans" (Brennan 1983, 23). Not everyone, however, agrees
that the danger is the same. While acknowledging the similarity,
Edward Kenyon (1986), author of *The Dilemma of Abortion*, notes
that most scientific advances can be used for good or evil and
should not be discarded simply on the grounds that they may be
misused. If we keep the ideal of informed consent foremost, he
argues, then this eugenic nightmare will not repeat itself
(132–33).

On the other hand, the eugenic goal itself, even without state
enforcement, carries a coercive element. With the establishment
of more accurate and widely available prenatal diagnostic tech-

niques, it is all too likely that "pressure will be put on parents to make the right decision," eugenically speaking (Allen, 1979, 37). Many Americans believe that our constitutional "right to privacy," as put forth by *Roe v. Wade* in 1973, will prevail over the need for "protection of the public from disease" (Green and Capron 1982, 495–96). However, it should be remembered that the present right to abortion, as stated by *Roe v. Wade*, is based on the depersonalization of the fetus. Denying the fetus the status of personhood rather than strengthening the woman's right to voluntarily undergo prenatal diagnosis and selective abortion, could actually threaten women's rights if the emphasis is on eugenics. "In a situation where the fetus has no inherent rights and genetic health becomes an overriding value," Lebacqz (1973) cautions, "compulsory amniocentesis and abortion is a logical outcome" (124). Eugenics, therefore, coupled with the present depersonalization of the fetus, rather than increasing a woman's autonomy, could very likely trap her into "forced choices," whether legal or social.

Genetic Variability and Species Adaptability

Some geneticists oppose the eugenic goal, not because of the compulsory element involved, but because they feel the goal itself is intrinsically misguided:

> Within our species, differences in gene frequencies from one population to another should not be seen as a lamentable basis for hierarchizing into 'inferior' and 'superior' groups, but rather as a deposit of richness. . . . Genetic load is the price in genetic disease for conserving adaptability in the species (Lebel 1978, 33–34).

Genetic variability is, therefore, not something we should weed out through eugenic abortion but an "investment in future adaptations . . . It is a load, we should be ready and willing to bear" (Lappé 1972, 423). Furthermore, there is a real danger, Lappé cautions, that separating humans on the basis of their eugenic worth will lead to a deterioration of the medical ideal of "nondiscriminative prenatal and postnatal care" (ibid., 426).

This "lack of respect for the diversity of nature itself," theologian Matthew Fox (1983) maintains, stems in part from our rather narrow Judeo-Christian image of God as a "normal" male and our profound failure to celebrate the image of God in "the diversity of nature or creation itself" (296).

Conclusion

In summary, the eugenic argument for prenatal diagnosis and selective abortion cannot be used to justify the present programs of prenatal diagnosis and selective abortion. Not only is the present objective of eugenics a doubtful goal in terms of the future genetic health of humankind, but, because voluntary prenatal diagnosis and selective abortion work directly contrary to the eugenics goal, the only way to justify selective abortion based on eugenic grounds is to introduce a compulsory element. Compulsion in a liberal democracy is justified only when it is the only way to serve a greater good, such as the protection of individual human dignity and rights. The eugenic justification involves infringement on the freedom of would-be parents as well as on the rights of the fetus and others who may fall outside socially established norms. The eugenic justification turns prenatal diagnosis and selective abortion not into a choice but into a tyranny of the survival of the gene pool and the "normal" over the survival of human freedom and diversity.

The Fetal-Wastage Justification

Selective Abortion as a Means of Assisting Mother Nature

The fetal-wastage justification of selective abortion is a variation of the eugenics argument based on nature, rather than humans, as the genetic engineer. Close to two-thirds of all pregnant women spontaneously loose their embryos by the twelfth week of gestation (Edmonds et al. 1982), and more will miscarry during the latter two trimesters. All in all, it is estimated that as few as 22 percent of all conceptions ever make it to birth (Lebel 1978, 14).

The rate of loss for embryos and fetuses with chromosomal and genetic defects is apparently much higher than the rates for normal embryos and fetuses. Up to 60 percent of spontaneous abortuses have been found to have chromosomal abnormalities (Boué et al. 1975, 11). For reasons yet unknown, the 45, X genotype (Turner syndrome) is the most common chromosomal abnormality found in spontaneous abortuses, accounting for almost 20 percent of all cases. More than 99 percent of conceptions involving a 45, X genotype end in spontaneous abortion (Rogers and Shapiro 1986, 349). Of those that survive into the second trimester, about two-thirds will spontaneously miscarry before term (Hook et al. 1989, 855). On the other hand, there is little evidence that 47, XXX, 47, XYY, or 47, XXY genotypes are more likely to spontaneously abort than are normal fetuses following a midtrimester amniocentesis (ibid.). The excess rate of spontaneous midtrimester abortion (i.e., the rate above normal for this time in gestation) for a 47, +18—Edwards syndrome—fetus is slightly less at 63.8 percent, while the chance of a fetus with Down syndrome (47, +21) spontaneously aborting in midtrimester is 25.6 percent above the average (ibid.).

Given these figures, it is has been hypothesized that most of the remaining abortuses probably also had some sort of genetic defect (Callahan 1970, 116). While this seems to be a reasonable conclusion, some people take it even further, moving out of the realm of scientific description of a natural phenomenon and into the realm of value judgments by concluding that selective abortion is a means of "expediting mother nature, for," as Mary Seller (1976) puts it, "nature makes a definite statement about the fate of abnormal fetuses" (139). Thus, selective abortion is viewed in terms of fulfilling some sort of "natural law" by carrying out what nature failed to do in a particular case—a means of "weeding out conditions which natural selection would in any case discard" (Lebel 1978, 14).

Given the fact that about three embryos/fetuses are spontaneously lost for every one that makes it to birth, the loss of an embryonic life comes to be regarded as a necessary process in the production of a normal child. For example, Rebecca Cook

(1985), of the Columbia University School of Public Health, sees little difference, ethically speaking, between the spontaneous abortion of fetuses with disorders and selective abortion. If we tolerate this loss by chance, then we are being inconsistent, she concludes, if we will not tolerate it as a deliberate process (214). In fact, the loss of these fetuses, whether through natural or induced abortion, is regarded as a means of enhancing life.

Using an argument similar to the reproductive-compensation argument, Cook (1985) writes: "The availability of prenatal diagnosis followed by selective legal abortion, is the condition of creation of healthy human lives. . . . Refusing selective abortion is to sacrifice the [normal] lives denied existence by legal prohibition of abortion" (216–17). Selective abortion is now given the status of a life-giving process, whereby fetuses with disorders, who were overlooked by nature in the natural "weeding out" process, are removed or sacrificed to make way for healthy normal children who otherwise would not have a chance to be born. Thus, in the total picture, there is a quantitative gain rather than an overall loss of human life.

In this regard, it is interesting to note that the word *amniocentesis* comes from the Greek *amnion,* meaning "lamb," and *kentesis,* meaning "puncture." "The image of the sacrificial lamb conjured up by the Greek etymology of 'amniocentesis' is more than accidental," Lappé (1973) points out. "In order to allow the birth of those free of genetic disease, it is necessary to kill those affected by it" (8). He notes how blithely, since the legalization of abortion, society has come to accept this equation (ibid.).

Do We Have a Duty to Unconceived Normal Humans?

Underlying the fetal-wastage position is the same assumption found in the eugenic argument: It is not desirable to have handicapped children around and, therefore, they should be eliminated, whether by social mandate or by nature, to make room for so-called normal people. Humans, like consumer products that are replaced or discarded if they are found to be faulty, are seen as means to certain ends rather than as ends in themselves.

This notion of humans as disposable runs contrary not only to medical tradition but also to the basic beliefs of liberal democracy and the Judeo-Christian tradition. It cannot be sustained without first denying the personhood and moral value of the fetus with a genetic disorder and, second, by presupposing that we have a moral obligation to unconceived "normal" fetuses.

There seems to be a rather odd unspoken assumption here that there is somewhere a warehouse of "normal" preconceived children just clamoring to be conceived and that we are somehow harming them by not allowing them to be conceived. If one carries this reasoning to its logical conclusion, it appears that there is a duty not only to abort fetuses with genetic disorders to make room for normal fetuses but also to conceive as many children as possible because not to do so is to "deny possible children the prospect of life" (Cook 1985, 216).

This belief that possible and as yet unconceived children, as long as they are "normal," have a right to life is difficult to sustain, because one of the conditions normally assumed necessary for being the bearer of any rights is that one at least exists. Logically, "what does not exist cannot be the subject or bearer of anything" (de George 1981, 202). If this is the case, then it makes no sense to speak about duties of any sort to nonexistent beings (or, more accurately, nonbeings). "We owe them nothing and they have no legitimate claim on us for the simple reason that they do not exist" (ibid.). From this, it follows that parents do not have a moral obligation to unconceived children.

No one or no generation, therefore, can be expected to sacrifice their lives for future, nonexistent beings. Thus, there are no moral grounds to justify the sacrifice of existing fetuses, even if they do have a genetic disorder, solely for future, nonexistent normal fetuses or children.

The claim that we have a duty to increase the number of normal people in the world is further weakened by the arguments of the crisis environmentalists and the family planners who regard many of the present problems of the world, such as pollution, depletion of resources, and poverty, as a direct result of overpopulation (Dyke 1977, 34–37). Although these two groups differ on what is the most desirable means to reduce population growth, both believe that parents have a moral duty to limit the size of their families.

Discrimination against High-Risk Fetuses

There are two other questionable assumptions of the fetal-wastage argument. First, there are plenty of fetuses, so the loss of a few isn't really all that bad because they can easily be replaced. Second, being a member of a medical high-risk group diminishes one's moral worth. This sort of misguided reassurance—that it isn't so bad to lose a child because you can always have another one—is sometimes offered to couples who have just had a miscarriage or lost a sick or severely handicapped child. If all humans really are created equal, as our Declaration of Independence claims, then the use of odds of survival as a reason for depersonalization betrays the very basic moral principle of equality of all persons by making some (healthy people) "more equal" than others.

This numbers game can also lead one to some rather odd conclusions about who should be aborted. The percent of 45, X (Turner syndrome) embryos and fetuses who spontaneously abort is apparently much higher than for most other chromosomal disorders that clinically have much more severe effects on the individual. Yet most people would argue that the abortion of a female fetus with Turner syndrome is less justifiable than the selective abortion of a trisomy 18 (Edwards syndrome) fetus, most of whom die shortly after birth.

Discrimination against members of high-risk groups is also directly contrary to the ethos of the medical profession; it is precisely those people in high-risk groups who have traditionally been the focus of medical care. The percentage of people with acquired immunodeficiency syndrome (AIDS) or some types of cancers, such as childhood leukemia, who will die as a result of their affliction is even greater than the percentage of embryos with genetic disorders who spontaneously abort.

Nature, too, one could logically infer, makes a "definite statement" about the fate of these other afflicted people. If spontaneous abortion should be viewed as nature eliminating the abnormal, why can't cancer or other diseases, such as AIDS, be seen as nature exhibiting an intention to eliminate a certain segment of the population? Indeed, the nature's-intentions argument has been used to oppose funding for more research for AIDS by claiming, much to the chagrin of most medical professionals, that AIDS is nature's way of dealing with homosexuals and that we should not interfere with the natural weeding out process of this so-called aberrant element in human society (see Paul Cameron, *Family Research;* Newsletter of the Family Research Institute, Inc., Washington, D.C., for an example of this type of reasoning).

As a rule, however, when it comes to postnatal fatal or debilitating diseases, we generally regard someone who "beats the odds" as showing a strong will to live and regard their survival as an event to be celebrated, rather than as grounds for euthanasia because the majority of victims of this particular condition are naturally "wasted" or killed by it.

Confusion of Natural with Desirable

The naturalistic approach to selective abortion "confuses the distinction between biological events which medical practice has traditionally attempted to stop, and the traditional bias for the preservation of human life, which has characterized the profession" (Lebel 1978, 14). The medical profession does not, with very few exceptions, capitulate in the fact of their ignorance in treating afflicted people and propose instead to assist nature by eliminating those that they cannot help. Indeed, much of medicine involves interfering with what might be termed "nature's purposes" and does not at all equate natural with desirable. Lejeune (1970) writes, regarding selective abortion as a continuation of a natural process:

For millennia, medicine has striven to fight for life and health and against disease and death. Any reversal of these terms of reference would entirely change medicine itself. It happens that nature does condemn. Our duty has always been not to inflict the sentence but to try to commute the pain (128).

Conclusion

The fetal-wastage justification of prenatal diagnosis and selective abortion, like the eugenics justification, not only involves a tyranny of the "normal" but also makes the claim that there must be a certain standard of health as a prerequisite for continued medical care, an assumption that is, as Lejeune (1970) and others point out, contrary to the traditional medical ethos.

The fetal-wastage argument also confuses natural with desirable. This assumption, while being questionable in other areas of human existence, is contrary to the traditional goal of medicine, which is to actively interfere with nature when it causes pain and suffering to humans.

8

Social-Burden Justification for Selective Abortion

The social-burden argument justifies selective abortion by point-ing to the harms caused by the disproportionate demands that people with serious genetic disorders make on public resources. However, like the eugenic argument, the social burden argu-ment can only be supported if one accepts that it is morally acceptable for society to discriminate against fetuses on the basis of handicap, a position that is considered morally repugnant in the treatment of born people. The argument is further weakened by the fact that the handicap experienced by most people with genetic disorders is, for the most part, a result of oppressive and discriminatory social structures rather than an inherent aspect of their condition.

The Argument

Our Duty to Promote the Common Good

Even if one rejects the biomedical justifications of selective abortion, society's interests can still be invoked to justify selec-tive abortion if the costs to society of caring for people with genetic disorders can be shown to be a heavier burden than the collective members of a society should reasonably be expected to bear. In these cases, society might have reasonable grounds for regulating reproduction (Joseph Fletcher 1979, 124). As parent-citizens, it is argued, people have a duty to act for the common good and to cooperate in promoting this good by not bringing to birth children who will be an intolerable burden on society.

Selective abortion is regarded by many as an acceptable means to avoid these burdens and reduce overall human suffering. In addition to the burden the disorder places on the fetus in terms of the pain and anguish suffered and a severely compromised "quality of life," the adverse effects on the family, both emotional and financial, and the cost to society, primarily in terms of the burdens placed on societal resources, are two reasons most frequently cited for the justification of both selective abortion and selective infanticide (Shaw et al. 1977, 593).

In the United States, where family autonomy is a strong ideal, family and individual considerations are generally held to be most important (ibid.). In socialist societies, on the other hand, the order of these priorities is more likely to be reversed, with the interests of society being given priority over the rights of the individual family members. The social justification of selective abortion is "pragmatic, rather than humanistic," in its orientation (Murray 1974, 196). It is oriented toward the collective good rather than the satisfaction of individual interests. Those who accept this justification are, consequently, willing to limit the range of choices for individual citizens in certain circumstances because they believe that other values, such as the reduction of avoidable anxiety and suffering, and social and economic costs are more important.

When the adverse social consequences of a particular disease are severe enough, the state's interest in promoting the health and well-being of its citizens can override or limit a citizen's right to privacy and self-determination. Mandatory, rather than voluntary, participation in programs designed to reduce the social burden of a disease is justified on the grounds that one can generally expect greater compliance under mandatory legislation (Powledge 1974, 30). The expected compliance for compulsory phenylketonuria (PKU) testing of newborns in Massachusetts, for example, was about 90 percent (ibid.).

Compulsory vaccination for certain debilitating diseases, such as polio and smallpox, quarantine of those with contagious diseases, premarital testing for sexually transmitted diseases, carrier testing for sickle cell anemia, and compulsory screening programs in hospitals for PKU have all been made mandatory in different states at different times.

Health as a Precondition for Social Worth

One of the reasons the state claims an interest in protecting the life of the fetus in the first place is the contributions, economic as well as cultural, that these individuals may someday make to the community (Rush 1983, 133). Sumner Twiss (1974) explains this model in an article on the different models of genetic responsibility.

> In order to meet present and future social needs, it should be recognized that society has a stake in maximizing the number of useful people with "social worth" who have the capacity to satisfy such needs. Conversely, society has a stake in minimizing the number of people likely to become public charges and therefore burden society's resources. Thus it might be argued that in order to further the common good, society may, and perhaps should, undertake measures to ensure that each individual is born as healthy as possible and to avoid so far as possible the costs of caring for the genetically defective (256).

In our society health, as is evidenced by the boom in health clubs and health foods, is often seen as a "precondition for an even more important and highly held value, individual achievement" (Sorenson 1974, 170). Because one's social (and personal) worth is tied up with one's state of health in an achievement oriented society, people with disabling handicaps generally suffer from social stigmatization and discrimination to an even greater extent than do members of minority groups (ibid., 172).

Cost-Benefit Calculations

The perceived burden to society of individuals with genetic disorders is usually measured in monetary cost-benefit terms.

Even though the number of individuals born with genetic disorders may be low, the cost of caring for these people can be very high. Therefore, the expense and social inconvenience of keeping alive an individual with a genetic disorder must be weighed against the needs of the many.

Also, the cost of prenatal diagnosis has to be taken into consideration. Prenatal diagnosis, as a procedure, can be regarded as cost-effective only if it is followed by selective abortion of fetuses with genetic disorders.

In keeping with this approach, elaborate cost-benefit analyses have been performed for various genetic disorders to demonstrate how selective abortion would significantly reduce financial burdens to the state as well as individual members of society. For example, Milunsky (1973) estimates that the cost of full-time institutional care for a person with a disorder such as Down syndrome who lives to the age of fifty is "about thirty-two times the cost of prevention through prenatal diagnosis and therapeutic abortion" (166–67). The cost of maintaining a child with Tay-Sachs disease in an institution in 1986 was approximately $2,250 a month (Colen 1986, 40). The majority of this expense is often paid through publicly funded programs, such as Medicaid.

Another outstanding benefit to society of selective abortion occurs if the aborted fetus is subsequently replaced with a normal fetus (Blank 1982, 363). Because selective abortion is frequently followed by reproductive compensation, socially mandated prenatal diagnosis and selective abortion would not only serve to reduce the burden severely handicapped people place on societal resources but also would actually lead to an enhancement of the social good by maximizing the number of useful people with "social worth." Consequently, a mandatory program of prenatal diagnosis and selective abortion cannot be criticized on the grounds that it prevents parents from exercising their right to have a family, because they are free and in fact encouraged, except in rare instances in which both parents are affected homozygotes, to try again for a "normal" child.

Mandatory Selective Abortion and the Social Good

A program of mandatory prenatal diagnosis and selective abortion, although it would very likely be resisted initially by those who place individual freedoms over concerns for the social good, is a real possibility in the United States. The woman's right to an abortion in the latter part of her pregnancy is already limited by *Roe v. Wade* because of the state's interest in protecting potential human life. By logical extension, it could be argued that the state may also claim to have a compelling interest in eliminating particularly burdensome potential lives.

The savings to the state of a mandatory program of prenatal diagnosis and selective abortion, as has been pointed out, could be considerable. Such a program would not be without precedence. Legislation of the state's interest in the health of future citizens is already exemplified in laws restricting marriage of those who are found to have specific types of venereal disease. How the Supreme Court might weigh the state's monetary interests against the claim that mandatory prenatal diagnosis violates an individual's right of privacy or bodily integrity remains an open question. In a time of increasing costs of social service programs and decreasing budgets, "mandatory amniocentesis may in fact approach mandatory abortion" (Green and Capron 1974, 76).

Analysis

Making Cost-Benefit Calculations

The social cost-benefit argument, while it appears to provide a reasonable justification of selective abortion, turns out not to be as easily calculable or unbiased as it first appears. In fact, it is questionable whether it is even possible, in the majority of cases, to accurately analyze social worth (Twiss 1974, 257).

The selective abortion of fetuses with disorders that have relatively predictable prognoses, such as Tay-Sachs disease, appears to be relatively easy to justify if one accepts the basic premises of the social burden argument, because of the heavy financial burden these children put on medical and social resources and their presently predictable lack of potential to make any cultural or monetary contributions to society. In calculating burden, however, it is not the medical severity of a genetic disorder that should serve as the primary factor in deciding whether the state has a legitimate interest in the abortion of a fetus with a genetic defect, but rather the total burden that child will, during his or her lifetime, place on social resources as opposed to the contributions he or she may make.

The state, for example, would have a less compelling interest in passing legislation regarding the selective abortion of infants with anencephaly than those with Tay-Sachs disease because, except for expenses incurred in prenatal care and delivery, anencephalic infants rarely survive more than a few hours after birth and hence use little of society's valuable resources. On the other hand, society also would have no interest in preserving the life of fetuses with anencephaly because there is no chance they will make any significant material contributions to society.

While the costs of caring for children with these two disorders are relatively easy to calculate, for most genetic disorders the calculation of potential social benefits and burdens is not so easy, because the majority are "notoriously variable" in their expression (Powledge 1974, 49). The task of drawing the line between a socially tolerable burden and one that is unacceptable becomes especially formidable in the face of such unpredictability. The severity of spina bifida, for example, is very difficult, if not impossible in many cases, to predict even after birth (Kolata 1980, 8). Decisions about the social worth of an affected child's life before birth are even more of a guessing game. While some children with spina bifida die despite the tremendous medical resources used to save them, 70 percent of those who do live to adulthood are employed in normal full-time occupations (Laurence and Beresford 1976, 197).

Down syndrome is another disorder that is a favorite target of social cost-benefit analysis. Although Down syndrome has a less variable prognosis than spina bifida, it does not always or even usually lead to institutionalization or lifelong financial dependence. Many adults with Down syndrome work at productive, albeit simple, jobs in the community.

The benefits associated with abortion for sex selection for X-linked disorders is even more difficult to assess. In the case of Duchenne muscular dystrophy, the state would have to calculate whether the average burden associated with providing services for a person with Duchenne muscular dystrophy would outweigh the equal probability that a male fetus might be normal and develop into a socially useful member of society.

Pertinent to such a calculation is the question of whether the money and resources saved by not having to provide care for a person with Duchenne muscular dystrophy for, on average, fifteen years (Riccardi 1977, 82) would justify the loss of an equal number of people who might put in forty to forty-five years of productive work in the community. In addition, most people with Duchenne muscular dystrophy, although physically impaired, do not suffer from any type of mental impairment and sometimes make significant contributions to society—contributions that would be lost through a program of mandatory selective abortion.

Genetic disorders with a late onset, such as Huntington disease, present the cost-benefit analyst with a similar set of problems. Individuals with this genetic disorder generally lead a productive life until middle age, at which time gradual deterioration sets in, in most cases necessitating extensive care and usually institutionalization. In calculating the social burden of Huntington disease, the years of productivity have to be weighed against the cost of care after the onset of the symptoms.

Thus, for the majority of genetic disorders, the uncertainty of the prognosis makes calculation of the social worth of an affected fetus purely on the probability of a particular outcome "a notoriously perilous undertaking" (Twiss 1974, 257).

The proper allocation of social benefits is a concept "rich in ambiguities." Should we be more concerned about "extended highway systems," resources for "luxuriant leisures," or "national defense" than "providing health care for persons with genetic defects?" (Gustafson 1974, 214) Even if we do mandate selective abortion, there is no political guarantee that resources saved by reducing the number of births of children with genetic disorders will be directed toward better health care or other worthy social goods.

Should resources for the support of those with genetic disorders ever become an unbearable social burden, then, when there is an uncertain prognosis, infanticide or adult euthanasia, once the individual is no longer productive, seems to be a more rational choice of action from a social cost-benefit perspective. However, until the point when there is an actual burden present, it is difficult to justify.

Implications for Infanticide and Euthanasia of Individuals Who Are Social Burdens

The line between normal and abnormal or acceptable and unacceptable social burdens is not the only line that must be drawn if we as a society are to select who should live and who should die. A line also must be drawn with respect to time. Once we have established a criterion that justifies the selective abortion of a fetus with a particular genetic disorder, what's to stop us, Lebacqz (1973) asks, from using the same arguments to justify infanticide of those disabled newborns who were not identified by prenatal diagnosis (123)? If we are dealing not with a fetus or a newborn with spina bifida but with a four- or fourteen-year-old child, it should be asked, "Why should not the social costs to society, 'tilt against treatment' in these cases as well?" (Heymann and Holtz 1975, 400)

Joseph Fletcher (1973) maintains that the grounds used for ending the life of a "terribly defective fetus" in utero ought, if we are to be consistent in our moral reasoning, also to oblige us to end this same sort of existence later in life (115). By applying the same yardstick of universality, the tables can be turned by pointing out that if we are unwilling to commit infanticide on the grounds that these infants will be a burden, then we should also be unwilling to commit selective abortion on these same grounds (Ramsey 1970b).

Several people, including John Fletcher (1981a), contend that the reasons used to justify selective abortion will never cross the line of birth to justify infanticide of these same individuals. He believes that the adoption of a social policy of selective infanticide of newborns with genetic disorders, as opposed to a social policy of selective abortion, would not be prudent because it would undermine the optimal moral condition for the "beginning" of life: "the experience of trust . . . a society that supports acceptance of defective newborns, where reasonably possible, does more to nurture patterns of acceptance in parents and thus reinforces the child's basic trust in the world's trustworthiness" (77).

In addition to his medically incorrect assumption that life does not begin until the moment of birth, many people take exception to Fletcher's double standard regarding the acceptable limits of treatment of born as opposed to unborn humans. For example, Rosalyn Darling (1979), in a study of twenty-five families of children with severe genetic disorders, concluded that prenatal diagnosis, like selective infanticide, undermines trust between parents and children. If this is the case, then Fletcher's argument regarding the clarity of the line that separates the two procedures loses much of its force.

Regarding John Fletcher's lack of serious concern about the potential dangers of the slippery slope that might exist between selective abortion and selective infanticide, we should not forget that as recently as the early 1960s the line between therapeutic abortion and elective abortion was seemingly secure and a policy supporting abortion on demand was unthinkable for the majority of Americans (Atkinson and Moraczewski 1980, 107).

Some philosophers and physicians believe that we are already on a slippery slope that is eroding our attitudes toward born people with genetic disorders (Kass 1973). Surgeon R. B. Zachary (1977) writes:

> It has often been said by those who oppose abortion that the disregard for life of a child within the uterus would spill over

into postnatal life. This suggestion has been "pooh-poohed," yet in spina bifida there is a clear example of this. The equanimity with which the life of a 17-week-gestation spina bifida infant is terminated after the finding of a high level of alpha-fetoprotein in the amniotic fluid has, I think spilled over to a similar disregard for the life of the child with spina bifida after birth (1462).

While several studies have been done on attitudes toward people with handicaps (Yuker 1988), few data are available on attitude changes over time. In the past decade, there has been a decline in government spending for social programs for the disabled and a growth of a new conservatism with emphasis on an individualism that encourages ostracization of the handicapped (Stubbins 1988, 30). A recent report by the U.S. Census Bureau revealed that "disabled Americans are less likely to hold jobs now than they were earlier this decade, and those who do work have lost earning power" (*Providence Journal*, August 16, 1989, A-7). However, it is difficult to know whether this development is directly related to changing attitudes regarding selective abortion and infanticide, or is the result of other variables.

If we really believe that the worth of a human should be assessed on the basis of his or her potential burden and contributions to society, then if a person's net worth falls below a required minimum, that individual's "direct killing can be justified and even declared obligatory" (Atkinson and Moraczewski 1980, 106). In fact, the reasons for abortion for a genetic disorder become an even more compelling justification for infanticide because of a genetic disorder. In the case of infanticide, there is less risk of eliminating an individual because of a false-positive test result. Given the uncertain prognosis of many genetic disorders, there is also the opportunity to make a more accurate assessment after birth of the infant's potential to be socially useful.

Therefore, the time line regarding the elimination of an individual who is or might be a social burden seems to be as arbitrary, and perhaps dependent on current social attitudes, as that between acceptable and unacceptable social burdens.

Assessment of Non-Monetary Social Burdens

Burden to society can also be measured in other types of harm rather than purely monetary losses. Using this same principle of relief of burden and suffering to society, "we could," one author writes, "dispose of numerous unwanted persons—the mentally handicapped, the senile, the criminal and so on—since all would be considered by some as causing suffering and being a burden to family and society" (Monteleone and Moraczewski 1981, 54).

Males with the XYY syndrome, for example, although phenotypically normal and capable of supporting themselves monetarily, are unusually prone to antisocial and criminally aggressive behavior. While the incidence of the XYY syndrome in newborns is about one in one thousand, the incidence of XYY males in the prison population is about twenty in one thousand (Hook 1973, 139). Consequently, besides the obvious monetary burden of supporting a person in prison (about the same as the cost of sending someone to Harvard), there is an added harm in terms of the threat to the safety and property of other members of society. Is the probability of harm to society under these circumstances enough to tip the scales in favor of selective abortion of XYY males?

Before one dismisses such a scenario as highly unlikely in the United States, at one time compulsory newborn screening programs for the XYY genotype, much like the compulsory screening programs for PKU, were seriously considered by some hospitals. Screening programs for the XYY genotype were dropped not because they infringed on the privacy of parents but because of the uncertainty of the prognosis and the fear that labeling a child as an XYY male could actually bring about more harm in terms of promoting a self-fulfilling prophecy and lead to an increase, rather than a decrease, in the probability of antisocial behavior (ibid.).

Regarding selective abortion of XYY males on the basis of their potential threat to society, it has frequently been noted that not only are XYY males more prone to violent behavior, but the entire male (XY) population is statistically more prone to violence than are women (Allen and Allen 1979). For example, rarely are there more than one or two females on the "25 Most Wanted" list put out by the FBI. The number of male prison inmates, despite the fact that at least white males as a group are socially and economically privileged in our society, far outnumbers the number of females in prison.

What, then, are the social implications for the use of the criterion "proneness to violent behavior" as a reason for the selective abortion of males in general (assuming there is an adequate sperm bank or enough males for reproductive purposes)? While it may seem absurd to us in a male-oriented society to regard the Y chromosome as a defect, for several centuries "femaleness" (XX) was regarded by many learned men as a birth defect.

Exactly where do we draw the line between genetic disorders that do or do not warrant abortion because of the risk that the bearer might be a threat to other members of society? While most of us would agree that having a male genotype alone is not sufficient, how about proneness to mental illness? Just recently, the genes have been isolated that seem to predispose a person to manic-depressive behavior (Lappé 1987, 5). To abort these fetuses would undoubtedly benefit society by decreasing the demand on public resources, such as mental institutions and other social services. However, while this may also benefit society in terms of eliminating some potentially very dangerous people, such as Hitler, "it would also potentially deprive us of great poets like Sylvia Plath or politicians like Winston Churchill, each of whom may have suffered from bipolar manic depression" (ibid.).

How should the loss of one be weighed against the loss of the other? How can these nonmonetary benefits be quantified to facilitate decision making in these different and difficult situations? Until this calculation is done, social cost-benefit analysts are on shaky ground when it comes to the decision as to who should live and who should die.

Choosing the Decision Makers for Formulating Social Policy

An important question, too often overlooked, regarding cost-benefit analysis of social worth is, Who should act as the agent of the state in making these life and death decisions? Parents, because of their emotional involvement, often allow family considerations to overrule social considerations. The family, obviously, cannot be relied upon to always make life-and-death decisions about their own children based solely upon the minimization of social burden and the maximization of social benefit.

Elected politicians are not a good choice either because they generally do not have any training in the science of genetic disorders or in the economics involved in making a decision about their degree of social burdensomeness.

Handing over the authority to make these decisions to a special committee of physicians, while seemingly a more obvious choice, is also problematic in that physicians have a strong bias for healthy children and tend to be overly pessimistic in their prognoses of untreatable genetic disorders (Weir 1984, 129). Regarding spina bifida, for example:

> Many doctors believe it would be better if all children with neural tube defects were never born and they are likely to communicate this attitude to parents. . . . Physicians and parents often have quite different views of the value of life for spina bifida children. They [the physicians] only see them as sick children (Kolata 1980, 9).

Darling (1979) likewise found that "a life defined by physicians as intolerable might come to be defined in a very different manner by parents. . . . the social worlds of parents and physicians vary considerably" (239). In fact, in her study she found that the greatest interactional difficulty reported by parents after the birth of their child with a severe genetic disorder involved not an ignorant public but physicians and other medical personnel (203).

While physicians have typically tended to judge social worth based on their own achievement-oriented value systems, which are often utilitarian in nature (Peterson 1981, 98), recently, fear of so-called wrongful life or wrongful birth suits has motivated physicians to an even greater extent to "err" on the side of a pessimistic prognosis (Weir 1984, 129; Johnson and Elkins 1988, 41).

For those women who do not choose to abort their fetuses with defects, pessimistic prognoses may become self-fulfilling prophecies if infants with bleak prognoses fail to get adequate medical care, or educational and employment opportunities necessary to realize their potential, thus perpetuating the belief that they were not worth salvaging in the first place.

Professionals who provide rehabilitative services for people with handicaps may also be poor choices for public policy making regarding the social potential of people with genetic disorders. Like physicians,

> professionals [in the rehabilitation community] define the problems, the agenda, and the social reality of disabled people, in ways that serve their own interests more closely than those of their clients. . . . Clients often define what troubles them by interiorizing the attitudes and values of their professional helpers (Stubbins 1988, 23).

While we claim to be a democracy, civil rights advocates of affirmative action programs point out that it is evident that the United States is also very much a "meritocracy" run by a financially and socially successful elite from the professional and upper classes. Because of this, "persons who are permanently handicapped may suffer from a feeling of exclusion from participation in the political realm" (Cassel 1982, 643). Thus, the political decision-making process regarding who is a social burden and what sorts of people should be allowed to be born into this society is already biased against people with handicapping genetic disorders before it even begins.

While the cost-effectiveness for society of allowing children to be born with disabilities is a common enough topic of discussion, the social cost-effectiveness of the unaffected replacement children who frequently follow a selective abortion is rarely questioned. In a society that already has enough people, it should not be so readily assumed that a replacement child will necessarily be a social asset. "In keeping the ledger, the costs to society of his care and maintenance cannot be ignored. . . . Who is a greater drain on society's precious resources, the average inmate of a home for the retarded or the average graduate of Berkeley?" (Kass 1985, 92).

Indeed, one might feasibly argue that highly intelligent and physically healthy people have far more potential to squander valuable societal resources and cause harm to others than do people with disabling genetic disorders. The need for public money and expensive medical resources to live is not the only way in which a person can be socially "defective" or a drain on society. "How many of us," Kass (1985) ponders, "are not socially 'defective' and with none of the excuses possible for a child with PKU?" (94). It is not people with Down syndrome who are creating nuclear weapons, dumping toxic waste in our waterways and air, selling cocaine and cigarettes to children, squandering millions on lavish parties and expensive homes and yachts—thus tying up valuable property and resources that could be used for the public good while returning nothing in the form of productive labor—or using their political position to steal from public treasuries. Yet no one has ever suggested euthanatizing these so-called enterprising people or the selective abortion of fetuses of the idle rich as a means to preserve or reclaim valuable public and natural resources.

Handicap as a Social Construct

Joseph Stubbins, in his article "The Politics of Disability" (1988), argues that the disability experienced by people with genetic disorders is primarily social rather than a direct consequence of their physical or mental condition.

> Disabled people are a disadvantaged minority, just as women and some racial groups are. . . . To be disabled is to belong to an oppressed minority. The essence of disability is the *social and economic* consequences of being different from the majority. Being female rather than male or being black rather than white are

symptoms of being disadvantaged. The disadvantages inhere in social relationships (24).

In a study of career patterns of persons labeled as mentally retarded, Mercer (1965) likewise found that the very definition of mentally retarded is rooted in professional middle-class values. This approach, known as the "social systems perspective," views deviance as a label that emerges within the context of social interactions, in contrast to the conventional clinical perspective, which views deviance as an attribute of the deviant persons (18). The sociohistorical perspective also views "the negative stereotype about handicapped people" as being "the product of social labeling of a powerless minority group" (Lubowe 1989, 93).

Applying the social system perspective to families of children who are mentally retarded, Mercer found that the higher the status of a family—economically and professionally—the more likely parents were to concur with widely accepted definitions of mental retardation and to be pessimistic about the future of their mentally retarded child. Low-status families, on the other hand, were much more accepting of their mentally retarded child and could envision them playing normal adult roles (33). It is also interesting in this regard that working-class families are more likely to become active crusaders and advocates for their handicapped children than are parents from the middle and upper classes (Darling 1979, 231).

Just as "handicapped" as a deviant condition is in great part a socially determined status in a perfection- and achievement-oriented society, in a male-dominated society where women enjoy few opportunities, social burdensomeness or deviance can be defined in terms of one's sex. Northern India is one of many areas of the world with a strong social bias against females. An estimated eight thousand to ten thousand female feticides were carried out in the Bombay area alone between 1978 and 1982 (Wertz and Fletcher 1989, 25). Until 1983, when prenatal diagnosis for sex selection was barred in government hospitals, sex selection accounted for the majority of prenatal diagnoses in Bombay.

In the United States, on the other hand, the primary reason for seeking prenatal diagnosis is the detection of chromosomal anomalies, such as Down syndrome, rather than the XX genotype.[1] Is our perception of or moral consensus about which chromosomal pattern constitutes a serious social burden any less biased than that of those in Northern India who seek prenatal diagnosis?

In our presumably more egalitarian society (at least regarding sexual differences), sex selection is not considered justified on social grounds. In fact, the frequent use of the term *feticide* in reference to the abortion of a female fetus and *selective abortion* or *termination* in reference to a fetus with a disorder implies that killing takes place only if the fetus is normal—as defined by those in power in our society.

Regarding female feticide, John Fletcher (1986) argues that the state should discourage selective abortion of females because it is "an unfair use of resources," it implies that "undesired gender is equivalent to disease," and it "offends the commonly held principle of equality between sexes" (851). One can only wonder why the selective abortion of fetuses who are mentally retarded or physically handicapped doesn't likewise "offend the commonly held principle of equality" between all people and, hence, ought to be discouraged for these very same reasons?

While many people argue that prenatal diagnosis is most easily justified for "serious and fatal genetic diseases" (Wertz and Fletcher 1989, 24), the reality of the situation is that most of the conditions, such as Down syndrome and spina bifida or sex chromosome anomalies, that prompt selective abortion are not usually fatal. In fact, geneticist W. Fuhrmann (1989) predicts that, with the increased use of commercial laboratories, which often do not provide genetic counseling as do hospital clinics, for prenatal diagnosis, "an unavoidable consequence will be a rising number of pregnancy terminations for minor defects and

---

[1] When illegitimacy was considered an inexorable social stigma, the burden of illegitimacy was also regarded by many as a "reasonable" justification of infanticide (Damme 1978).

mistaken diagnosis, in order to avoid physician liability, in the sense of defensive medicine" (384).

Much of the social burden of people with handicaps comes not from their intrinsic lack of potential but from a lack of opportunity to participate in a productive and meaningful way in an achievement-oriented society. The perception of the seriousness of a particular genetic or chromosomal pattern depends in great part on the opportunities that society provides for people with those particular karyotypes, whether it be 46, XX in India or 45, X or 47, +21 in the United States.

Beatrice Wright (1988), in a study of attitudes toward people with disabilities, found that in the United States we have a "fundamental negative bias" toward people with handicaps that "steers perception, thought and feeling along negative lines to such a degree that positives remain hidden. [This bias] is a powerful source of prejudice that ill serves those who are already disadvantaged" (3).

Lack of access alone, in terms of wheelchair ramps for people with spina bifida or Duchenne muscular dystrophy, are very effective in handicapping these people in terms of their opportunity to participate in the mainstream of society (Glasser 1985). Similarly, our workplaces do not accommodate people like those with Down syndrome, who are often excellent at simple routine tasks and whose cheerful dispositions make them pleasant colleagues. Instead of focusing on their positive qualities, they more often are shuffled off to sheltered workshops by well-meaning social service agencies.

Social conditions that define and, to a great extent, create what is a handicap, therefore, have an enormous impact on those who are labeled handicapped and "can be a source of untold suffering." In the same way culturally defined labels of what is appropriately masculine and feminine have been the cause of much discrimination and suffering for women in the past (Cassel 1982, 642).

Professor of epidemiology and biostatistics Abby Lippman (1991) writes, " In today's Western world, biomedical and political systems largely define health and disease as well as normality and abnormality" (16). A social definition of disease and its consequent social burden says more about the "dis-ease" of those in power around people who are different than about those who are relegated by them to the fringes of society. People with genetic disorders are defined as social burdens because it is professionals—whether physicians or politicians—who define the terms of participation in our society. If we had in our society a "greater tolerance and provision for pluralism" (Darling 1979, 239), rather than a demand for perfection, the problems of people with handicaps in our society would be greatly reduced. A society that creates the very conditions that lead to the victimization of a specific group of people, whether women or people with genetic disorders, and then uses these conditions as an excuse to deny these people life or entrance into that society, is engaged in the worst form of victim blaming.

Public Pressure to Choose Selective Abortion

Even if the utilitarian cost-benefit type of argument is limited to the elimination of humans with disorders detected before birth, the general acceptance of this type of reasoning, even without mandatory legislation, places a subtle and insidious pressure on parents of fetuses with potentially costly disorders to abort them for the alleged good of society. Public opinion is a powerful force. Even "good, intelligent people who prefer to respect the dignity of each human being," Christian ethicist Bernard Haring (1971) writes, "would, with scarcely any reflection, agree to an abortion if there seemed to be danger that a child be born deformed or otherwise socially unacceptable" (17–18).

Because of the expense involved and the inconvenience to other members of society to provide services for people with handicaps, children born with severe genetic disorders "are frequently regarded as 'limits' that prevent the full flowering of a society dedicated to expanding our range of choices" (Hauerwas 1986, 15). Consequently, selective abortion has not just come to be accepted as one of a range of acceptable choices but has been actively promoted by many people "partly because of a belief that handicapped people cost more than they're worth" (Meehan 1984, 159).

Rothman (1985) warns that while the new technologies may appear to increase one's options, the increasing pressure to undergo prenatal diagnosis and the gradual erosion of the possibility of having and accepting a child with a handicap may have an unintended consequence in reduction of choice by making giving birth to a child with a disability socially unacceptable. In this sense, selective abortion is less of a free choice than elective abortion, in which the social costs of the choice are not as evident and the woman is given greater rein to choose free of societal pressures. An exception might be in the case of poor minority women and unwed teenage mothers, two groups traditionally discriminated against in our society, to whom elective abortion, like selective abortion, is often subtly encouraged (and even passed off as stemming from benevolent and paternalistic concern) by those in more fortunate circumstances as the socially responsible choice.

As with the eugenics argument, the social burden argument is criticized as being reminiscent of the reasoning used by the Nazis:

> During Hitler's regime hundreds of thousands of retarded children and other "unfit" persons were annihilated, and this attitude prevails today among some . . . even in free countries. The ideal of utility dominates to such an extent that even a society built on respect for all persons tends to countenance some form of annihilation for those who, from the viewpoint of economic progress, are considered "unfit" (Haring 1971, 18).

The attitude that it is one's social duty to undergo selective abortion is likely to become even more prevalent with the growing awareness that resources on this planet are limited and the accompanying societal concern to use these limited resources as effectively and efficiently as possible (Sorenson 1974). With easier access to and the development of safer and earlier prenatal diagnostic techniques parents who do not utilize these advances will likely be socially ostracized (ibid., 177–78).

As far back as 1976, the National Institute of Child Health and Human Development suggested that "sound medical practice would dictate that all pregnant women above the age of thirty-five should be offered amniocentesis" (Atkinson and Moraczewski 1980, 20). More recently, it has been predicted that "in the 1990's amniocentesis may very well become a standard, routine part of all prenatal care" (Rothman 1985, 189). In fact, some writers (Fletcher 1983c, 143; Johnson and Elkins 1988, 409) express concern that justification of selective abortion of fetuses with genetic disorders on the basis of their potential financial or social burden to society may eventually lead to a policy of mandatory genetic screening and prenatal diagnosis.

The state of California, for example, mandates that alpha-feto-protein (AFP) testing be offered to all pregnant women. If the woman does not want to undergo testing, she has to sign a refusal form. If the test is positive, the woman can refuse an abortion (Hubbard 1985), but it is with the knowledge that she is carrying a potentially socially burdensome child.

While this practice may sound relatively benign, some people believe it is a subtle (and often unconscious) means of putting pressure on women to consider selective abortion of their socially unacceptable children.

Even when access to AFP testing is not mandated by law, for those women who agree to AFP testing, on the grounds that it is routine for all pregnant women, the pressure to follow up a positive result with further testing can be subtly coercive. For example, I was invited to sit in on a counseling session with a woman who had had a positive result of a routine AFP test. It was obvious that she did not want an amniocentesis and would not consider an abortion should the amniocentesis be positive. The counselor, who prided herself on her nondirective approach, did not let the woman go until she finally gave in and submitted to an amniocentesis, which was scheduled for that very afternoon. The woman's reluctance to have an amniocentesis was continually interpreted (or misinterpreted) by the counselor as ignorance on the part of the woman about the ease of amniocentesis and the hardship of having a child who had a genetic disorder.

"A woman who decides not to have prenatal tests or not to abort a fetus who she knows has a disability," Ruth Hubbard (1985), a Harvard University biologist writes, "takes on responsibility for the social, medical, and economic problems she and her family may experience as a result. It is in incongruous to call that making a choice" (575).

John Fletcher (1983c), who supports a woman's right to choose selective abortion, expresses the fear that, because of the cost-benefit advantages of prenatal screening, "a climate of moral blame" may be cast around parents who do not comply. To what extent, he asks, should society be expected to bear burdens brought about by parental decisions by those who do not conform to social norms?

Whether or not prenatal diagnosis becomes mandatory, societal attitudes toward those people with disabilities who manage to slip though the testing process would be less than sympathetic. One could hardly expect taxpayers to foot the bill for the care of these children (Allen and Allen 1979). While prenatal diagnosis and selective abortion may bring freedom from the burdens of caring for a child with a genetic disorder, "How soon," Bruce Hilton (1972), of the Hastings Center for bioethical research, asks, "will this freedom become a responsibility . . . in the eyes of society. . . . The sympathy towards parents 'afflicted' with a mongoloid child will change in the day when we know they chose to have the child" (9).

It is becoming more and more common for older women who have children who are mentally retarded to be regarded with "a good deal of suspicion, if not outright hostility" because they should have taken the proper steps to avoid having had a retarded child (Hauerwas 1986, 204). In cases in which the parents decide to give birth to such a child, social agencies might plausibly argue that they do not have an obligation to help support a child whose birth could easily have been avoided.

Darling writes:

> A common experience reported by parents [of children with
> severe birth defects] was one of being blamed rather than helped
> by societal agents, of being made to feel that because *they* had
> given birth to a defective child, they should somehow provide for
> their children's unusual educational, physical, or other needs (178).

Thus, acceptance of the social justification of selective abortion places the cost-benefit analyst, who argues at the same time
that the state should help with the care of handicapped people,
in a quandary. If one believes that the public should share in the
financial burden of supporting a child with a genetic disorder, at
the same time, this opens

> the door to a claim by public agencies to have a voice in the deci-
> sions of parents; that is, since the "public" is going to bear part of
> the cost, and since the "public" does not readily recognize a duty
> to bear costs that are avoidable, a public authority might claim a
> right to prohibit parents from bearing children who are a great
> expense to the state or to philanthropic institutions (Gustafson
> 1974, 218).

Even with prenatal testing, there will be mutations for disorders not tested or some parents may unknowingly be carriers of
a particular recessive gene for which there are no tests or for
which tests were not performed because the parents were
thought to be at low risk for that disorder. Therefore, there will
always be disabled fetuses who will slip through the holes in the
screen of genetic testing. There are also myriad other nongenetic
factors that can cause retardation and disfigurement in the
fetus—factors for which, in the climate of moral blame and general ignorance about the mechanisms of inheritance, the mother
will probably be held responsible.

Social Acceptability and Self-worth

From the point of view of the child with a handicap, "his
recognition that society blames his parents for having him

would be an awesome awareness, and could not have but a profound effect on his appreciation of himself" (Atkinson and Moraczewski 1980, 109). On the reverse side of the coin, those children who successfully passed the gamut of tests would be aware that they were alive only because they met certain standards prenatally.

Given this, they might reasonably conclude that their social worth is tied up with maintaining this minimal level of social acceptability. Indeed, there is not one of us who is not at risk, through accident or illness, of becoming a grave burden on society. One can have a perfect baby only to have him or her fall and sustain a head injury that "condemns" the child to a life of mental retardation. A young person may become restricted to a wheelchair because of a sports or automobile accident. Even presidents and millionaires are not invulnerable. How are we to handle these unpredicted social and personal tragedies? We probably would allow these unfortunate people to remain in our midst because of our bias in favor of born people. In a society that values people on a cost-benefit basis, however, the label "burden" and the resentment of those who have to pay taxes for the support of these people, would be felt by both parents and children.

An attitude of not wanting to be inconvenienced by fetuses with handicaps, many argue (e.g., Atkinson and Moraczewski 1980; Darling 1979; Hauerwas 1986; Kass 1973; Lebacqz 1973; Monteleone and Moraczewski 1981), will surely spread and affect our attitudes toward born people with handicaps who are not just potential but actual burdens on society. The present social policy of restricting elimination of potentially socially burdensome people to the time before their birth, though it may appear to protect the policy makers from being disposed of themselves should they too become disabled, is shaky because it is supported with weak and inconsistent reasoning—reasoning that is likely to come tumbling down on the very people who created the structure.

The "mentality of disposing of genetically defective infants communicates worthlessness to the already existing handicapped persons whose self-images can be severely traumatized by the realization that society doesn't want them" (Monteleone and Moraczewski 1981, 55). In such a climate, those who live and cope with the burdens of genetic disorders may feel more demeaned and become resigned to a life of quiet despair and guilt, or they may feel "compelled to counter the pressure on them and their descendants 'to be eugenically responsible' with moral claims of their own for fair treatment and restraint from punishment" (Atkinson and Moraczewski 1980, 148).

Counter Moral Claims

These counter moral claims are based on the recognition that there are important values other than social cost-efficiency. Disillusioned with the values of a perfection-oriented society, parents of children with handicaps "often enter into a protracted period of 'crusadership' in which they attempt to create solutions for their child that society lacks" (Darling 1979, 24).

One counterclaim these parents and their advocates put forth is that judging people primarily in terms of their social utility entails a blatant disregard of the belief in the unconditional and equal dignity of all people—a value held in high esteem in democratic societies. How can we accurately quantify, in a cost-benefit analysis, the harm done by the erosion of this and other important moral values against the monetary benefits of not keeping alive a nonproductive person with a genetic disorder?

Also overlooked in these social cost-benefit formulas are long-cherished moral qualities, such as compassion, sharing, and the capacity to give and receive love, to trust, to be courageous, and to be patient. The use of such terms as *products of conception, defective fetus* and *defective neonate*, or *damaged goods* belies a crass consumerism when it comes to nascent human life. To insist that the value of a fetus is entirely dependent on social worth, a "value attributed to it by a market society at the going price," political scientist Jean Bethke Elshtain (1984) points out, "preserves consumer sovereignty and untrammeled choice but strips us of our terms of moral evaluation" (56).

Rothman (1985) makes an especially cogent plea against the introduction of the capitalist values of the marketplace into human reproduction, as it would be destructive to the very value of respect for one another upon which our democratic society rests. Prenatal diagnosis and selective abortion in a commodity-oriented culture, she warns, actually limits genuine choices rather than providing the consumer-parent with "untrammeled choice." The evolving American value system regarding children and parenthood, Rothman continues, "represents further movement towards the commodification of life, towards treating people . . . as commodities" (188). Prenatal diagnosis and selective abortion especially, she argues, encourages this "commodification of the fetus" (ibid.).

Christian ethicist Stanley Hauerwas (1986) believes that the key moral question is not whether we have the monetary resources to "integrate those whom we perceive to be particularly different from the rest of us . . . [but] do we have the moral resources?" (183) Unlike monetary resources, moral resources, like the biblical fishes and loaves, are multiplied by use. In this sense in this day and age, it has been argued, we cannot afford to be morally indifferent to those who are needy.

Author Pearl S. Buck (1968), the mother of a child born retarded because of PKU, writes of her experience:

> In this world, where cruelty prevails in so many aspects of life, I would not add the weight of choice to kill rather than to let live. A retarded child, a handicapped person, brings its own gift to life, even to the life of normal human beings. That gift is comprehended in lessons of patience, understanding and mercy, lessons which we all need to receive and to practice with one another whatever we are (xi).

John Rawls (1971), a leading contemporary social and political philosopher, argues that where there are social and economic inequalities, they should not be arranged so as to benefit those in power or even the majority, as the cost-benefit analysts would have it, but so that "they are both (a) to the greatest benefit of the least advantaged and (b) attached to offices and positions open to all under conditions of fair equality of opportunity" (83). Given that at any time any one of us might become social burdens and because few people would want themselves or those they love to be disposed of should they fall into such unfortunate circumstances, rational people would choose to live in a society where there is assurance that those who are least advantaged will be cared for and not abandoned by society.

When the two come into conflict, the value of nonabandonment generally overrides that of the social cost-benefit burden of rescuing a distressed person. "No advanced society," Heymann and Holtz (1975) write, "now allows some of its citizens to die to save the others the cost of furnishing minimal, custodial care" (402). As a society, we are prepared to pay a high price to reassure one another that no one will be abandoned in times of desperate need. Society's obligation not to abandon its members in time of need is not generally based on a person's awareness of this right, as we consider abandonment of infants and other helpless persons to be a heinous, immoral act. Thus, we will spend, without objection, hundreds of thousands of dollars to rescue an injured hiker or a downed pilot stranded on a mountain top, to save a person from a collapsed building, or to rescue a baby from a well, even when the odds are high that the distressed person has suffered costly injuries and may have severely impaired social usefulness as a result of the misfortune. "With the possible exception of the politically charged abortion issue," Heymann and Holtz (1975) write, "there is no precedent for a governmental or private decision to withhold available medical resources even from a class of those in need" (404).

The duty of a liberal democratic state to promote the fundamental principle of justice by providing equal care and protection for all its members is severely compromised by the social justification of selective abortion. If we accept this reasoning, care and protection become conditional upon how much a person can do for the state. According to fascist or totalitarian definitions, the roles of the state and the citizen are reversed in the cost-benefit argument and individuals are viewed not as ends in themselves but as means to an end. Individual humans do not have intrinsic worth but have only instrumental worth in terms of their usefulness or calculated benefit to the smooth functioning of the state machine.

In such a society, even when blatant monetary cost-benefit considerations are made secondary, life is still judged as good or bad in terms of "such characteristics as intelligence, independence, self-direction and self-control, productiveness and physical normalcy and attractiveness" (Atkinson and Moraczewski 1980, 106). While couched in nonmonetary terms, what is being conveyed is that the valued individual is one who can take care of his or her own affairs and support himself or herself and so not be a burden on society or be displeasing to others.

Intervention on the Grounds of Potential Burden

The social justification for selective abortion is at odds with the traditional goal of state intervention in medical care. The aim of public screening for disease in the past has been to identify those suffering from a disease so that the affected person can be treated and/or steps can be taken to prevent the affected person from transmitting the disease to other members of society. Thus, screening was "an admirable method of combating disease" (Powledge 1974, 25). With prenatal diagnosis and selective abortion, however, the concern is not the care of the person but "the prevention of the person" (ibid., 46).

While rejecting the utilitarian cost-benefit reasoning of the social burden justification as insufficient on its own to justify selective abortion, public policy analyst Robert Blank (1982) nevertheless believes that "eventually some trade-off between individual and society benefits must be reached" (358). When and under what conditions should these trade-offs be made?

Given the fact that the burden to society, except in the rare instance of fetal therapy funded by public monies, does not begin until after the birth of the child, and also given the uncertain prognosis of most genetic disorders, one might argue that the state does not have the right to actively intervene until the time that there is an actual burden or threat. Traditionally, the prospect of future burdensomeness, in terms of disease or criminal inclinations, has not been considered sufficient to justify the placement of restrictions on a person let alone his or her death. We cannot euthanatize elderly people because they might become demented or a burden on society, nor can we lock up people because they might commit a crime. The principle of not penalizing people because they are a potential threat to others in society, in fact, is so firmly a part of our justice system that we cannot even lock up or effectively restrain a potentially dangerous person even if he or she is actually threatening to kill another person.

State intervention on the grounds of membership in a particular high-risk group, therefore, is discriminatory at best. The state is no more justified to quarantine homosexuals or intravenous drug users on the grounds that they are members of groups at high risk for AIDS or to imprison a poor African-American man because he is in a high-risk group for crime than it is to order the abortion of all fetuses with Down syndrome or spina bifida on the grounds that they might become a social burden.

For the "champions of the individual in an age of conformity," bioethicist Tabitha Powledge (1974) urges, we should not lose sight of the fact that "we really are all unique: in our fingerprints, our biochemistry and even our disease" (44). Most of us believe that it is unfair that our worth as a person and member of society be gauged not according to our own merits, but on the achievements and shortcomings of a particular group to which we happen to belong. Yet, many of us do this to people who are handicapped without giving it a second thought (Wright 1988). This tendency to equate people who have a genetic disorder with the disorder itself, rather than seeing them as unique individuals, is evident when people say "it's" a "Tay-Sachs baby" rather than a "baby with Tay-Sachs disease" or a "Down fetus" rather than a "fetus with Down syndrome." Because of our language, the important distinction between the disorder and the fetus or person is easy to overlook.

Conclusion

Even given that state regulation (or social pressure on parents) to abort a child who would be a heavy burden on social resources is cost-effective, the erosion of other moral values upon which our democratic society is built would be even more costly in the long run. While the preservation of valuable resources may someday become an issue, it is not at present an issue in the United States or other Western nations. Daniel Callahan (1973) of the Hastings Center for bioethical research maintains that an affluent society should be able to "absorb the costs of caring for defective individuals" (24). Not doing so is not so much a statement about the use of scarce resources as a statement about our priorities as a society and the worth of people with genetic disorders.

If we should someday find ourselves in desperate times when resources are severely limited, one might conceivably justify withholding medical treatment (or fetal therapy) that involves a scarce medical resource from a fetus or born person who is actually dying of anencephaly, Tay-Sachs disease, a severe form of spina bifida, or Huntington disease, (assuming that some form of palliative care is still administered to the dying persons). It would still be difficult, however, to justify the active killing, through selective abortion, of humans who *might be*, but are not yet, social burdens; nor could one justify selective abortion (or euthanasia) when the burden imposed or potentially imposed on society is a burden not inherent in their condition or only in their condition but one created or amplified by restrictions established by those in power on the potential of these people to participate in society.

9

Family-Burden Justification for Selective Abortion

The presence of a genetic disorder in the fetus is one of the most frequently cited mitigating circumstances that is thought to override the normal prohibition against abortion. So far, however, both the argument based on eugenic concerns and that based on social burden have failed to provide sufficient moral justification for selective abortion.

A third argument based on the burdensomeness of the disorder to the family overcomes some of the problems of these arguments—particularly regarding the infringement on the freedom of the family from mandatory testing and abortion. The family-burden justification, because of the struggles and hardships all too often faced by families with a child with a genetic disorder and the sympathy one cannot help but feel for many of these families, is one of the most compelling of the arguments given for selective abortion.

The Argument

Relevant Moral Principles

In the United States, when the rights of society and the rights of individual parents conflict regarding selective abortion, the standard of parental or familial good is usually given priority (Kass 1985). Although in certain circumstances, it is argued, parents may have a duty to society to avoid the birth of a severely defective child, in the last analysis it is the parents' right to determine, "according to their own wishes and notions of what is good for them, the genetic quality of their offspring" (Twiss 1974, 258).

"This principle of respect for the autonomy of patients," John Fletcher (1986) writes, "has the most universal acceptance by practitioners in prenatal diagnosis and is the most relevant resource for the many conflicts that accompany abortion choices" (843). One of the trends that has shaped this attitude is the increasing awareness of women's rights (Lebacqz 1973, 110). The majority of American genetic counselors believe that the selective abortion decision belongs "solely to the mother" (Kass 1985, 85), thus defining family rights even more narrowly in terms of the woman's autonomy.

A second moral principle that is used to support the family-burden justification of selective abortion is that of nonmaleficence or "Do no harm." Selective abortion, it is claimed, is a means to protect the family from the financial and emotional stresses that are so often associated with bearing and caring for a child with a genetic disorder. Special pleas are made, particularly on the behalf of families who are already caring for a child with a serious disorder. In fact, to avoid such a burden to one's family, according to Fletcher (1986), may even be seen as a positive duty under certain circumstances.

> If one can know with reasonable certainty and safety that the fetus is affected by a serious and untreatable disorder, it clearly follows that one has a moral duty to obtain the knowledge, unless weightier moral reasons exist to the contrary. . . . What ought to be done about the diagnosis is, however, tempered by concerns that arise from respect for the principles of autonomy, beneficence and justice (847).

Harms to the Family

There is no doubt that families often suffer greatly as a result of having a child with a serious genetic disorder. The nature and severity of the disorder and the particular burdens it might impose on the family, therefore, should be taken into consideration when making a decision about selective abortion.

Regarding severe disorders, such as Tay-Sachs disease, ethicist James Gustafson (1974), who rejects selective abortion in most cases, argues that the parents of a fetus with Tay-Sachs disease are morally free to seek selective abortion to avoid their own suffering and that of their fetus.

Ellen, the mother of a child with Tay-Sachs disease, speaks of the almost unbearable suffering she and her husband underwent during the years spent watching their son slowly die:

> I can't stand it any more! But that was my pain. My pain was, "If you're going to die, die, and a lot of us who have children who are terminally ill say, well, 'If you're going to die, die, don't wait three years, or five years—if you're going to go don't make it hard on everybody'" (Colen 1986, 38).

Another factor to be considered is the material resources of the particular family. The financial cost of caring for a child with a genetic disorder can be astronomical, especially in the United States, where medical care is not socialized (Burton 1975, 125). Approximately 70 percent of families in the United States with a child who is chronically disabled have "significant financial problems as a result of the child's disorder. . . . Many of the costs of caring for a chronically disabled child are hidden—special diets, architectural modifications, maintenance of a wheelchair or other orthopedic aids, travel to treatment sites, or days lost from work" (Ireys 1981, 333). In many families, the father, and often the mother as well, may have to take an extra job to help cover medical and other associated expenses (Erbe 1974). Even for those families who have private medical coverage, the continuing costs of medical care are often not covered. "The very Judeo-Christian meaning of life," bioethicist Richard McCormick (1981) maintains,

> is seriously jeopardized when undue and unending effort must go into its maintenance . . . if the financial cost of life-preserva-

tion care was crushing, that is, if it would create grave hardships for oneself or one's family, it was considered extraordinary and nonobligatory (163).

Other problems encountered by parents stem from having to cope with the many practical, daily difficulties associated with caring for a child with a genetic disorder. Learning and putting . into practice the necessary skills to care for the special needs of these children can be time-consuming and exhausting. Frequent trips to the hospital can be disruptive to the family routine. A child with spina bifida, for example, may need as many as twenty operations to correct common orthopedic problems associated with the condition (Ireys 1981, 338). Siblings, especially, are likely to suffer, as parents have to spend more time away from home working and making trips to the hospital.

Nonvisible disorders, such as sickle cell anemia, hemophilia, or cystic fibrosis, can be disruptive in other ways because of the unpredictability of the crises, in terms of their timing, duration, and intensity, as well as the often unrealistic hope when everything is going well that their child is "all better."

Parents of children who are mildly mentally retarded may have difficulty finding adequate social and educational services for their child, as most institutions are geared toward either normal children or severely retarded or emotionally disturbed children (ibid., 340). This may partly account for the finding that there is a somewhat higher rate of severe family disruption or breakup when the child is only slightly handicapped as opposed to when the child has a severe handicap (Strong 1983, 169; Ireys 1981, 327).

In addition to anxiety, exhaustion, financial loss, and disruption of family life, these families often suffer from a loss of self-esteem (Heymann and Holtz 1975, 407). Members of the family of a child with a serious genetic disorder frequently experience "cosmic guilt" and shame associated with visibly being carriers. This realization may at times "acquire the status of a severe personal problem if individuals interpret nature's machinations as punishment resulting from their own conduct"

(Sorenson 1974, 176). Mothers especially may try to overcompensate for their guilt by overindulging the child and consequently neglecting their husband and other children (Buresh 1981). "Parents may also feel extreme guilt in feeling that the child's death may be a relief," thanatologist Stephen Lubowe (1989, 91) writes. This may, in turn, be reflected in injuries to the child's personality.

> Guilt, along with anxiety, may lead the parents to have excessively high standards for muscle performance, social behavior and cleanliness. An opposite extreme to over-demanding child-rearing is the doting overprotective parent who allows the child to become physically inactive or obese. The child may also be allowed to become emotionally dependent, hypochondrical and spoiled (ibid.).

Institutionalization of the child, while a superficial solution to these problems, usually only serves to further increase the parents' guilt. Even when parents know intellectually that they are not personally responsible for the child's disorder, it is still difficult for parents to "wash away the deep anxieties and unjustified feelings of guilt or shame they experience" upon the birth of a "malformed child" (Volpe 1984, ix).

Social Stigmatization

The great stigma attached to the parents and siblings of a "severely retarded or grossly malformed child," it is argued, adds to the justification of selective abortion because abortion can be regarded as "necessary to preserve the mental health of the mother" (Rush 1983, 135). In addition to personal guilt and shame, the stigmatization of people with serious handicaps by other members of the community comes to be shared through association by all members of the family. This phenomenon is known as "stigma transference" or "courtesy stigma" (Darling 1979, 32). Because of this, "handicapped children and their families often find themselves either without any consistent network of community support or with outright rejection from their neighbors" (Ireys 1981, 331).

Stigmatization is usually most keenly felt by parents in dealings with medical and social service professionals. In her study, Rosalyn Darling (1979) found that the most common complaint of these parents was that the "medical treatment their children received had often been delivered in a rude and dehumanizing way" (150). Their children were frequently treated by medical professionals as things rather than people (152) and the parents were often treated in a "blaming way, especially if they refused institutionalization for their children" (203).

The problems faced by families of children with genetic disorders can sometimes seem overwhelming in the face of the paucity of support that our society offers them. The most basic social and educational services taken for granted by parents of normal children often have to be fought for by parents of children with handicaps, thus adding to the stress, exhaustion, and time away from other members of the family. Uninformed teachers may interpret a child's physical handicap, such as Duchenne muscular dystrophy or spina bifida, and rejection by peers as evidence of mental retardation. Segregation in "special skills" classes can further add to this sense of isolation and inferiority (Lubowe 1989, 92).

Given society's stigmatization of people with serious handicaps and the lack of adequate social services to meet their needs, all the parents in Darling's (1979) study worried about their child's future. This was especially true of parents of children with Down syndrome when the parents had the child late in life. Most parents hoped that if something happened to them and they were no longer able to care for their child at home, their child would not be institutionalized but would be able to live in a group home or sheltered workshop. At the same time, they were realistic about the scarcity of good group homes. In making a decision to selectively abort their fetus (whom they named "XYLO") who was diagnosed as having Down syndrome, Rayna and Mike Rapp (1984) asked themselves:

As we ourselves age, to whom would we leave the person XYLO would become? Neither Mike nor I have any living kin who are likely to be young enough, or close enough to take on this burden after our deaths. In a society where the state provides virtually no decent humane services for the mentally retarded, how could we take responsibility for the future of our dependent Down syndrome child (98)?

The accumulation of all these burdens can lead to the breakdown of the family unit. In the United States, the divorce rate among families of children with genetic disorders is as much as four times higher than the national average (McCormick 1974). For those families that stay together, severe marital discord is also significantly higher (Strong 1983, 168). Even when the family stays intact, parents of children with genetic disorders such as Down syndrome exhibit "considerably higher levels of anxiety, hostility and depression" than do parents of children without disabilities (Sorenson 1974, 176).

When there is such a threat to the integrity of the family unit, it is concluded, the prevention of serious harm to the family can outweigh the parental duty to protect a particular fetus—even when the parents "regard the fetus as fully human" (Fletcher 1986, 827). In fact, the well-being and the physical integrity of the family are so important, some argue, that it can, in some cases, even override the right to life of a newborn with a serious genetic disorder (Strong 1983, 169).

Because of all these harms to the family, Seller (1976) claims that an abnormal fetus can be seen as actually threatening the life of the mother, inasmuch as her life involves having to care for a handicapped child. Indeed, it might be argued, the presence of a handicapped child threatens not only the life of the mother but also of the whole family and society as well (ibid.).

The tremendous burdens placed on parents of children with genetic disorders impose Samaritan-type duties on a woman and her family that are not expected of others in similar situations. Consequently, it is unjust for anyone to demand that these parents make such extraordinary sacrifices. It would be morally commendable if they willingly took on such burdens, but it is not obligatory.

Nondirective Counseling

Most people who support this justification place a high value on family and, in particular, maternal autonomy. The family is seen as being the most capable unit for making a well-informed and morally correct decision regarding the outcome of the pregnancy. Parents, Twiss (1974) argues,

> are in the best and perhaps unique position to assess the total impact that a genetically defective child may have on themselves and their families, to make realistic predictions of what will contribute to or detract from the welfare and happiness of themselves and their families (259).

"The insinuation of the physician's prejudices into the decision-making process of the counselee," warns Aubrey Milunsky (1986), editor of the well-known medical text *Genetic Disorders and the Fetus*, "constitutes a moral affront to individual privacy and reproductive autonomy" (9). Consequently, prenatal genetic counselors are instructed to be as "impartial and objective" (8) as possible—in contrast to the traditional physcian-patient relationships in which the physician "heals by decision" (Lebel 1978, 28). Support for this approach is drawn from several sources, including the "medical consumerism movement, the feminist movement, [and] the American value of individualism" (Rothman 1986, 41).

A woman is generally recommended for prenatal diagnosis and genetic counseling by her obstetrician. The counselor may be either a trained genetic counselor with an MS in genetic counseling or an obstetrician who specializes in prenatal diagnosis. In some cases, a team approach may be used. The role of the prenatal genetic counselor vis-à-vis the parents is simply to provide the "fundamental necessity for truly moral choice: full and accurate knowledge" (Lebel 1978, 38). This includes, ideally, not only providing that parent with technical information but also "bringing out moral, sociological, ethical, theological aspects of the decision she faces" (ibid., 15). While proponents of nondirective counseling admit that no counselor can claim to be completely neutral, they believe that they can still be non-directive enough so that the parents can make a genuinely autonomous moral choice based on an assessment of the burdens that having that particular child will place on the family.

Analysis

The Myth of Neutrality

Not everyone agrees that neutrality in prenatal genetic counseling is achievable or even possible to approximate. Johnson and Elkins (1988), for example, question whether counseling physicians, because of their medicolegal concerns, are ever able to present a balanced picture, as their goal is to get the patient to take the test (409). Even Milunsky (1986), after urging the prenatal genetic counselor to always take a nondirective stance, betrays this bias when he then continues: "The difficulty lies mainly in trying to remain impartial while aiming to prevent the occurrence of genetic disease" (9).

Farrant (1985), in a study of attitudes toward amniocentesis, found that for most physicians the primary goal of diagnosis is detection of and abortion of fetuses with disorders. Another study found that a woman is more likely to decide to have an abortion if her obstetrician relates the results of her tests than when a geneticist does (Lippman 1991, 36). In fact, some physicians don't even bother informing parents of a negative diagnosis, instead telling them to assume everything is okay if they aren't contacted by a certain date (Richards 1989, 177). Consequently, the covert purpose of prenatal genetic counseling often becomes the subtle manipulation of the parent(s) into making the decision that is most advantageous for the physician while, at the same time, letting the parents think they are the ones who actually made the final decision. To facilitate this goal, tests may be presented to pregnant women in a misleading or ambiguous way. Because most women are more concerned with reassurance than the detection of abnormalities (Farrant 1985), the tests may be described by physicians as tests to "make sure your baby is alright." This communication may be interpreted by the parents as a procedure to prevent an abnormality rather than one that may reveal an abnormality (Richards 1989, 172).

Rothman (1986) describes a counseling session she attended in which the counselor was discussing amniocentesis with a reluctant thirty-nine-year-old woman. The counselor tells the woman, "One-in-140 will have mongolism and we want to make sure you're not that one." When the woman still resists, the counselor spends a great deal of time reassuring her that amniocentesis is not painful. The woman tells her she doesn't want the test, to which the counselor replies "Think of the advantages." When the sister, who has accompanied the woman, jumps in and tries to convince her sister to have the test, the counselor interrupts saying: "A woman has to decide for herself. No one can decide for her. It has to be a very personal decision" (48).

It is generally assumed by physicians that a woman will choose to have some form of prenatal diagnosis, that it is standard medical practice, especially if she is older or at risk for a genetic disorder, such as Tay-Sachs disease (Rothman 1986, 51). Many women simply go along with whatever their physician says to do (ibid., 42). Almost all the women in Rothman's study reported that their husbands, like their physicians, strongly encouraged them to have amniocentesis (ibid, 53). The husband, she found, is more likely to describe himself as the "realist" in the family and to align himself with "the doctor, with science, with the larger society" (ibid., 212). Another study likewise found that when it came to making the final decision about having a selective abortion, the husband was most often the one who was certain, while the woman wrestled with the choice (Furlong and Black 1984, 21).

Women who hesitate or refuse to undergo prenatal diagnosis are expected to justify their decision (Rothman 1986, 63). While the risk associated with amniocentesis is a widely used and socially acceptable excuse for refusing amniocentesis, women's own reasons—"their feelings, their intuitions, their sense of discomfort—these are not acceptable" (ibid., 79). Even with procedural risks, the perception of risk differs among individuals. Studies show that obstetricians are willing to pay a higher penalty in terms of risked miscarriages than are women (Richards 1989, 174). Thus physicians often downplay the risk of the procedure. In fact, Farrant's study revealed that 24 percent of the women undergoing amniocentesis were unaware of the risk of miscarriage and that another 86 percent were unaware of other possible side effects (Farrant 1985, 111).

Opposition to midterm abortion is not always acceptable as an excuse because a woman should still want prenatal diagnosis for "reassurance"—the assumption on the part of the medical profession being that, of course, people would want information if it is technically available (ibid., 82). To not want such information is to act irrationally—"to bury one's head in the sand." "The social pressures to participate in screening programmes and to terminate an affected pregnancy are considerable," writes child care and development specialist Josephine Green (1990). "Women may, as a result, experience considerable stress and find themselves acting against their own moral convictions" (1076). While hailed as an advance to promote women's reproductive freedom, if earlier, less invasive prenatal diagnostic tests (such as chorionic villus sampling or a maternal blood test) become widely available, the last socially acceptable reasons for refusing prenatal diagnosis may disappear, and women may have even less freedom to say no.

Because only a minority of women have made any sort of decision, before receiving the results of prenatal diagnosis, on what they will do in case of a positive result (Interview, Prenatal Diagnosis Center, Inc., Lexington, Mass., August 9, 1989), how parents learn about their fetus's condition cannot help but influence their decision regarding selective abortion. The manner in which counselors or physicians present the information—the order in which they present it, the information they choose to impart, and their personal perception of the burdensomeness of a genetic disorder—necessarily involves a value judgment. "It is hypocrisy to pretend," James Neel (1971) writes in an article written for genetic counselors on the ethical issues involved in prenatal diagnosis, "that the emotionally involved, nonmedically trained parents will reach a decision by themselves" (220).

The attitudes of women who were seeking amniocentesis toward children with genetic disorders differ from that of the medical professionals (Rothman 1986). For example, in Rothman's study, less than half of the women said they would abort for mild retardation (ibid., 164). However, few parents are likely to choose to carry an XYY fetus to term if they are told that he will "probably become a criminal" (Neel 1971, 225) or that their fetus with Down syndrome will "be a vegetable" (Buresh 1981, 63).

Most of the counselors interviewed by Rothman (1986), on the other hand, reported that they would have abortions for most abnormalities, including the possibility of mild retardation; half said they would abort for *any* abnormality (46). As one counselor explained to her, "I wouldn't have anything that was not perfect, not normal, anything with ifs, ands or buts" (47). Rothman also noted a tendency on the part of the counselors to "paint retardation in the darkest terms possible" (162). Not one of the counselors said anything optimistic about raising a child who was mentally retarded. Buresh (1981) also found that the physicians, in discussing the prognosis of Down syndrome, focused only on the negative aspects of the disorder and seemed to be unaware of the positive aspects or potential of people with Down syndrome (406–7). This bias probably stems, in part, from the lack of training most physicians have in the nature of genetic disorders (Johnson and Elkins 1988; Buresh 1982).

Just as or even more significant than the issues that are raised are those that are not raised. One of the complaints of patients undergoing selective abortion is the lack of "written information about psychosocial effects" (Edwards et al. 1989, 22). Physicians frequently fail to inform parents of the psychological stress that accompanies prenatal diagnosis and the high incidence of marital stress and depression following a selective abortion (Leibman and Zimmer 1979, 132–33). In fact, Rothman (1986) noted that most physicians avoid *any* controversial issue. The majority avoid the issue of abortion in preamniocentesis sessions, unless it is brought up by the patient (39). Most physicians justified this oversight by reassuring themselves that "most people don't want to know" (ibid.). When the woman herself does bring up the possibility of abortion, the methods of midtrimester abortions are rarely discussed (ibid.).

Because medical professionals are trained to see prenatal diagnosis, abortion, and genetic disorders as individual physical problems with individual physical solutions, rather than seeing them in a wider psychological and social context, they generally have little knowledge of possible social solutions to some of the problems associated with caring for a child with a genetic disorder. The negative attitudes of physicians toward children with genetic disorders is a major source of feelings of uncertainty and hopelessness experienced by parents when they learn about their child's disorder (Van Riper and Selder 1989, 64–65). Parents, therefore, are typically given little or no information about the resources available in the community for a child with a particular handicap or alternative ways to care for their child, including the possibility of adoption (Weir 1984, 259). This is a serious oversight, given that the most frequently cited reasons for choosing selective abortion stem from fears regarding lack of social and financial support for the child and the family.

Parents as the Decision Makers

Even it were possible to provide parents with full and unbiased information, they are usually in a distressed emotional state after receiving a positive prenatal diagnosis that is hardly conducive to clear decision making. While the provision of "full and accurate information" is necessary for a truly moral choice (Lebel 1978), one can hardly conclude from this that "full and accurate information" alone will lead to a "truly moral choice," a conclusion that seems to be taken for granted by some advocates of nondirective counseling. To assume this is to ignore the whole moral evaluation process that includes being able to assess the situation from an unbiased position to the extent that this is possible.

The diagnosis of a genetic disorder in a fetus, like the birth of a child with a serious genetic disorder, sets into motion a grieving process and a prolonged period of sadness, anxiety, and anger that can last for months and even years. The first reaction of most parents upon hearing of their newborn's handicap is "shock, disbelief and disappointment" (Darling 1979, 59). Although they eventually undergo a "process of resocialization," based on interaction with their own child and other families of children with handicaps whereby they come to define their child positively, the initial stages of shock and denial can last for days or months (Darling 1979, 222–23; Martinius 1986, 199). During this period of grieving, parents are "typically incapable of assimilating information" (Fost 1981, 321).

These initial negative feelings are for the most part transitory. In a study of parents of children with Down syndrome, the initial reaction to the birth of the child was highly negative. However, in the course of caring for their child and becoming more certain and aware of the nature of the condition, parents "reported that the positive consequences of [their life transition association with Down syndrome] far outweighed the negative ones" (Van Riper and Selder 1989, 75). The transitory nature of the initial negative feelings is also supported by the observation that not a single organization of parents who have mentally or physically handicapped children has ever endorsed abortion of the handicapped (Martinius 1986, 177). Indeed, many organizations, such as the Spina Bifida Association, not only are vigorous in discouraging abortion of fetuses with spina bifida but their members also have a standing offer to adopt newborn babies with spina bifida, if necessary.

Because of the late time in pregnancy when prenatal diagnosis is usually performed, parents may feel pressured to make a quick decision about their fetus's future at a time when, emotionally, they are least prepared to make a competent, well-reasoned life-and-death decision. Typically, a decision to have a selective abortion is made within a day or, at most, a few weeks after receiving a positive diagnosis.

The diagnosis of a genetic disorder is not the only crisis faced by pregnant women. There is a sense in which every pregnant woman undergoes a "crisis" (Martinius 1986). Feelings of "ambivalence, anxieties, fears, and unconscious impulses of rejection" are normal during any pregnancy (ibid., 198). On top of all this, the "genetic anxiety" that is now experienced by most couples could even further cloud or impair parents' ability to make an autonomous decision (Johnson and Elkins 1988).

The usual experience of obstetricians and pediatric surgeons in telling the family about the diagnosis of a fetal malformation "may be that of destroying the parents' expectation of a normal child" (Martinius 1986, 197). Given the confrontation with a discrepancy between a parent's idealized child and a fetus with a disability, this normal ambivalence toward pregnancy can easily turn to open rejection of the fetus. It is common for parents to overreact upon being "informed of a fetal malformation, in the form of a demand for immediate abortion" (ibid., 200). This initial overreaction is one of the most troubling problems in prenatal diagnostic counseling (ibid.).

The impulse to reject any fetus who is not normal might, in the future, be compounded by the fear that a deliberate choice not to abort a fetus with a known serious disorder could result in that child's later bringing suit against his or her parents (Beeson et al. 1983, 236). This possibility was brought up in the *Curlender* case (1980), although it was shortly after prohibited by California statute.

This initial rejection is also "demonstrated by the occasional demand for immediate termination of pregnancy in the face of minor anomalies diagnosed by prenatal examination, anomalies which may well be correctable and not even disabling" (Martinius 1986, 198). In fact, according to geneticist Marc Lappé (1987), a woman's choice to have a selective abortion is "affected far more by the certainty of the diagnosis for a particular disorder, than by the variability of the prognosis for the fetus" (8). Thus, the extent of the burden the disorder might impose on the family is often a secondary consideration in the decision to have a selective abortion. Physicians, J. Martinius (1986) suggests, could try to "compensate for the agitation" by explaining the problem, possible interventions, and ways to cope with a child with a handicap. While this is the optimal method of disclosing the news of a positive diagnosis it is, unfortunately, not the norm (197).

Parents, consequently, are asked to make a decision about the life of their fetus and to make an accurate assessment regarding their capacity as a family to cope with the burdens (and joys) associated with raising a child with a genetic disorder at a time when their grief and their negative feelings toward the pregnancy are at their peak. Given this, "it seems especially disingenuous and even irresponsible for physicians and scientists," Kass (1985) contends, "to finesse the moral question of genetic abortion and its implications and to take refuge from the issue of who decides behind the not-yet-broadened skirts of pregnant patients" (86).

Passing off "mistakes" made by distraught parents by saying "The freedom [of parents] to err is of high value in the genetic counseling job" (Lebel 1978, 30) is to make light of the life of another human being and to be insensitive to the grief and trauma many parents experience after going through a selective abortion. In other situations that involve the medical destruction of a human life, such as euthanasia or capital punishment by injection, there is no celebration or valuing of the "freedom to err." Instead, every effort is made to ensure that the margin of error is as small as possible. The same consideration should be given to fetuses who have genetic disorders.

In a society that values autonomy, it is often automatically assumed that the greater the range of choices, the better it is for the person making the choice. However, the mere possibility of choice can also increase the tragedy of the final choice, as it did in *Sophie's Choice* when Sophie was forced to accept responsibility for choosing which of her two children would die at the hands of the Nazis. Such choices, Rothman (1986) believes, are "a mockery of the concept of choice. It is a lesser-of-two-evils choice . . . a no-choice choice" (179). In drawing a parallel between Sophie's choice and the choice of selective abortion, she writes:

> There is an underlying element in both, the element of forced choice. In choosing between the tragedy of a disabled, defective, damaged, hurt, "in-valid" child, the tragedy of aborting a wanted pregnancy, a woman becomes responsible for the tragedy of her choice. Whichever "choice" she makes, it is all the worse for having been chosen. If she chooses to keep the pregnancy and have the baby, she is responsible for its suffering. . . . If she chooses to abort it . . . then she grieves for the loss of a baby none the less because she has chosen its loss (180).

Most women who have a selective abortion view it as their only choice rather than as a true choice between viable options. It is an experience of being "trapped" rather than a "rational seeking of information and choices" (ibid., 181). The pro– abortion rights stance—that it is solely the mother's needs that matter and hence solely her choice—fails to take account of the fact that children are born into a family, or some similar network of social relationships, and not into an isolated private relationship with one woman.

Birth and parenthood are social rather than private events. If a woman or parent has a positive duty to avoid harm (the duty of nonmaleficence) to her family and yet neglects to seek prenatal diagnosis or wants the child because she personally feels able to cope with the child, how is the value placed on respect for her autonomy to be balanced against her obligation to be fair to the other members of the family and to avoid harm to them? With the responsibility for making the choice resting primarily on the mother, the birth of a child with a serious genetic disorder, may come to be seen as an act of irresponsibility on her part.

To privatize the decision also privatizes the blame and responsibility for the final decision. Not only might this have the effect of creating resentment in the family, if there is disagreement or ambiguity regarding the final decision, but the cost of raising a child with a genetic disorder could become even

more burdensome as insurance companies adopt this line of reasoning. One of the future costs of having prenatal diagnosis
readily available might be intense pressure by insurance companies on pregnant women to undergo testing. If a genetic
disorder is detected and the woman refuses to terminate the
pregnancy, insurance companies might legitimately be able to
refuse to pay for all subsequent health costs for the mother and
child on the grounds that a genetic disorder is no longer an
"unknown contingent" but a knowable condition that can be
avoided (Baum 1989, 15). "After all," Rothman (1986) points out,
"she chose to have the baby. She could have avoided this
tragedy, but chose not to" (227).

Hidden Costs to the Family

While much has been written about the obvious harms
caused to a family by the presence of a child with a genetic disorder, others contend that there are other, more subtle harms to
the family from prenatal diagnosis and selective abortion that
have not been considered in the overall calculation.

Many people, for example, believe that the mere presence of
choice in decisions involving abortion eliminates, or at least significantly reduces, the anguish or grief suffered by the family.
Often, genetic counselors and physicians expect women to be
grateful for the abortion rather than saddened by it (Rothman
1986, 231). However, the anticipation of death or loss does not
necessarily diminish the actual grief after the loss occurs
(DeSpelder and Strickland 1987, 222). Even in cases of potentially fatal genetic disorders, such as anencephaly or Tay-Sachs
disease, the real issue is the method and timing of death rather
than the avoidance of death and grieving.

The response to elective abortion has been characterized as
"mild to transient grief." In contrast, with those who have selective abortions because of genetic abnormalities, the response is
best described as "moderate to severe, and prolonged"
(Edwards et al. 1989, 22). Genetic counselor Tabitha Powledge
(1983) reports that mourning the loss of a fetus through selective
abortion is almost identical to mourning the death of a newborn

infant (40). Others have also found that women who underwent selective abortion go through the same grieving process as other bereaved parents (Borg and Lasker 1981; Blumberg et al. 1975). This grief is "long-term" and often only "emerges fully after discharge from the hospital and lasts well beyond the interest and stamina of supportive family members and friends" (Weiss et al. 1989, 1009). A study of women who had abortions following ultrasonic disclosure of a fetal malformation experienced, as a result of the abortion, "long-lasting," and "severe psychological trauma" (Jorgensen et al. 1985, 31).

Unlike the death of a born child, grieving may be inhibited by the fact that it involves a "disenfranchised" death—that is, a death or loss of life that is not generally acknowledged by society (DeSpelder and Strickland 1987, 219–20). A father of a fetus who had Tay-Sachs disease tells of the intense pain and grief he and his wife experienced after a selective abortion:

> My wife and I often felt like lepers, as if no one could bear to touch our loss . . . others seemed oblivious to our experience. . . . There were days when we felt especially bereft, and when people seemed especially silent or unfeeling that we began to question our right to mourn (Silver 1986).

Parents and families are denied the support from social conventions and rituals that comfort and assist other survivors in their grief. Vincent Rue (1984), who studied the effects of abortion on fathers, notes that in abortion "emotional resolution is nearly impossible because there is no visible conclusion—just a memory. Because the unborn child was denied humanity, he or she is denied a grave or a marker. The grieving process is left unfinished" (226). Grieving the selective abortion of a wanted pregnancy, like the raising of a child with a handicap, can also create a rift and stress between parents (Rothman 1986, 207).

Indeed, it has been found that the grief associated with a selective abortion "becomes incorporated into one's very being" (ibid., 215). Even when good support groups are available, "there will be families who are extremely traumatized by this process and psychiatric help may be required" (Maidman 1989, 19). Geneticist Janice Edwards and her colleagues (1989), in their work with patients in a "moderately-sized genetic center," found that "psychiatric and marital problems requiring professional intervention occurred with frequency among our participants" (34).

In Rothman's (1986) study, women who had selective abortions reported that having another baby, while a source of comfort and joy, does not make up for the lost baby (216). "If there is any lesson we can learn from women's greater openness about reproductive tragedies," Rothman writes, "it is that pregnancy and babies do not cancel each other out. For their mothers, fetuses are not often 'fungible,' as some philosophers claim: interchangeable and replaceable" (80).

The actual abortion procedure can also be a source of intense suffering for those involved. Medical personnel, as well as women can be traumatized by second- and third-trimester abortions. Professor of obstetrics and gynecology Jack Maidman (1989) points out that the medical staff as well as the woman can suffer great psychological trauma from the abortion process.

> The staff's problems in the termination of pregnancy are extremely complex. Most doctors and nurses who work in pregnancy termination facilities were trained to think of themselves as healers and life-givers, not terminators of life. They also suffer burnout, guilt and grieving. The second trimester terminations produce reactions that are even worse, since the products of conception at this stage of gestation are more easily identifiable (16).

Because of this, most physicians prefer to induce abortions by injection of prostaglandins or saline solution. Although it may be more traumatic for women because they have to go through labor and the delivery of a dead fetus, it is less emotionally harrowing for the medical professional than a dilation and evacuation (D&E) (Rothman 1986, 195). Warren Hern and Billie Corrigan (1978) of the Boulder Abortion Clinic in Colorado report that they have observed intense reactions in both themselves and their colleagues to abortions with the D&E method, which is used in about half of all mid-trimester selective abortions. They believe that this is primarily because of the "violence of the procedure" and the "visual impact of the fetus." In a speech given to physicians at a meeting of Planned Parenthood, Hern and Corrigan (1978) told their audience:

> We have reached a point in this particular technology where there is no possibility of denial of an act of destruction by the operator. It is before one's eyes. The sensations of dismemberment flow through the forceps like an electric current (5).

Conflicts experienced by medical personnel include denial, projection, intellectualization, disturbing dreams, and disruption in their own interpersonal relationships. The nurses, who have to deal with disposing of the aborted fetus, often suffer the most, although both nurses and physicians report suffering from "abortion burnout" (Arnold 1984, 3). Other adverse reactions include "dread, depression, anxiety, guilt and identity crises related to the role conflict of healer and abortionist" (Leibman and Zimmer 1979, 128). Many medical personnel cope with the trauma by avoiding all but necessary contact with the woman. Thus, they are often psychologically unavailable to offer the emotional support that the woman needs when undergoing a selective abortion (Rodman et al. 1987; Furlong and Black 1984).

Women undergoing selective abortion frequently report that the medical staff consistently refused to recognize the humanity of the fetus, instead referring to "it" as "fetal tissue" or a "Down's fetus" (Levine 1979, 114). Katharine Levine (1979) writes of how isolated and betrayed she felt—"alone except for the baby in my uterus"—in her labor (114). She was treated curtly and even rudely by the staff that breezed in and out at long intervals to check her progress, not willing to acknowledge the suffering she was going through. Another woman, who had a saline abortion, described her experience as being full of contradictions and alienation: No cheerful nurse attending me or explaining the frightening process the saline had set in motion. They waited at the station in the hall. No one ever examined me. . . . I felt morally defiled, guilty, forced into an association with the death of what I loved and wanted. . . . Why was I convinced that the nurses were repelled by me when I was in labor . . . ? (Maloy 1988, 70)

In a follow-up study of women who had abortions for NTDs one woman commented, "I felt that the medical profession had lost interest in me. The baby was terminated, so 'end of problem.' For me the problems were just starting" (White-Van Mourik et al. 1990, 502). Thus, the claim that selective abortion is acceptable while infanticide (the other medical solution for relieving a family of the burden of caring for a child with a disability) is not, because the latter leads to "the potential brutalization of those who participate in it" (Fletcher 1986, 846), needs to be reevaluated in light of the possible harmful effects of selective abortion itself on those, family as well as medical personnel, who are directly involved.

Studies suggest that the prenatal diagnosis procedure itself may be harmful, not only to the woman but, as was pointed out in an earlier chapter, to those fetuses without disorders who are not selectively aborted as well as to their siblings. However, even if the woman chooses to abort the fetus, possible harms to the siblings as well as to the woman may still occur. In a study of what they termed the "aborted sibling factor," Anita and Eugene Weiner (1984) concluded that "there is increasing evidence that even very young children may be aware of maternal abortions despite family attempts to maintain secrecy" (209). While most parents who seek prenatal diagnosis tend to assure themselves that their children "would be so grateful for being born healthy that no real threat would be perceived," this idea underestimates "the power of the human mind to imagine and enlarge on reasons for rejection" (John Fletcher 1972, 478).

In another study on the impact of selective abortion on the family, it was revealed that almost all the parents, even when their children were very young and had not been informed about the abortion, noted some sort of change in their children's behavior around the time of and in the weeks following the abortion (Furlong and Black 1984, 25). These changes included regressed behavior, sadness, disappointment, and feelings of guilt.

Those children and other members of the family who have the same genetic disorder as the aborted fetus may interpret the abortion as rejection (John Fletcher 1972, 470). This could increase their insecurity and be a blow to their self-esteem. With the recent development of a test to prenatally detect the gene for Huntington disease, parents with a family history of the disorder are placed, Hubbard (1985) writes, in the

> outrageous position that they themselves are healthy and do not know whether they in fact will have the disease, they must decide to test their future child prenatally and terminate the pregnancy if the test reveals the presence of the gene for Huntington disease. If it does and they decide on abortion, they are as much as saying that their life has not been worth living because they will sicken and die at some undefined future date (and isn't that not true of all of us?). If they do not abort they are knowingly wishing a cruel, degenerative disease on their future child. This is an obscene 'choice' that no one should have to make (574).

In fact, the question has been raised as to whether physicians should even consent to parents' requests to perform prenatal testing for Huntington disease, as it breaks the "primary principles of confidentiality, privacy and individual justice that are owed to those children" (Bloch and Hayden 1990, 1).

Even normal children cannot help but feel insecure knowing that a younger sibling died because he or she was not "normal." What might happen to them if they should get sick or have an accident and no longer measure up? With prenatal diagnosis, parental love is no longer unqualified. Pediatrician Philip Ney (1983) warns:

> Children are becoming increasingly aware . . . that they exist only because their mothers chose them and chose them only

because they were desirable. Since their fate once hung on their desirability they tend to feel secure only when they are pleasing to their parents (171–72).

Ney (1979) also believes that abortion increases the likelihood of child abuse because "abortion truncates the developing mother-infant bond, thereby diminishing her future mothering capacity" (26). It also weakens the traditional taboo against the use of violence toward our own children and other weak and defenseless members of society. A study at Johns Hopkins University of women who came to the attention of the hospital because of child abuse found that previous reported abortions was one of the independent medical factors that was significantly associated with child abuse in women (Benedict et al. 1985, 217). Another study found that abortion may interfere with the maternal-infant bonding process with subsequent infants (Klaus and Kennell 1976), a factor that may contribute to the likelihood of abuse.

In a survey of the social well-being of the nation, Marc Miringoff (1989) found that the social well-being of the American child has been on an "overall downward trend since 1973" (7). The problem area that has worsened most significantly, he notes, is child abuse. While the dramatic increase in child abuse in the past few decades has been attributed by some people to better reporting procedures and a worsening economic climate, these two factors do not tell the whole story, given that the general social health index for the nation did not start to decline until late in the 1970s and that most of the improvement in reporting techniques took place in the early 1980s rather than in the mid-1970s (Miringoff 1989, 7). While the legalization of abortion is likely not the sole cause of the rise in child abuse, it is hard to ignore the correlation between the two. The use of abortion, including selective abortion, as an "easy" means to solve immediate problems, needs to be more carefully assessed in terms of the harm that the practice may be causing our children when parents attempt the same problem-solving strategy with their troublesome born children.

Conditionality and Parental Obligation

By incorporating "the issue of abortion right into the route to motherhood, it institutionalizes conditionality in mother love" (Rothman 1986, 85). Prenatal diagnosis, therefore, changes the whole experience of parenthood. The increasing use of prenatal diagnosis by parents may have the effect of diminishing that sense of parental love and concern that children need for optimal development (Fletcher 1972). Does the "procedure itself," John Fletcher (1972) asks, "because it inclines the parents to contemplate the abortion of the fetus before they are fully informed as to the results of the test, erode that 'basic trust' which is . . . [according to Eric Erickson] the first task of the budding personality" (473)?

Before prenatal diagnosis, caring for one's own child was one of the few areas of commitment that was unconditional. While women with unplanned and unwanted pregnancies might justifiably claim that they are not bound by this obligation because they never agreed to the pregnancy (and the parenthood that it entails) in the first place, women seeking prenatal diagnosis cannot claim to be exempt, as the very act of asking for prenatal diagnosis rests on a commitment to and acceptance of the pregnancy.

It is normally assumed, except in very exceptional circumstances, that a parent cannot allow a dependent child to die simply because that child's death would serve the needs of others in the family (Santurri 1985, 132). Why shouldn't similar duties to one's child be present during pregnancy? (Gustafson 1974, 220). If family burden is not a more compelling concern than the life of the child after birth, then, if we are to apply consistent moral reasoning, it shouldn't be able to override the same child's (fetus's) right to life before birth, unless there are morally significant differences between the two situations. Degree of burden is not significantly greater before birth. In fact, the burden of caring for any child, let alone a child with a serious genetic disorder, is much greater after birth than before (Sherlock 1987, 215).

If we were dealing with a two- or three-year-old child or a teenager who became disabled through injury or a genetic disorder that was not detected prenatally or at birth, we would clearly expect the parents to bear the burden of the cost of maintaining the life of their child. In a similar manner, parents might experience tremendous anguish (and even great financial cost) in having to cope with an obnoxious and unruly teenager, but they cannot seek to avoid this cost or burden by severing all ties with their child—at least not until the child is eighteen. To unconditionally bear the unexpected burdens associated with parenthood is not usually considered extraordinary "good Samaritan" behavior but simply part of the expected obligation parents have to their children. Acceptance of the risk of undertaking parenthood entails agreement to care for and support the child, regardless of how inconvenient or burdensome they may be or become.

The ultimate cost of making concern for one's children conditional on their state of health might be even greater than the benefits derived from being able to set limits on the degree of burdensomeness each family is willing to bear. "Each of us would loose a great deal," Heymann and Holtz (1975) write,

> if the idea were accepted that the family exists as a unit only insofar as its continued existence is of benefit to each individual member. Indeed, our individual characters are importantly shaped by a sense of the family commitment to share each other's good and bad fortune (408).

The Quest for a Perfect Baby

Several people have expressed concern that prenatal diagnosis, and the consumer mentality surrounding it, might encourage parents to seek the so-called perfect baby and to have less tolerance of those who are handicapped (Baum 1989, 13). However, others argue that the increasing intolerance of parents for children with defects is a healthy trend. Littlefield (1969), for example, argues that with overpopulation the world no longer needs all the children "we are capable of bringing into it—especially those who are unable to compete and will be an unhappy burden to others. If the size of our families must be limited," he argues, "surely we are entitled to children who are healthy rather than defective" (723).

If parental, or in particular maternal autonomy, is the sole criterion in making a decision about selective abortion, then other ethical principles and values, including what is best for the family and the fetus (in terms of fetal health and well-being) can be ignored and the decision made purely on whim (Weir 1984). It is simply unrealistic to dismiss interference in family choices by assuming that "altruism in families is strong," as Duff and Campbell (1976, 492) do. That parents are not always altruistic is evidenced by the fact that the most common cause of death among six- to twelve-month-old infants in America is being killed by their parent(s) (Ney 1979, 25).

There are times when parental desires and the best interests of their children come into conflict. While legal protection of the child has been extended to protect the high-risk neonate against the desires of the parents to deny him or her life or medical care, the present standard of prenatal care is to "give the mother's and family's interests precedence when they conflict with the interests of the fetus" (Fletcher 1983c, 154).

Sumner Twiss (1974), who tentatively supports the family-burden justification, sees this as a serious criticism of the argument. Neither children nor fetuses, he maintains, are the property of parents (253).

The consumer view of parental autonomy with respect to the selection of which fetuses should live is problematic in that it "suggests children are like property, that they exist for the parents" (Kass 1985, 95). Children are coming to be seen in terms of an investment. We speak of being able to afford another child, much as we talk about being able to afford a second car or some other luxury item (Rothman 1985, 188). "In this value system . . . ," Rothman (1985) writes, "we are learning to see our children as products of conception. . . . We work hard, some of us, at making the perfect product, what one of the doctors in the childbirth movement calls a 'blue ribbon baby'" (188). At one time, obstetricians simply had to deliver babies; now they are expected to deliver healthy, "trouble-free" babies. To do otherwise is to invite a lawsuit.

"The allure of a genetic test for a normal, or in the future an *optimal* baby," Lappé (1973) writes, "threatens to reinforce an inexorable trend in Western society towards typecasting the less-than-optimal into categories for assortment and ultimate disposal" (8). Indeed, the very health, intelligence, and normality of the unborn children of middle-class parents, have now become what many of "these parents use to formulate their *own* sense of adequacy and success" (ibid.).

In a society in which the very essence of humanness is defined in terms of the traits of the so-called normal adult, we increasingly tolerate children only as potential adults. "We put up with their 'childness' only because we think it will soon be over and they will be like us" (Hauerwas 1986, 185). However, children who are retarded or severely handicapped can never enter this adult world of adequacy and success, as now defined in our society. "They" will never be like "us."

Prenatal diagnosis and women's increasing dependency on medical professionals for information about the quality of their fetus can also lure women into the false hope that, with prenatal diagnosis and proper care, they can be assured of having problem-free children. Once control of the quality of one's child was offered as a possibility, the medical professionals were expected to live up to their advertising "promises" (as perceived by the consumers of prenatal diagnosis). It is common today to hear older woman say they would never have dared to attempt a pregnancy were it not for the availability of amniocentesis.

Yet, prenatal diagnosis is not foolproof. Many of these women think that their only fear is Down syndrome. However, even with recent advances, only a small percentage of genetic disorders can be identified by prenatal diagnosis (Baum 1989, 10). Also, even when the diagnosis is clear, the prognosis most often is not. Prenatal diagnosis alone, for many genetic disorders, is a poor predictor of later burdensomeness.

Measuring the Burdensomeness of a Disorder to the Family

The very "notion of parental good," Kass (1985) reminds us, "is very ambiguous and subjective and subject to change" (95). Guidelines for what is too great a burden, according to the family-burden justification, becomes relative to what each particular family perceives as a burden. For some parents, the burden on the family of raising a child of the undesired sex may be regarded as an intolerable burden, while other parents are willing to voluntarily, through adoption, take on the care of a severely handicapped child.

Perception of burden often has more to do with external circumstances than the fetus's condition. For example, acceptance of a child with handicaps is inversely related to one's socioeconomic status. Burton (1975) also found that parents' ability to cope with a child with a serious handicap was directly related to their "contentment" to live on a "day-to-day basis" (231). Parents who were highly motivated and achievement oriented (as American parents tend to be) were likely to experience more feelings of resentment and frustration (ibid.).

Parents who were religious, on the other hand, found it easier to cope with the demands of living with a child with a genetic disorder. In Burton's study, 72 percent of the mothers and 40 percent of the fathers reported that their religious beliefs and membership in a supportive religious community greatly assisted them in coping with the disorder and in accepting the situation (234).

The Burden of a Fetus of the Undesired Sex

Medical professionals define normal or nonburdensome in medical terms. However, burden to the family (or burden in terms of compelling a woman to continue carrying a fetus she doesn't want) can also be defined in terms of fetal sex or race. Yet, the majority of people, while seeing abortion as justifiable for even minor genetic and chromosomal disorders, believe that the use of prenatal diagnosis for sex selection is wrong (Fletcher 1986, 847).

In a society that claims to value family autonomy in these matters, why should this be the case? The burden associated with having another daughter can be far greater for some families than that associated with raising an XYY son who, in many countries (including our own), is probably less likely to face social discrimination and more likely to be financially independent than a daughter. If it is solely up to parents to decide what, for each of them, is normal or what is outside their limits of acceptability and hence too much of a burden, why can't these genetic limits be defined in terms of sex? After all, medically speaking, femaleness and maleness are diagnosable chromosomal conditions.

The family is not a private, autonomous unit but a group existing within a particular social context. In some countries, the birth of a girl is almost always regarded as a tragedy. In a patriarchal society, such as India, the birth of a female child can ruin a marriage or cause extreme financial hardship. In addition to a substantial dowry that the bride's family must pay to the bridegroom's family, "it is not unusual for the bride's parents to finance the bridegroom's studies or professional training . . . indeed, very many families get enormously indebted because of the dowry pressure and the debt is often carried on to the next generation" (Roggencamp 1984, 270).

Gender, like disability, is a social construct that influences our perception of people with these labels. Rothman (1986) writes, "Each society and social grouping establishes definitions of normal, of acceptable variations from normal, and of deviant or stigmatized variations from normal. . . . Some societies clearly mark males as normal, females as 'other'" (225). Lest we forget the role cultural expectations play in one's definition of a genetic disorder, we should be reminded that females were once regarded as "misbegotten males" (Aristotle and Thomas) who are "made of blood without soul" (John Marston) and, unlike men, are not made in the image and likeness of God (Augustine) (Fox 1983, 268). Now it is children with disabilities who, society tells their progenitors, are defective, are tragic mistakes of nature, rather than persons also made in the image and likeness of God.

These social constructs are constantly being affirmed by one's social milieu—in its religious symbolism and myths, in the media, and in the kinds of social support available (or unavailable) to different groups of people. For example, worldwide surveys indicate that nearly everyone would prefer their first-born child to be a son (Hoskins and Holmes 1984, 237). The United States is no exception (Wertz and Fletcher 1988). In fact, in the United States, "women experience the gender of their fetuses in ways similar to the way they experience their potential disability" (Rothman 1986, 226).

Even now it is difficult for parents to find stories for their daughters in which females were portrayed as people in their own right, rather than as appendages to men. While we've gotten past this to some extent, the so-called normal American family is still portrayed as having only healthy, nondisabled children, despite the fact that 7 to 10 percent of all children in this country suffer from some sort of disabling chronic illness—usually as the result of a genetic disorder (Kleinberg 1982, 5). The television series "Life Goes On," which features a son with Down syndrome, is an outstanding exception.

While many feminists ardently protest the "systematic eradication of women through the practice of selective abortion of female fetuses" in countries such as India (Roggencamp 1984, 266), is this any less justifiable than the systematic eradication of fetuses with Down syndrome or spina bifida or even fetuses with relatively minor sex chromosomal anomalies? Powledge (1981) argues against the use of prenatal diagnosis for sex selection on the grounds that it is the "original sexist sin . . . destroying an extant fetus for this reason is wrong because [it] makes the most basic moral judgment about the worth of a human being rest first and foremost on its sex" (196–97).

Again, the question must be asked: Why is judgment about one's moral worth or degree of burdensomeness based on sex discrimination morally unacceptable, but not judgment about the worth or right to life of their fetus based on potential intellectual capacity or ability to walk unassisted? If burdensomeness to the family is a morally legitimate reason for selective abortion, then it ought to apply equally to burdensomeness caused by having a child of the undesired sex.

For medical professionals in countries such as the United States, who claim to value maternal autonomy, to deny or discourage parents who are seeking prenatal diagnosis for sex selection because they believe that raising an unwanted daughter is not a burden, but to encourage prenatal diagnosis for NTDs or chromosomal disorders on the grounds that raising an unwanted child with a handicap, such as spina bifida or Down syndrome, is too much of a burden for any family, is both paternalistic and a betrayal of their own middle- and upper-class values regarding (in theory at least) the equality of the sexes but not the equality of handicapped and nonhandicapped people. To allow, and even encourage, families to discriminate against their fetus by selectively aborting him or her only when the discrimination is labeled socially acceptable demonstrates inconsistent moral reasoning rather than true respect for family autonomy.

Culture and Family Burden

While some people claim that abortion is ultimately feminist in that it serves the needs of women, these needs are to a large extent created by a society that is hostile toward women and children. Burton (1975) found that in the United States the hardship experienced by the family of a child with a serious handicap stems primarily from economic privations rather than the need to care for the child. In countries where medical care is subsidized, such as Northern Ireland, financial loss is "of least consequence in measuring burden to family" (126). In her study of fifty-two families living in Northern Ireland, Burton found that "only a relatively small percentage of parents felt that their sick child's illness had prevented them from accomplishing either a viable marital relationship, a satisfying parental relationship, or their basic aims in life" (231). This difference is reflected in the finding that, while the majority of American women opt for abortion when they learn that their fetuses have spina bifida, only about 40 percent of their counterparts in Britain and Ireland do so (EUROCRAT Working Group 1991, 52).

Burton's (1975) study of Irish families also revealed that, rather than permanently disrupting family relationships, "64% of the study's mothers and 53% of the fathers felt that their shared task had drawn them closer together" (231). Studies in Great Britain also report that "some parents and families become closer and more mutually supportive during the treatment of a chronically ill child and that siblings of such a child are not more likely to respond in maladaptive ways" (Ireys 1981, 330). Thus, much of the burden caused by disruption in family relationships in the United States may result primarily from the extraordinary financial burden imposed on families with children with genetic disorders.

The Burden of a Death in the Family

Different cultures have different mythologies surrounding death and dying that shape individuals' perceptions of children who are severely ill or dying. At one time in Western society, dying was considered a "more or less public ceremony" (DeSpelder and Strickland 1987, 62). It was an opportunity not only for the dying person to review his or her life, but also for all participants to reflect on their unique nature, goals, and destiny.

With the advent of a more materialistic approach to life, death, because it was seen as the cessation of meaning, came to be feared and viewed as something to be avoided. Those who were sick and dying were isolated from the rest of the community. Better that those who might make us uncomfortable with their death or precarious state of health die or rather be "terminated" in the privacy of their mother's womb so that their death does not have to be seen or acknowledged publicly. The most significant change in this new approach to death "may be the dying person's sense of his or her meaning for others. Feeling that he or she has scarcely any significance for other people, the dying person today may feel truly alone" (ibid., 70).

In response to our strong cultural bias against the dying, Kass (1985) suggests that the experience of living with a seriously handicapped or dying child might actually be a positive experience in that it could "help the healthy siblings learn how to cope with adversity" (95). Many families have mentioned that the challenge of living with a child with a serious genetic disorder, such as muscular dystrophy, and seeing them overcome hurdles in their lives can be a rewarding experience (Burton 1975, 231).

Realistically speaking, though, in a society that is embarrassed by the sight of death and dying and does everything it can medically to interfere with and dehumanize the natural dying process of children with fatal genetic disorders, it is hard to imagine the possibility of a "good death" or "benemortasia," as Dyke (1977) calls it (81). The mother of a child who died of Tay-Sachs disease wishes that she had chosen abortion or infanticide had it been available as an option: "The pro-lifers are out there saying, 'You only care about your own pain,' which is very real, but we didn't want to see him be uncomfortable and die that way—it was a very undignified way, we felt . . . to die" (Colen 1986, 38). Thus, while parents may want to act beneficently toward their child, selective abortion might, tragic though it may seem, be viewed by parents as the lesser of two evils—as the best way to handle the dying process of a fetus or child in a society that is hostile toward those who are ill and dying.

Conclusion

Despite its obvious flaws, the family-burden justification is one of the most compelling justifications of selective abortion, whether it be the selective abortion of female fetuses in India or the selective abortion of fetuses with medically defined genetic disorders in the United States. While the burdensomeness to the families of these children is to a large extent a culturally determined construct, the burdens to the family are still very real, given the nonsupportive social context in which they must care for and nurture their socially and physically unacceptable children. There is little doubt that it is unfair that a few families are unequally burdened with the correction of these injustices. It is also unjust for other members of society, including lawmakers, to compel parents to unconditionally commit to a relationship with a child to whom society has made no more than a token commitment.

For the family involved, the cost of acting beneficently toward their socially unacceptable fetus is often extremely high, both emotionally and financially. The dire consequences suffered by many of these families cannot be dismissed by anecdotes about families who grew together as a consequence of their experiences with their fetus or by platitudes about the joys of raising a child with Down syndrome.

Nevertheless, parents cannot use society's irresponsibility as an excuse to back out of their own personal moral responsibility for their offspring. Because the harms to the family originate primarily from unjust and oppressive social structures, the family-burden justification becomes a moral demand on all members of society to work toward changing these social structures rather than a morally acceptable reason for parents to act out, as "harmlessly" and privately as possible, society's oppressive attitudes toward certain classes of fetuses and born people. The family-burden justification instead ultimately points away from privatizing the family's decision and toward greater social responsibility and social change.

10

Quality-of-Life Justification for Selective Abortion

The quality-of-life argument has grown primarily out of the debate over the euthanasia of newborns with genetic disorders rather than within the context of selective abortion. This argument focuses on the best interests of the fetus rather than on any burden or inconvenience others—be they parents, siblings, or society in general—may feel as a result of the fetus's disorder (Arras 1984). One's right to life, it is maintained, should not be overridden because of contingent factors such as one's parents' financial resources, their religious and social standing, or their personal preference for a perfect child. Justice demands that all persons receive equal consideration. The fetus, like other persons, should be treated as intrinsically valuable rather than as a means to the ends of others. Thus, this argument seems to overcome the most obvious shortcoming in the social- and family-burden justifications for selective abortion—namely, that they are discriminatory against both fetuses and born people who are handicapped.

The Argument

Life as a Relative Good

While all human life is seen as good, it is precious only as the condition of other values. Because life is only a relative good, the duty to preserve life is a limited one. The normal conceptual connection between life and good is shattered in the presence of a severely retarded, profoundly damaged child (Arras 1984). The greatest evil is not death but rather unremitting pain and suffering. If we believe that pain and suffering are evil, then we have a moral duty to do what we can to eliminate these scourges.

This concept of life, Richard McCormick (1981) believes, as opposed to the view that life is an absolute or intrinsic good, is more consistent with the Judeo-Christian tradition (162). When a genetic disorder creates so much suffering and hardship that it threatens the very possibility of meaningful human relationships—which are the condition for "growth in love of God and neighbor"—the preservation of that life, he argues, distorts the very meaning of life (164). The call to love one another as God loves us sometimes demands that we make the hard decision to bring such a life to a closure.

Pediatricians Raymond Duff and A. G. M. Campbell (1976) also believe that this kind of respect for the quality of an infant's life—what they term a "person-oriented philosophy"— represents an advance over the traditional "disease-oriented" philosophy of medicine, which "supports a total crusade against disease" (488). The person-oriented philosophy, unlike the traditional philosophy, "regards some kinds of severely compromised living as worse than death" (487). There are times, therefore, when we have a moral duty, and perhaps it should also be a legal duty, to end the life of a fetus with a severe genetic disorder.

Selective abortion in modern society is regarded as the equivalent to the infanticide of deformed infants in primitive societies. Both practices show "the same great respect for the quality of human life" (Neel 1971, 222). The quality-of-life argument, therefore, rather than demeaning the life of the fetus, as do most of the other arguments used to support selective abortion, shows the greatest respect for the fetus's moral worth. "Judging that it is better to die rather than to live on," ethicist Joseph Margolis (1978) writes, "does not entail that life is not worthwhile or not worth living or worthless"(187). At times, ending a life of suffering and meaninglessness is preferable to living, especially if the fetus is going to die a painful death anyway. Indeed, a life that is still worth living might justifiably be ended in "order to close that life in the most favorable way" (184).

Selective Abortion as Preventive Medicine

In medicine, there are times when harm must be done to a patient (the fetus in this case) to prevent an even greater harm from occurring. Selective abortion, which is a harm, may be seen as a type of preventive medicine performed out of concern for the fetus with a severe genetic disorder to spare that fetus the much greater harm of a life of meaningless suffering. It is not merely *preferable* that this fetus not be born, it is *"wrong* to [knowingly] cause a person to be born" under these circumstances (Engelhardt 1982b, 186). Parents who intentionally give birth to a child with a disorder such as Down syndrome are committing a harm against their child by "inflicting grievous injury at will" (Fletcher 1979, 126). The obligation to put the best interests of the fetus first in these circumstances overrides parental autonomy. Parents and physicians have a moral duty not to prolong a life when it can be determined that the quality of that life will have a "substantial negative value for the person involved" (Engelhardt 1982b, 187). The concept of "wrongful life," although not yet put into law in any of the states, is the legal embodiment of this position, in which birth itself is seen as an injury or harm for which the parents, if they were aware of their fetus's condition, can be held liable "for the pain, suffering and misery which they wrought upon their offspring" (*Curlender* 1980).

Fetal Euthanasia

Because the good of the fetus is of primary importance in this argument, Susan Nicholson (1981) refers to selective abortion as "fetal euthanasia." It is a euthanasia decision in that it is made with the intention of humanely ending the life of a human so that he or she will not be condemned to endure a life of suffering. Applying the Catholic argument, which states that people are not obliged to "use extraordinary measures[1] . . . except where the preservation of their life or health is required to attain some greater good" (78), Nicholson argues that pregnancy in the case of a severely affected fetus may be withdrawn as an extraordinary measure because it merely makes the continued existence of the fetus intolerable. Just as "a parent may have a malformed infant mercifully removed from an incubator, then a woman may have a malformed fetus mercifully removed from her uterus" (90). The usual arguments against involuntary euthanasia do not hold here because with the fetus, unlike an adult or older child, there is an absence of any wish for life or death (76). In the absence of such wishes, it is up to someone else, like the parents or a third party, to make the decision on behalf of the fetus.

Assessing Quality of Life

While continued life is obviously in the interests of the normal child, this is not so clearly the case when the child has a serious genetic disorder (Gustafson 1974, 207). In these cases, the burden of the disorder must be weighed against the benefits of nonexistence. The most obvious burdens are those that are inherent in the disorder itself. The seriousness of the disorder is clearly relevant in making a moral distinction between those fetuses that should be selectively aborted and those that should not.

In setting up guidelines for third trimester abortions, Dr. Frank Chervenak and his colleagues (1984) came up with two criteria that they believe must be met for the abortion to be morally justifiable:

1. The fetus is afflicted with a condition that is either (a) incompatible with postnatal survival for more than a few weeks or

---

[1] Nicholson (1981) defines extraordinary measures as "those which cannot be obtained or used without excessive expense, pain, or other inconvenience, or which, if used, would not offer a reasonable hope of benefit" (78).

(b) characterized by the total or virtual absence of cognitive function; and
2. highly reliable diagnostic procedures are available for determining prenatally that the fetus fulfills either condition 1a or 1b (502).

Anencephaly, they believe, is one of the few genetic disorders that fulfills both of these conditions. In the case of anencephaly, prenatal death does not constitute a harm because there is not and never can be any cognizance of harm or benefit on the part of the fetus.

Others are not as stringent in establishing limits on the range of genetic disorders that qualify for selective abortion. John Fletcher (1986), for example, believes that trisomy 13 and trisomy 18, two disorders with reliable prenatal diagnoses that are incompatible with extended survival after birth, should be added to the list of disorders that meet the above two criteria (828). [2]

James Gustafson (1974), on the other hand, suggests that the quality of a fetus's life should be evaluated, not only in terms of that fetus's survivability after birth, but also in terms of his or her normal development after birth. One needs assurance that there is at least a probability of some sort of meaningful and rewarding life (207). This possibility does not exist, for example, for fetuses with Tay-Sachs disease because they will live out the majority of their life in an "inexorable course of deterioration" (ibid.), the harms of which outweigh the benefits of their normal development during the first six months. In cases such as these, "it is meaningful to speak of selective abortion not as abandonment of parental care, but, on the contrary, as the very manifestation of such care" (Santurri 1985, 133).

In addition to considerations of pain and survivability, "the presence or absence of such characteristics as the ability to think,

---

[2] Neither Fletcher (1986) nor Chervenak and colleagues (1984) are arguing from a quality-of-life perspective. However, their criteria have been used by some to support a quality-of-life justification for selective abortion.

to communicate, to give and receive love," Arras (1984) adds, "seems to be highly relevant" (31). In order for life to be worth living, there must be a "threshold of meaningful human life" or "basic humanity" (32) that must be met. For example, death would be in the best interests of a fetus whose life, even though it might be a long life, will be impaired by profound brain damage and whose "days will be measured by operations and whose pain will be unrelieved by the communication of human sympathy" (26). Some quality-of-life philosophers maintain that this "minimum standard of human health and potential" should be backed up by law (Joseph Fletcher 1979, 123). Humans who fall below this standard should have a "right not to be born" (ibid., 125). To fail to abort them is to deny them this right.

Those burdens indirectly related to the disorder, such as lack of family and societal support, are somewhat more controversial among those who support the quality-of-life justification. It is not the source of the burden, it might be argued, that is the issue here but the cumulative effect of these burdens on the fetus that matters. Taking all these potential burdens into consideration, Anthony Shaw (1978) came up with the following quality-of-life (QL) formula to determine which neonates should be denied treatment:

$$QL = NE \times (H + S)$$

NE refers to the natural physical and intellectual endowment of the child; H, the contributions to the individual by the home; and S, the contributions to the individual by society. In a similar vein, Richard Brandt (1978) proposed the creation of a "happiness curve" for neonates. For those who fall below a certain level (where unhappiness outweighs happiness), he suggests infanticide (49). By applying either of these formulas to selective abortion, the number of fetuses who might qualify as candidates could be greatly increased.

Making the Decision

The decision-making process is complicated by the fact that the fetus cannot consent or even (presumably) have any wishes regarding life or death. If the quality-of-life justification is to be used to sanction selective abortion, society must first have in place an objective set of appropriate guidelines specifying the range of malformations that warrant selective abortion. However, even if these guidelines could be agreed upon, this still leaves open the question of who is going to make the final decision in a particular case.

Nicholson (1981) believes that once these parameters are in place, the final decision should rest with the parents (82). Others disagree, pointing out that neither the attending physician nor the parents have enough objectivity to make such a decision. Joseph Margolis (1978) argues that the decision should be made from the viewpoint of a reasonable, mature person and what he or she would personally regard as a life not worth living. The parents are hardly likely to be impartial, and the physician's loyalty is likely to be with the parents. The final decision, therefore, should be subject to an impartial institutional review or court to ensure that it is made solely with the interests of the child in mind. Because selective abortion is legal at present, regardless of the type of genetic disorder, this decision making has not become an issue. However, there is an increasing tendency, when there is a question of whether it is justified to euthanatize a particular neonate with a genetic disorder, to turn to the courts to "enumerate those conditions which make life not worth living" (Dougherty, 1985, 115). This might well become the case with selective abortion, if abortion on demand should be outlawed at some future date.

Analysis

Selective Abortion as Medical Treatment for the Fetus

One of the assumptions implicit in this argument is that those parents who do not abort their disabled fetus have somehow imposed the tragic condition upon the fetus—that they have victimized the fetus—and are, therefore, responsible for the resultant suffering (Carmenisch 1976, 39). In this description, selective abortion is viewed as therapeutic for the fetus, and the woman's body is viewed as a kind of life-support machine that should be withdrawn if the treatment makes the fetus's existence intolerable.

However, this is an incorrect description of pregnancy. Pregnancy is not a form of treatment or extraordinary treatment because gestation is an ordinary part of everyone's early development. To see pregnancy as a medical treatment is to play into the tendency in the past few decades to medicalize pregnancy— to view it as a medical problem with medical solutions rather than as a natural process (Arditti et al. 1984).

Another odd assumption of the quality-of-life argument is that death is a therapeutic benefit to the fetus, in that it is done for the sake of the fetus. While it is clear how the death of the fetus may benefit the family or society, the benefit to the fetus is not quite as clear. The whole concept of benefiting the fetus by aborting him or her is problematic in the sense that the treatment (abortion) destroys the beneficiary of the act (Carmenisch 1976). Does it even make sense to speak of benefits without a beneficiary? Because the alleged benefit of nonexistence and the reduction of suffering it brings for the fetus occurs in the absence of his or her continued existence, during which the beneficiary could experience the results of that choice, then to whom do we have this duty or obligation?

While nonmaleficence—"Do no harm"—is one of the key moral principles in the medical profession, nonsuffering and health are not normally sought at any cost as the highest good. Rather, medical professionals attempt to reduce harm and suffering on the assumption of the beneficiary's continued existence. They seek minimal pain compatible with continued existence, but this is not what is being chosen in the case of selective abortion.

The confusion in the application of the "Do no harm" principle stems from making the condition, rather than the being, the focus of concern. With selective abortion, to eliminate the condition—the suffering—we eliminate those who suffer. "In the case of what other diseases," Kass (1985) asks, "does preventive medicine consist in the elimination of the patient at-risk? . . . The very language used to discuss genetic disease leads us to the easy but wrong conclusion that the afflicted fetus or person is rather than has a disease" (89). Because of this confusion the usual analogy between selective abortion and other types of preventive medicine, such as efforts to deal with the suffering caused by polio, AIDS, cancer, or heart disease, breaks down.

A linguistic confusion also exists in the quality-of-life argument as a result of the equivocal use of the term *suffers from* (Hauerwas 1986). Because those who have a genetic disorder "suffer from" that disorder in the sense of "experiencing any process" (*Webster's New World Dictionary* 1987, 597), some people assume that they "suffer from" the disorder in the other sense of the term—namely, "undergoing or enduring pain, loss or injury" (ibid.). From this, they jump to the conclusion that it would be better for the person with the genetic disorder not to exist at all than to have to "suffer from" such a disorder.

While confusion arising from the use of terms such as *suffer from* might be understandable, the brutality of the abortion procedure itself betrays the claim that the focus is solely on the welfare of the "suffering" fetus or on ending that life "in the most favorable way."[3] In second trimester abortions especially, the concern is primarily with killing the fetus rather than the comfort of the fetus or even the mother in many cases (Reardon 1987, 97). Indeed, if the midterm fetus can experience suffering, the abortion procedure itself is probably the cause of the greatest pain and suffering that will ever be experienced by the fetus, who, it is claimed, is being beneficently and lovingly put out of his or her supposed misery. Thus, talk of abortion for the sake of the fetus calls into serious question one of the most ardent claims of this argument: that it places a high value on the personhood and moral worth of the fetus.

---

3 None of the proponents of the quality-of-life justification of selective abortion made any mention of the type of techniques used in abortion.

Assessing Quality of Life

While concern for achieving a good or quality life might be commendable, the goal itself is extremely vague and open to subjective interpretation. With the exception of very severe disorders at one end of the quality-of-life continuum, and nonhandicapping genetic disorders, such as sex chromosomal disorders, at the other, there is considerable disagreement among supporters of this justification about which genetic disorders warrant selective abortion. Tay-Sachs disease and anencephaly are the two disorders that are most frequently mentioned to justify abortion. Survivability is generally cited as the primary value in these cases, with a normal, pain-free existence being a secondary consideration.

However, if six months of a normal, pain-free life does not make it worthwhile, as in the case of Tay-Sachs disease, then just how long must a life last to make it worthwhile? Few people believe it is justifiable to euthanatize someone who, for example, has just been diagnosed with terminal cancer but is unaware of the diagnosis and will have six symptom-free months ahead of her or him before the dying process begins, yet many of these same people believe that it is justifiable to abort a fetus with Tay-Sachs disease using the quality-of-life argument. This implies that six symptom-free months as an adult are intrinsically more meaningful than six symptom-free months as an infant, which is contrary to the claim of the quality-of-life justification that all people, regardless of age, are of equal moral worth.

Even given that people of all ages are of equal moral worth, there are still problems in this calculation. For example, is there some ratio of "normal" to "abnormal" years of life that can be used to determine whether meaningful life is present? If in the case of Tay-Sachs disease a ratio of about 1:5 "normal" to "abnormal" months is not sufficient to make that life meaningful, then do three to four years of "normal," symptom-free life also fail to justify the life of a child with Duchenne muscular dystrophy who, on average, will live another sixteen or seventeen years not only with the symptoms but usually with knowledge of the disorder and the slow deterioration?

Also, how should the intensity of suffering during these dying years be calculated into the formula? The dying process of a person with Huntington disease, for example, is filled with more suffering and anguish, and is often far more prolonged—sometimes lasting up to twenty years or more (Bergsma 1973, 487)—than that of a child with Tay-Sachs disease. In fact, it is questionable whether children dying of Tay-Sachs disease suffer much at all as a result of the dying process, thus making the argument that we are aborting them for their own sake somewhat suspect. For example, Ellen, a woman whose child, Justin, died of Tay-Sachs disease, made the observation that the "pain of Justin's deterioration" was hers and her husband's pain rather than Justin's. "I don't think he ever physically suffered. . . . It was [our] pain" (Colen 1986, 37).

Because of this, Daniel Callahan (1971) rejects the quality-of-life justification of abortion for fetuses with Tay-Sachs disease. "No one should be fooled," he writes, "into thinking we were really acting for the sake of the child, nor . . . be fooled into thinking that we were doing anything other than taking the life of the fetus in order to preserve the welfare of the parents" (7–8).

The selective abortion of a fetus with anencephaly, on the other hand, which is often cited as the most clear example of a justifiable use of the quality-of-life argument, upon closer inspection, simply does not qualify as fetal euthanasia—abortion performed out of kindness or concern for the fetus. On the contrary, the selective abortion of a fetus with anencephaly is based on the *lack* of any such obligations (present or future) to the fetus. Where the prognosis is so bleak and the nonexistence of any cognitive functioning so certain, there is no issue of either benefiting or harming the fetus or of determining what sort of quality of life that fetus does or will have. In the absence of any moral obligation to the fetus, the concern is for the mother's quality of life and the burden that carrying such a fetus places on her. In these cases, "pregnancy termination may benefit the pregnant woman by reducing the period of time during which she would suffer the psychological pain of carrying a fetus with a hopeless prognosis" (Chervenak et al. 1984, 501). It is not done to benefit the fetus.

Selective abortion for the sake of the fetus is also problematic in that before birth the prognosis associated with most genetic disorders is highly speculative. Even at birth, there is sometimes substantial disagreement among physicians about the prognosis of an infant with a genetic disorder (Sherlock 1987, 382). With potentially debilitating disorders, such as Down syndrome and spina bifida, two disorders frequently targeted by prenatal diagnosis, the diagnosis is "so uncertain, any supposition about the quality of such a life will be sheer guesswork and a policy based on it difficult to sustain" (ibid., 258).

With spina bifida, the prognosis is widely variable before birth, ranging from symptoms incompatible with prolonged survival to a life with no visible handicap at all. Even people who are seriously handicapped by spina bifida, rather than living the "miserable and unhappy" lives that most people imagine them leading, are for the most part "happy people who can respond to concern for their personal welfare" (Zachary 1982, 358). While some degree of mental retardation and physical handicap is almost always present with Down syndrome, because most children with this condition are happy and "derive great satisfaction from their lives," their "riddance," Arras (1984) concludes, cannot be justified as serving the children (30). "The main difference separating them from us," he suggests, "lies not in our capacity for enjoying life and for having love, but rather, it has been plausibly suggested, in 'their congenital inability to hate'" (ibid.). If this is the case, we should ask ourselves who has the real handicap—people with Down syndrome or "normal" people—if the real "meaning of life," as McCormick (1981) claims, lies in our ability to lovingly relate to God and other people? Yet, the judge who presided in the 1983 Baby Doe case (regarding the withdrawal of nutrition for a newborn with Down syndrome) ruled that "a minimally acceptable quality of life was not present in a child with Down syndrome" (Elkins et al. 1985, 492).

Although suffering is frequently cited as one of the main factors that can seriously compromise one's quality of life, suffering, unlike physical pain, is a relative phenomenon that is extremely difficult to measure objectively. What different people find to be sources of fulfillment or suffering is highly personal and varies greatly from one individual to another. Although suffering can include physical pain, it is not limited to it. Some patients report suffering when it is least expected; others do not suffer when it is assumed by others that they are suffering greatly (Cassel 1982).

According to Sherlock (1987), people with lower degrees of cognitive and social abilities "do not usually suffer very much" and are probably "little aware of the lives they could be leading were it not for their affliction" (81). It is *knowledge* of one's deficiency that is the source of most suffering. While the majority of nondisabled people believe that it is the profoundly retarded who are most likely to lead lives of meaningless suffering, both John Lorber (1973) and Norman Fost (1976) report that with potentially crippling conditions, such as spina bifida, the suffering is generally *greatest* among those with the highest intelligence. If the purpose of euthanasia "is to prevent the survival of those who suffer the greatest anguish, then," Fost (1976) writes, "a selective policy would withhold treatment from those whose prognosis for intelligence is best" (26). Because most physicians and parents are unwilling to go along with this policy, one might then ask what exactly is the nature of this "suffering" from which we are so nobly saving these so-called unfortunate fetuses and newborns?

It is also frequently assumed that having a badly deformed body is a source of great psychic suffering for the person with the handicap. "Normal," or the "natural standard" (Kass 1985, 97), becomes equated with "good." Surely, no one should have to suffer the "indignity" and burden of being "trapped" in a terribly deformed body. This assumption is usually supported by reference to psychoanalytic theory that postulates that there is a strong relationship between one's feelings about one's body and one's degree of adjustment and personal happiness (Darling 1979, 34). However, this relationship has not been borne out in studies of children with severe handicaps (ibid., 35). In a study comparing the level of self-esteem of twenty-nine congenitally blind children with the same number of sighted children, no significant difference was found between the two groups (Zunich and Ledwith 1969, 771).

Regarding the widespread belief that a person with a genetic disorder would rather not have been born, Lejeune (1970) found that, while the majority of patients with a severe genetic disorder (if they can express their feelings) regret the affliction, they "do not regret being themselves and being alive" (124). In another study of 222 successive suicides, not a single case of suicide was found among anyone who [had] any congenital anomalies" (Callahan 1970, 113).

The one exception to this are patients who are in the early stages of Huntington disease. In these cases, the suicide rate is from seven to two hundred times the normal rate, depending on the country (Swavely and Falek 1989, 112). This finding supports Sherlock's (1987) claim that it is knowledge of one's deficiency that is the source of greatest suffering, as these suicides generally take place when deterioration has set in but cognitive dysfunction is still minimal and patients are well aware of what is happening to them. One might predict similar suicide rates among previously "healthy" adults who become severely disabled because of accidents or combat.

Another major point of disagreement among supporters of the quality-of-life justification concerns the extent to which burdens external to the individual, rather than directly related to the disorder, should be counted in calculating one's quality of life. Socioeconomic burdens, parental rejection, lack of adequate institutional care, or opportunities for a minimally satisfactory life can all add up to substantial burdens that might culminate in a life of misery, suffering, and isolation from meaningful human contact, and even a painful and brutal death in the case of child abuse, as surely as can the physical or mental disability itself. Thus, it is not the source of the burden, some argue, that is at issue here but the cumulative effects of these burdens on the fetus.

While some advocates of the quality-of-life argument object that the inclusion of social and family burdens would be extremely unjust because they "are not the fault of [the] children" (Arras 1984, 28), the burden of suffering because of the inadequacies of one's parents or society is just as real. Indeed, we should also be reminded that the genetic disorder is not the fault of these children or their parents. Although it is true that we have a duty to work toward increasing opportunities for happiness for all people, if we accept the quality-of-life argument, why should those who presently lack the opportunity for happiness, because of oppressive social or family structures, have to suffer while waiting for social reform or for cures? One might argue that children with Tay-Sachs disease suffer because of the lack of a medical (external) solution to their problem. Yet, it is not being suggested that we put these children through years of "suffering" while waiting for a possible cure. Why, then, should other children with genetic disorders be made to suffer while waiting for cures? To compel an individual to live a meaningless life of suffering because the source of the burden is external, if one adopts the quality-of-life reasoning, is not to respect the fetus as an end in itself. If life is a good only as the ground of other values and if conditions are such that the realization of these values seems impossible, then, if the focus is truly on the best interests of the fetus, we have a moral duty to end the life of that fetus regardless of the source of the burdens.

Advocates of the quality-of-life justification, if they are consistent in focusing only on the burdens suffered by the individual, find themselves in the paradoxical position of tacitly condoning social discrimination—a position that they claimed to be avoiding. "If intolerable burden is really the critical issue," Edmund Santurri (1985) points out, "why not cast the net more widely to include even those genetically normal fetuses whose lives will be made miserable by social circumstances. Is the prospect of a life in South Africa, for instance, grounds to abort a black fetus? Does being Jewish in Nazi Germany count? If not, then what precisely is the difference between these cases and the genetic abortion being advocated?" (138)

The quality-of-life argument might also be used to justify the abortion of female fetuses in India where many females live a life of misery, suffering, and rejection. In New Delhi alone, four hundred to five hundred dowry deaths occur each year, where the new wife is burned to death by her husband because he is not satisfied with the extent of her dowry (Roggencamp 1984, 271). The abortion of a fetus to spare him or her possible future abuse stemming from parental rejection is another frequently used variation of the quality-of-life argument in the United States.

While children with handicaps are more vulnerable to abuse (Barbara Devens, lecture on "Child Abuse and the Medically Special Child," University of Rhode Island, July 1987), the prevalent notion that "abortion prevents the birth of abused and unwanted children is empirically incorrect" (Sherlock 1987, 211). E. F. Lenoski (1976) found that 90 percent of abused children were "wanted" fetuses and that abused children are more likely to be named after one of the parents, thus suggesting that parents who set very high standards for their children might be more likely to abuse them when they fail to live up to parental expectations. Unfortunately, the consumer mentality that often accompanies prenatal diagnosis encourages parents to set high standards for their children. However, this does not necessarily mean that the fetus who is diagnosed as having a genetic disorder will end up being an abused child. Even when the child has a serious genetic disorder, there is no accurate way to predict how the parents will react to the child after birth. Parents may grow to love and cherish a child with a handicap who was initially unwanted, or initial rejection may be increased by exposure to the child (Callahan 1970, 113).

A major problem with the use of abortion to spare the unwanted fetus, whether a female in India or a fetus with Down syndrome in middle-class America, from a life of physical and emotional abuse is that it is a form of victim blaming, rather than a solution to child abuse and, consequently, merely further legitimates the rejection and mistreatment of these classes of people. Because of the irreconcilable conflict between the values of beneficence and justice, the quality-of-life argument fails as a viable justification of abortion. "In the long run," Karen Lebacqz (1973) concludes, "this violation of fundamental rights of equal treatment is a more serious threat to the 'quality of life' of all of us than the birth of numerous children with defects will ever be" (126).

Deciding When to End a Life of Suffering

Another problem with use of the quality-of-life justification for selective abortion is that, with few exceptions, most genetic disorders do not seem to be a handicap in the uterine environment—at least among those who do not spontaneously abort in early pregnancy. In their apparent concern for relieving the suffering of these fetuses, advocates of the quality-of-life argument for selective abortion make a subtle shift from talking in the present tense about the present quality of life of the fetus to talking in the future tense. There is no indication that the majority of fetuses with genetic disorders, such as spina bifida or Down syndrome, which might cause great suffering after birth, let alone disorders with symptoms that do not manifest themselves until long after birth, are in pain or are suffering before birth as a result of their genetic disorder (Callahan 1970). Thus, the analogy between selective abortion and euthanasia breaks down because euthanasia, which is defined as a means "of escape from some condition, usually terminal and felt by the patient to be intolerable" (Flew 1979, 114), is performed to relieve present suffering, not possible future suffering. [4]

However, while the quality-of-life justification cannot legitimately be used to justify the selective abortion of a nonsuffering fetus, it presents a strong argument for euthanatizing that same

---

[4] In fact, even a bleak prognosis at birth does not always indicate that the newborn is presently suffering because of the genetic disorder. Zachary (1982), for example, found that there is little evidence that newborns with severe spina bifida are in pain because of their condition (357). He claims that the large doses of painkillers administered to these infants as they are "allowed to die" is intended primarily to heavily sedate them so that they make fewer demands on the medical staff, rather than to relieve any pain the infants may be suffering (ibid.). Zachary further points out that painkillers are administered to babies in no apparent pain and asserts that the "direct purpose and effect [of these drugs] is the death of the child in a relatively short time" (ibid.). The passive euthanasia of newborns with genetic disorders, Heymann and Holtz (1975) maintain, is more a factor of the child's young age and the costs of treatment to family and society rather than concern for the quality of life of the child (399).

person later in life after the onset of debilitating symptoms. If selective abortion is truly an "act of love" (McCormick 1981), it is inconsistent to refuse to euthanatize a young child dying of cystic fibrosis or an adult with early symptoms of Huntington disease, but to claim at the same time that we have a moral obligation to euthanatize a nonsuffering fetus with the same condition. If life is a relative good and has value only as the condition of other values, when these conditions are not present, no matter what the stage of life, we have a duty to end that life. For those who protest, claiming that the born person has a higher moral status than the fetus, it should be pointed out that, on the contrary, the moral imperative to end the life of a born person who is suffering from a genetic disorder becomes even more compelling because the duty to respect the person and act beneficently toward the person becomes that much greater. Sherlock (1987) writes:

> It may be claimed that, having treated these children at birth and given repeated care afterwards, we have now created a social obligation to support them that does not extend to newborns [and fetuses]. . . . Even if we admitted that, *prima facie*, we ought to follow through on a social commitment to render care, it surely seems that if anything could defeat that obligation an admission that the child has a life not worth living surely would. If he does not have such a life, the case for letting such an infant die collapses. On the other hand, if such a life will be so bad that one ought to die rather than endure it, it seems cruel to force one to live it as a ten-year-old when a means of painlessly releasing the person from his or her misery is close at hand (86)

Our moral horror at euthanatizing, without their consent, older children or adults with debilitating genetic disorders runs counter to the claim by advocates of this justification that they regard all humans as having equal moral worth.

Who Decides for the Fetus

The quality-of-life justification of selective abortion is further weakened by the fact that someone else has to make the decision on behalf of the fetus. Arras (1984) argues that it is important to adopt the child's viewpoint rather than to substitute "the fears of normal adults for the genuine best interests of impaired children" (30). However, one simply cannot know how the fetus, especially in the absence of any obvious pain, would feel about being aborted. The question of whether a fetus with a severe genetic disorder would rather not be born is "insoluble in principle," because there is no way to predict how the fetus would feel or if he or she could know about his or her future (Callahan 1970, 113). In practice, any discussion of abortion for the sake of the fetus is done from the perspective of a born child or, more accurately, a healthy adult, but a standard based on healthy, normal development is hardly appropriate. The "reasonable person standard" will necessarily be prejudicial to the best interests of the child with a genetic disorder. As Arras (1984) himself points out, "Competent adults have naturally pitched their value systems on the solid ground of normalcy" (30).

Thus, the quality-of-life argument, when applied to selective abortion, is inherently paternalistic. While life for a person with a severe genetic disorder might be viewed by a nondisabled adult as being burdensomely boring or meaningless because of the limitations it imposes on that person, it would probably be boring only for the nondisabled person and not for the person with the disorder. "One who has never known the pleasure of mental operation, ambulation, and social interaction," John Robertson (1975) writes, "surely does not suffer from their loss as much as one who has" (254).

Of all the ill fortunes to which we may fall prey, "the loss of reason," it has often been noted "appears . . . to be the most dreadful" (Smith 1976, 1). What is the source of this dread? It is not the severely retarded who are in anguish. The dread that people experience in viewing others who suffer from these deficiencies is not the anguish of those who are severely retarded or physically handicapped but the anguish at the sight of those who remind us of our own vulnerability (ibid., 11).

According to Lubowe (1989), the "aesthetic repulsion toward disfigured people" and the anxiety the sight of them generates may also stem from our feelings of "helplessness in the face of both capricious life and death (92). Thus, the sources of the suffering that we claim to be beneficently eliminating for the sake of the fetus must be correctly identified. The misery and suffering wrought by a genetic disorder seems to be, to a great extent, the suffering the disorder causes the normal person—suffering that is projected onto the person or fetus with the genetic disorder—rather than any suffering felt by the person with the disorder.

Conclusion

While the quality-of-life argument might be applicable to euthanasia decisions about people (especially competent older children and adults) after the onset of debilitating symptoms, it cannot be used to justify selective abortion. Instead, it is one of the most deceptive of the justifications used to support selective abortion. "Whenever a strong group argues on behalf of a weaker group that their removal would be better than their survival," John Fletcher (1972) warns, "we should not be duly impressed" (482).

If we want to justify selective abortion, let us not delude ourselves into thinking we are doing it for the sake of the fetus and out of a great respect for the fetus but instead be willing to honestly examine our real motives. Lejeune (1970) once wrote that the real goal of "so-called premature euthanasia" is not "to spare seemingly unnecessary suffering to the *patient* [but] to prevent suffering to *his family and to society*"(122). Thus, the quality-of-life argument, rather than providing us with a sound moral justification of selective abortion, collapses back into the previously rejected justifications of selective abortion based on burdens to society and family.

11

Conclusion

The primary purpose of this book was to critically examine, from an informed position, the various arguments put forth in support of prenatal diagnosis and of selective abortion based on prenatal diagnosis. One of the early conclusions drawn was that while one could not prove beyond a doubt that the fetus was a person, in the moral sense of the term, there were also no sound reasons to eliminate fetuses from personhood and, therefore, deny them a right to life. Therefore, abortion—the taking of the life of a fetus—like the taking of the life of any person, has to be justified. The presence of a genetic disorder in the fetus is one of the most frequently cited mitigating circumstances that is thought to override the normal prohibition against abortion.

Five different arguments in support of selective abortion based on prenatal diagnosis were examined. The eugenic argument is weak, not only because of its dubious and ambiguous goals in terms of the future genetic health or normalcy of humankind but also because of the coercive element that would have to be introduced in the testing of all high-risk women and the compulsory abortion, particularly of all phenotypically normal carriers of deleterious genes. Another problem is that because virtually everyone carries at least a few deleterious recessive genes, we are all eugenically suspect. Consequently, the task of destroying all carriers becomes self-defeating or, if genetic testing focuses only on certain populations, such as blacks for sickle cell anemia, discriminatory. The fetal-wastage argument, on the other hand, not only confuses what is normal with what is desirable but assumes that a certain level of health is a prerequisite for continued medical care—both assumptions that run directly contrary to traditional medical ethics.

The three arguments based on the burdensomeness of the disorder were examined next. One of the major problems with the social-burden justification is that for most genetic disorders, the prognosis before birth is notoriously unpredictable, making any cost-benefit analysis highly speculative at best. In addition, like the eugenic argument, this justification places pressure on parents to abort, for the social good, their fetuses who have genetic disorders, thus creating a climate of blame around those families who fail to comply. This reasoning is even more troublesome in that society ordinarily does not consider potential future social burdensomeness to be a sufficient justification to end someone's life. The social-burden justification is also problematic in that handicap or social burdensomeness is to a great extent a culturally defined rather than a medical construct. The destruction of individuals who are social burdens primarily because of oppressive social structures that place restrictions on their participation in society smacks of the worst sort of discrimination and victim blaming. Finally, acceptance of the social-burden justification involves a serious erosion of other important values, such as the equality of all people, upon which a democratic society is built.

While the family-burden justification was one of the most compelling of the five arguments, it fails because it is based on the faulty assumption that a person can abdicate personal moral responsibility for their actions in the face of social irresponsibility. At the same time, while it claims to give highest priority to parental autonomy, the argument fails to take into account the stress parents are under when they learn of their fetus's disorder and the extent to which their personal decision and agony are in fact shaped by the biases and prejudices of the medical professionals and society at large. In privatizing the abortion decision, the care of those children who are born is also made a private family responsibility, or burden, rather than a collective social responsibility. The family-burden justification also fails to take seriously the potential harms of the prenatal diagnosis procedure itself as well as the harms of selective abortion to the woman, the family, the medical personnel involved, and those fetuses who survive the gamut of tests. In addition, by legitimating the consumer mentality that demands perfect babies ("products of conception") and the destruction of those ("defective goods") who fail to meet certain standards, it thereby destroys the unconditional nature of parental love and the parent-child trust that is built on this love.

The quality-of-life argument, which is based on the burdensomeness of the disorder to the fetus, on first inspection seems to avoid the charge brought against the previous arguments that they are discriminatory. However, besides the vagueness of the whole notion of quality of life and the problems inherent in the attempt to calculate another's quality of life, there are a number of very odd assumptions in this argument. One is that pregnancy is a type of medical treatment that should be withdrawn if it makes life unbearable for the fetus. A second is that death or nonexistence could be a benefit to the fetus. It was also pointed out that the majority of fetuses with serious genetic disorders are not suffering or in pain as a consequence of their disorder and that, therefore, talk of abortion for the sake of the fetus should make us suspicious that the true motives are not concern for the welfare of the fetus but simply a subtly disguised reworking of the arguments based on burden to society and the family.

While none of these arguments alone is able to support selective abortion, the possibility should be examined that when woven together the several strands might be strong enough to justify selective abortion. This could be done by taking a case that elicits our greatest sympathy and pity and leads us to consider that while selective abortion might not normally be justified, surely in this case it is.

Let us consider the following case. Rachel is a poor, single, African-American woman who was born with spina bifida. Her parents gave her up into foster care soon after her birth because they felt unable to care for a child with a handicap. Although she now manages to get around with the use of leg braces, because of her handicap, her lack of education (the local public schools did not have wheelchair access, so she has no formal education), and the unavailability of day-care facilities, Rachel is unable to get a regular job. Her first child, Lazarus, was also born with spina bifida. Not only is he confined to a wheelchair but he is retarded due to hydrocephaly, which was not treated after birth because Rachel had no medical insurance to pay for the operation. Despite the very small chance that Rachel's second child would also have spina bifida, she has just received the results of routine MSAFP testing, which indicates that there is a high probability that the fetus she is presently carrying also has spina bifida. Rachel is devastated. While she wants a second child, she doesn't know how she can possibly cope—financially and emotionally—with another handicapped child.

Despite the great sympathy we cannot help but feel for Rachel's predicament, even the several strands woven together still cannot justify selective abortion even in this case. Besides the possibility of adoption as an alternative to abortion, the abortion of this fetus because of handicap merely moves the problem of the discrimination already suffered by Rachel to an even more disenfranchised group—fetuses with genetic disorders. Also, use of the presence of a genetic disorder as a justification to abort Rachel's fetus devalues not only the fetus but Rachel as well and all others in our society who are handicapped. In doing so, it legitimates society's neglect of the needs of those who are handicapped.

The arguments put forth in support of selective abortion, while not strong enough to justify the practice, place a moral imperative on all members of society to work toward changing oppressive social structures—ecclesiastical as well as political and familial—that handicap people with genetic disorders. If the moral strength of a people is measured by how they treat the weakest and most defenseless, then selective abortion surely represents our failure as a society. Rather than being a solution to a problem, selective abortion is a tragic symptom of our individual and societal rejection and fear of those who are needy and those who are different as well as our lack of imagination to come up with just and nonviolent solutions to social problems.

Selective abortion is generally accepted by its proponents not as a positive good but as "a compromise in the ethics of relief of suffering" (Fletcher, 1983b, 234). This compromise, however, has been made far too readily and without an adequate concern for the moral implications and harms of the practice or a thorough study of other possible solutions. These solutions might include legal restrictions on selective abortion, although it does not necessarily follow that everything that is immoral should also be made illegal. While restriction of selective abortion might be a noble goal, to restrict it without also putting into place the social supports necessary for families to choose in favor of preserving the life of their fetus would be unfair to both the child and the family and an abdication of our collective responsibility as a society for the welfare of those in need. In this regard, the issue of who should decide when selective abortion might or might not be justified also needs to be addressed.

Lejeune (1970) once wrote that our response to selective abortion "must be guided by humility and compassion . . . humility because we must recognize we have no ready-made answers . . . [and] compassion because even the most disinherited belongs to our kin" (128). In the face of this challenge, we must not give up because of our own ignorance and attempt to eliminate those we cannot help. Rather, we must become advocates for those our society labels as the disinherited: fetuses and children with severe genetic disorders as well as their distressed parents. This willingness to change our attitudes must be accompanied by vigorous efforts to abolish those conditions that handicap children with genetic disorders as well as their families.

Where Do We Go from Here?

How might we, as medical professionals, social policymakers, religious organizations, families, and individuals, work toward the creation of a more compassionate society? This epilogue presents a list, albeit incomplete, of recommendations for these different groups.

Medical Professionals

The medical profession has traditionally located the source of problems within the individual and has regarded the social structure as irrelevant to diagnosis and treatment. While social structure may not be particularly relevant in the treatment of physically based conditions, uncorrectable genetic disorders are more of a social than a medical problem. Rather than institutionalize or abort those who do not fit into the system, medical professionals need to examine ways in which the system can be transformed or expanded to serve individuals with genetic disorders as well as their families.

Medical professionals also have to become more aware of how the practice of selective abortion threatens the most basic moral principles of medicine and society. The presence of a genetic disorder after birth is not generally considered sufficient grounds to actively cause the death of a nonsuffering child. Selective abortion and the accompanying idea that the genetically unequal can be treated unequally runs directly counter to the basic medical principle of equal treatment for all humans, regardless of their age, condition, or usefulness within a society.

In addition, the emphasis on parental autonomy and nondirective counseling turns the physician into a technician who is treating the desires of the patient (the parent in this case) rather than a professional making a medical judgment. Medical professionals who are presently participating in prenatal diagnosis and selective abortion procedures need to be asking themselves the question "what are we doing?" rather than fooling themselves into thinking they can claim moral immunity because it is the mother who makes the final decision. "All of us bear a responsibility in a democratic society," John Churchman (1989) writes, "at least in those areas where we can try to bring to bear some personal judgment and influence" (25). The nondirective approach to prenatal genetic counseling fails to take into consideration the possible harms of the prenatal diagnostic procedures themselves to the woman and family. Fletcher and Wertz (1987b) point out that "non-directiveness as a norm may have originated in part from lack of treatment options a well as from respect for autonomy. When no treatment exists it is easy to be non-directive" (309).

To accept selective abortion as a temporary expedient solution to one's helplessness in the face of severe genetic disorders runs the danger that it will blunt the moral consciousness of those involved rather than stimulate them to look for better ways to deal with the burden of genetic disorders. To eliminate those who cannot be helped by medical technology betrays the "Do no harm" principle of medicine and diminishes the role of the medical professional as a healer and a saver of life.

Selective abortion also fails to take into account the rights of the fetus and the role of the fetus as patient. An analysis of the concept of personhood yields no sound reason to eliminate fetuses from personhood and deprive them of the basic natural rights normally accorded to persons. Rather than simply take the easy way out when the interests of the fetus and those of the parent conflict by deferring to the desires of the stronger party, medical professionals need to reclaim a measure of professional autonomy and integrity, and be prepared to make a medical judgment that takes into consideration the benefits and harms of prenatal diagnosis and selective abortion for all involved. This approach is more consistent with the practice of medicine in other areas in which the medical professional may be working with more than one patient at a time, such as in family medicine, where the physician is faced with a case of suspected child abuse or in family counseling where there may be a serious conflict of interest between different members of the family.

In light of these considerations, the following is a list of recommendations for medical professionals:

1. Prenatal diagnosis should not be given routinely to all high-risk women nor should it be given on request. Although moral choices are influenced by the available technology, when there is a conflict between technology and morality, moral considerations should override the technological imperative. While the physician may have a moral obligation to provide prenatal diagnosis for disorders that can be treated in utero, the reassurance justification and the time-to-prepare justification, in light of the harmful emotional side effects of prenatal diagnosis, are not sufficient on their own to warrant the procedure. Prenatal diagnosis is a medical procedure, and physicians should use their judgment in deciding whether the woman requesting the procedure would benefit from it without at the same time causing undue harm to herself and/or the fetus.

2. Medical professionals should advise against selective abortion (even if it is legal) should a genetic disorder be discovered or suspected. Parents of fetuses with disorders incompatible with postnatal life, such as anencephaly, should not be pressured to seek an abortion but should be offered the option to continue the pregnancy because depression following a selective abortion is generally more serious than that following a stillbirth—probably because of the "role of decision making and the responsibility associated with selective

abortion" (Blumberg et al. 1975, 805). If abortion is chosen by the parents, the procedure should be performed in a manner that shows compassion for both the mother and the fetus. Imperfect though the fetus may be medically, it is still their child. To facilitate the grieving process, parents should be offered the chance to see and hold their child after the abortion. Funeral arrangements should be made, if so desired by the parents (Furlong and Black 1984, 23–24).

3. Medical professionals involved in prenatal care should receive more training about genetic disorders and the various resources available for parents who have a fetus with a genetic disorder. This training should include not only academic education but direct contact with families of children with genetic disorders and various social agencies that help these families. Current literature on the specific genetic disorders and information regarding local resources, including adoption agencies and quality residential schools, should be made available to the family.

4. A more interdisciplinary approach should be used in working with parents of fetuses with genetic disorders. Counseling for these parents and other members of the family should be ongoing throughout the remainder of the pregnancy (as well as after the birth of the child). Medical professionals should try to help parents see their fetus, not as "defective goods" to be disposed of but as a human being to be appreciated and loved by showing them ways in which they may help their child. Later counseling sessions should focus on the development of family and social support systems, strategies for coping, and the setting of realistic goals for the child. Bereavement counseling is also important to help the family work through the grief involved in the loss of their "idealized" child.

5. Hospice groups and support groups should be available for families of children who are dying of a genetic disorder, such as Tay-Sachs disease. Some hospitals are now encouraging parents to hold their dying newborns and even keep a Polaroid camera on hand to take pictures of the children for

the parents (Maidman 1989, 15–16). Medical professionals themselves also need to reexamine their handling of dying children and their families, especially the isolation of the dying child and the needless prolongation of the dying process by medical technology.

6. The trend toward putting more effort into researching genetic screening and less into research on cures for genetic disorders such as Tay-Sachs needs to be reversed. To concentrate on the former at the expense of the latter is to subscribe to an "ethics of despair" (Schweitzer 1987). More research is also needed on the side effects of prenatal diagnosis and selective abortion. Because of the privatization of abortion and the fear of appearing antifeminist, little research has been done on the possible harmful side effects of these procedures. The paucity of research in these areas as well as research on bonding between mothers and infants with genetic disorders (Elkins et al. 1985, 493) and on developmental stages and the potential of children with different genetic disorders has only served to diminish rather than enhance parental autonomy. More effort should also be extended to improve fetal therapy.

Social Policy

While changes in the medical profession are necessary, the interpretation of genetic disorders solely in terms of a medical model obscures the fact that the disadvantages stemming from genetic disorders are often more the result of social barriers and prejudices than of the handicap itself. Without concurrent social and political changes, the birth of a child with a serious genetic disorder, despite the best efforts of medical professionals, will too often remain a tragedy for most families. Such individuals and their families will find it difficult, if not impossible, to find personal justice in a society in which oppressive social structures severely limit their options and label them as "defective" members of society. As a society, we must demonstrate a willingness to support these families.

The following are recommendations for social changes:

1. There is a need for more day schools for children with disabling genetic disorders as well as for more research into the optimal learning style of these children. Educational services for families should begin shortly after the birth of the child.[1] Good residential schools that provide security and peace of mind for both the child and the family are also needed for families that feel unable to care for the child at home but do not want to be cut off completely from the care of their child.

2. There is also a need for more public education on the nature of genetic disorders. Because people with severe genetic disorders are so often isolated from the rest of society, negative stereotypes are easily perpetuated. The goal of better public awareness can be facilitated by working toward the integration of more children with handicaps into the public school system. The Public Education Act mandates that free education be provided to all children who have handicaps in the least segregated setting that can meet the child's academic and emotional needs. Education of the general public can be furthered by acknowledging the presence and achievements of people with genetic disorders in books, including textbooks, the news media, movies, and television shows. This is already happening in Denmark, where women and girls with Turner syndrome, as well as physicians, are actively educating the public about the nature of the syndrome (Neilsen 1989). Such education can help the person with the genetic disorder, promote the goal of increased awareness of the humanness and special gifts of those with a genetic disorder, and ease the fear about people who differ from the norm.

3. More group homes within the community are needed for adults with disabling genetic disorders. These homes should provide a secure and homelike environment and encourage

---

1 The Meeting Street School in Providence, Rhode Island, is an excellent example of a predominantly publicly funded educational organization that works with families and children with serious genetic disorders.

the residents to become as independent as possible. Apartment complexes that allow greater independence and privacy, while supplying necessary services for those with disabilities, are greatly needed—especially for married couples. Also, support groups should be made available for people with genetic disorders as well as their families and friends.

4. There should be greater incentives to integrate people with handicaps into the mainstream workforce rather than isolate them in sheltered workshops. The Rehabilitation Act of 1973, which mandates affirmative action hiring of people with disabilities by certain federal agencies, needs to be broadened and better defined. At the same time, we live in a society designed for the mentally and physically able. This design needs to be expanded so that those who fall outside general norms can also participate and seek fulfillment in our society. Dependence on social welfare is too often the result of discrimination and lack of suitable physical accommodations in the workplace rather than a consequence of the handicap itself. We must reject the stereotype of people with serious genetic disorders as eternal children or make political demands that they act out the role of a sick person if they are to get social benefits by providing more opportunities for them to work and live within the community and realize their potentials. To do this, we, as a society, also need to broaden our concept of quality of life to include not only financial power, intelligence, and physical beauty, but also other abilities, such as love and gratitude. This will enable us to make more room for those who are different and to benefit as a society from their unique contributions.

5. In framing a public policy for children with genetic disorders, the family unit must be taken into consideration. In the United States, because monetary expenses place an excessive and unjust burden on families of children with genetic disorders, and because the emotional burdens experienced by these families are so often tied up with financial burdens, societal responsibility for these children must include the provision of free or at least subsidized medical services. The

tremendous time and energy these families must now put into crusading for their children and trying to create solutions that society fails to provide adds substantially to other financial and emotional burdens. To relieve some of this burden, social services need to be improved and made more accessible and visible. There should also be an effort to move more social services from a medical setting into a community/ educational setting.

6. Services for children in general need to be improved. The unwillingness of society to take responsibility for the needs of parents and children (such as day care and maternity leave) adds to the burden experienced by parents of handicapped children with special needs. Children should be seen as a collective responsibility rather than as the private property of their parents.

7. Our society devalues women as well as children. In our social system, women are pitted against their children to compete for resources, such as social support, time, and even basic necessities such as food and housing. Women are constantly being asked to sacrifice their own needs for the sake of their children—indeed, the stereotype of the ideal mother in our society is a woman who is endlessly self-sacrificing. When one adds to this the devaluation of those who are handicapped, the sacrifices women are asked to make for their children with genetic disorders often become overwhelming. Women are in need of more empowerment in our society, but this empowerment, if we are to be a just society, cannot be at the expense of an even more disenfranchised group—the fetus with a genetic disorder. Therefore, if we are to keep the women's movement from becoming a "revolution that devours its own children" (Arendt 1951, 194), we must stop accepting social policies that pit these two traditionally disenfranchised groups against each other and instead work toward the establishment of social conditions in which both children and women can thrive without having to feed off of each other.

Religious Organizations

Religious organizations need to get rid of the stereotype of the divine as a "super-normal" white male and see God more "in the least of their brethren" by taking a stronger stand on issues of justice for women, children (both born and unborn), and those who are handicapped. If we are to grow as members of the human community and as children of God, we must learn to celebrate and respond to neediness rather than abort those in greatest need.

The following, therefore, are recommendations for the religious community:

1. Churches, synagogues, and other buildings used by religious organizations should be made more accessible to people with handicaps. Arrangements for transportation should be available for people with special needs. Congregations should be more aware of the special needs of families with children with serious genetic disorders by being willing to provide child care and emotional support.
2. Religious organizations can also function as educators to help the community accept and love those who are vulnerable and socially disenfranchised. In doing so, these organizations are truly doing the work of the evangelist. To reject those in need, as Hauerwas (1986) suggests so poignantly, is in the last analysis to reject God.

> The challenge of learning to know, to be with, and care for the retarded is nothing less than learning to know, be with, and love God. God's face is the face of the retarded; God's body is the body of the retarded; God's being is that of the retarded. For the God we Christians must learn to worship is not a god of self-sufficient power, a god who in self-possession needs no one; rather ours is a God who needs a people, who needs a son. . . . Like God [the retarded] offer us an opportunity of recognizing the character of our neediness (178–79).

The Family

Parents need to resist the eugenic/consumer mentality that values only "premium" babies. Selective abortion means selective acceptance and, consequently, entails a challenge to the tradition of unconditional parental love—one of the conditions thought necessary for the healthy development of the child. Consequently, the following are recommendations for families:

1. Parents who knowingly carry deleterious genes and are not willing to take the risk of giving birth to a child with a genetic disorder but still wish to have a child should seek reproductive alternatives, such as artificial insemination or adoption.
2. The notion of the child, especially the fetus, as the possession of the parents has served to work against giving up one's child for adoption and toward abortion as a solution when the family feels unable to cope with the demands of a child with a genetic disorder. A more positive attitude toward adoption needs to be fostered in society in general. Fulfillment of the special needs of a child with a serious genetic disorder is a task that many families are simply not in a position to undertake. In these cases adoption should be considered. Adoption procedures need to be reformed so that it becomes a positive choice for parents, rather than a source of additional guilt and failure. Many families are willing to adopt children with serious handicaps.[2] Birth parents should be allowed to participate in choosing a family for their child and, if desired, could be kept informed—perhaps through an intermediary—of the progress of their birth child. Residential schools for families who feel they cannot take on the full responsibility but still want to participate in the child's care should also be considered as an option.

---

[2] After the news of the euthanatizing by starvation of the newborn with Down syndrome at Johns Hopkins Hospital, Dr. Bartholomew received more than 150 letters from people requesting to adopt handicapped newborns (Allen and Allen 1979).

3. Most importantly, families of children with genetic disorders have to continue to boldly demand that society provide their children with needed services and recognition. It is hoped that some day the task of being an advocate for the disabled and disenfranchised will be taken up by more individuals and more social organizations, thus taking some of the pressure off of these already burdened families to have to actively crusade for services for their child—services that are automatically meted out by our society to nondisabled children.

The Individual

We, as individuals, need to deal more honestly with our own fear of being different and our own vulnerability and neediness. We all need to recognize that each of us is abnormal in some way—that perfection and normalcy are myths. We must break through the myth that life is good only if one is "a perpetual member of the Pepsi generation" (Hauerwas 1986, 201). In doing this, we will come to acknowledge that there are ways in which we are all handicapped mentally, physically, and/or emotionally, and that we are all vulnerable to becoming disabled ourselves. Only then can we begin to accept those who are different from us and those who are needy.

In working toward this goal:

1. We should seek to educate ourselves about genetic disorders and their effects on the individual, the family, and society. In doing so, we will become not only more tolerant of those who are different from us but better able to be available, if only as a listener and friend, to distressed parents.
2. We must strive to be less judgmental of families who are struggling with the dilemma of whether to bring a handicapped fetus to birth and put more energy into becoming advocates for those who are disabled by a genetic disorder. We should each, in our own way, actively work for social reforms and the rights of those who are disabled by genetic disorders.

3. Individuals who claim to be pro-life need to be willing to accept the full implications of their stance. Marty Bailey, the mother of baby "Jane Doe," said of the "right-to-lifers": "Where are they? They step into a life, do their thing and good-bye. . . . These people save a life, clap their hands after it's done and then they turn away" (Colen 1986, 193). This description of people who claim to be pro-life is all too often true. The present pro-life stance must be broadened to include concern for the "unwanted" and "socially unacceptable" child throughout the entire span of his or her life, not just before birth. Otherwise, like those politicians who claim to be pro-life while at the same time denying women and vulnerable children the social funds and programs necessary for a fulfilling life, too many people who rally against abortion will remain part of the problem rather than part of the solution.

4. In the same manner, pro–abortion rights advocates who support abortion as a solution to poverty and discrimination against women and children with handicapping genetic disorders need to reexamine their position in light of the evidence that the present tolerance of selective abortion and the privatization of the abortion choice may, in fact, be contributing to the isolation of and discrimination against these traditionally disenfranchised groups of people.

Appendix A

Fee Schedule for Prenatal Diagnostic Procedures

Genetic Counseling or	Mini	$50.00
Pediatric Diagnostic	Brief	$70.00
Evaluation	Intermediate	$90.00
	Extended	$110.00
	Long	$130.00

Amniocentesis $195.00

Ultrasound..$195.00

Follow-Up Ultrasound $100.00

Amniotic Fluid Cell Culture
   and Chromosome Analysis (GTG)..$520.00

Amniotic Fluid Cell Culture Only..$230.00

Amniotic Fluid Alpha-fetoprotein Analysis $40.00

Amniotic Fluid
   Acetylcholinesterase Electrophoresis.......................................$65.00

Amniotic Fluid Hemoglobin
   F Radial Immunodiffusion...$65.00

Maternal Serum Alpha-fetoprotein Analysis $40.00

Maternal Serum Alpha-fetoprotein
   and hCG Analysis $65.00

Blood Chromosome Analysis (GTG)..$380.00

Tissue or Biopsy Culture
   and Chromosome Analysis (GTG)..$520.00

Tissue or Biopsy Culture Only...$320.00

1/91

Appendix B

Hospital Consent Form for Amniocentesis

CONSENT FOR AMNIOCENTESIS

Date: _____ Time: _____ A.M.
P.M.

It has been explained to me and I have accordingly requested that Dr._____ and his/her assistants or designees attempt to perform an amniocentesis for diagnostic or therapeutic purposes. I understand that a needle will be inserted into the cavity of the uterus through my abdominal wall and that a portion of the fluid surrounding the baby will be removed for analysis.

The following points have been explained to me and I understand and accept them:

1. Amniocentesis is a technique which often is used in the management of pregnancy. The risk to the mother or fetus is considered low. Occasionally premature labor and/or miscarriage will occur after the procedure. Very rarely, a fetus may be injured by a needle puncture.

2. Attempts to obtain amniotic fluid cell cultures from the fluid are usually successful. Occasionally fluid cannot be obtained, or cultures do not grow and adequate studies cannot be completed and may need to be repeated.

3. The likelihood of misinterpretation of the biochemical and/or chromosomal findings is also small. However, a complete and accurate diagnosis of the condition of the fetus cannot be guaranteed.

I have read, or have had read to me, the above explanation. I understand it, and my questions have been answered.

Witness: _____

Title: _____

Signature:_____
(Patient)

Physician's Acknowledgement

The undersigned confirms that consent, as described above, has been given by this patient.

_____
(Physician)

Bibliography

Aberg, Anders, Felix Mitelman, Michael Cantz, and Jurgen Gehler. 1978. Cardiac Puncture of Fetus with Hunter's Disease Avoiding Abortion of Unaffected Co-twin. *Lancet* 2 (Nov. 4): 990–91.

Abernathy, Virginia. 1984. Children, Personhood and a Pluralistic Society. In *Abortion: Understanding the Differences*, ed. Sidney Callahan and Daniel Callahan, 117–35. New York: Plenum Press.

Allan, L. D., M. Tynan, and S. Campbell, 1980. Echocardiographic and Anatomical Correlates in the Fetus. *British Heart Journal* 44:444.

Allen, David F., and Victoria S. Allen. 1979. *Ethical Issues in Mental Retardation*. Nashville: Abingdon Press.

Allgeier, Albert, and Elizabeth Allgeier. 1988. *Sexual Interactions*. Lexington, Mass.: D. C. Heath and Co.

Ambani, L. M., R. S. Bhatia, S. B. Shah, and B. N. Apte. 1989. Prenatal Diagnosis of Tay-Sachs Disease. *Indian Pediatric Journal* 10 (Oct.): 1052–53.

Annas, George J. 1988a. Reaffirming *Roe v. Wade*, Again. In *Judging Medicine*, ed. George Annas, 174–79. Clifton, N.J.: Humana Press.

―――. 1988b. Righting the Wrong of "Wrongful Life." In *Judging Medicine*, ed. George Annas, 102–7. Clifton, N.J.: Humana Press.

Annas, George J., and Brian Coyne. 1975. "Fitness" for Birth and Reproduction: Legal Implications of Genetic Screening. *Family Law Quarterly* 9 (Fall): 463–89.

Arditti, Rita, Renate Klein, and Shelly Minden (eds.). 1984. *Test-tube Women.* London: Pandora Press.

Arendt, Hannah. 1951. *The Origins of Totalitarianism.* New York: Harcourt Brace.

Arnold, Mary. 1984. Abortion Burnout: Why Some Doctors No Longer Perform Abortions. *Catholic Twin Circle,* Aug. 5, 3.

Arras, John D. 1984. Toward and Ethic of Ambiguity. *Hastings Center Report* 14 (April): 25–34.

Atkinson, Gary, and Albert Moraczewski. 1980. Genetic Counseling, The Church, and the Law. A Report of the Pope John XXIII Medical-Moral Research and Education Center. Chicago: Franciscan Herald Press.

Augustine, St. 1955. *Enchiridon.* Translated by Albert Outler. Philadelphia: Westminister Press.

Baars, Conrad. 1979. Psychic Causes and Consequences of the Abortion Mentality. In *The Psychological Aspects of Abortion,* ed. David Mall and Walter Watts, 111–26. Washington, D.C.: University Publications of America.

Bakker, E., E. J. Bonten, H. Veenema, J. T. den-Dunnen, P. M. Grootscholten, O. J. van-Ommen, and P. L. Pearson. 1989. Prenatal Diagnosis of Duchenne Muscular Dystrophy: A Three-Year Experience in a Rapidly Evolving Field. *Journal of Inherited Metabolic Disorders* 12 (1): 174–90.

Bannerman, Robin, Dan Gillick, R. Van Coevering, N. L. Knobloch, and G. B. Ingal. 1977. Amniocentesis and Educational Attainment. *New England Journal of Medicine* 297 (Aug. 5): 449.

Barber, Bernard. 1976. The Ethics of Experimentation on Human Subjects. *Scientific American* 234:25–31.

Baum, Rudy. 1989. Genetic Screening: Medical Promise amid Legal and Ethical Questions. *Chemistry and Engineering News,* Aug. 7, 10–16.

Beauchamp, Tom, and LeRoy Walters. 1982. *Contemporary Issues in Bioethics.* 2nd ed. Belmont, Calif.: Wadsworth Publishing Co.

Beck, J. Robert, Andrea Jordan, and Frederick Meier. 1983. Modern Prenatal Diagnosis: The Ethical Dimension. *Lancet* 1 (Feb. 5): 303.

Becker, Howard. 1963. Outsiders: *Studies in the Sociology of Deviance.*
New York: Free Press.

Beeson, Diane, Rita Douglas, and Terry Lunsford. 1983. Prenatal
Diagnosis of Fetal Disorders. Part II: Issues and Implications.
Birth 10 (Winter): 233–41.

Benedict, Mary L., Roger B. White, and Donald A. Cornely. 1985.
Maternal Perinatal Risk Factors and Child Abuse. *Child Abuse
and Neglect* 9 (2): 217–24.

Benzie, R., M. J. Mahony, and D. V. Fairweather. 1980. Fetoscopy and
Fetal Tissue Sampling. *Prenatal Diagnosis* (special issue): 29.

Berg, Kare. 1983. Ethical Issues Arising from Research Progress in
Medical Genetics. *Progress in Clinical Biological Research* 128:261–75.

Bergman, B., U. Claesson, and J. Mark. 1991. Risk Evaluation in a Small
Series of Transabdominal Chorionic Villus Sampling.
Gynecologic and Obstetric Investigations 31:189–91.

Bergsma, Daniel (ed.). 1973. *Birth Defects Atlas and Compendium.*
Baltimore: National Foundation–March of Dimes.

Berini, Ruth, and Eva Kahn. 1987. *Clinical Genetics Handbook.* Montvale,
N.J.: Medical Economics Books.

Berne-Fromell, Kerstin, Gunilla Josefson, and Berndt Kjessler. 1984.
Who Declines from Antenatal Serum Alpha-Fetoprotein
Screening—and Why? *Acta Obstetrica Gynecologica Scandinavica*
63:687–91.

Biggers, John. 1983. Generation of the Human Cycle. In *Abortion and
the Status of the Fetus,* ed. William Bondeson, H. Tristam
Engelhardt, Stuart Spicker, and Daniel Winship, 31–54.
Dordrecht, Netherlands: D. Reidel Publishing Co.

Black, R. B., 1989. A One- and Six-month Follow-up of Prenatal
Diagnosis Patients Who Lost Pregnancies. *Prenatal Diagnosis* 9
(11): 795–804.

Blank, Robert. 1982. Public Policy Implications of Human Genetic
Technology: Genetic Screening. *Journal of Medical Philosophy* 7
(Nov.): 355–74.

Bleich, J. David. 1979. Abortion in Halakic Literature. In *Jewish
Bioethics,* ed. Fred Rosner and J. David Bleich, 134–77. New
York: Sanhedrin Press.

Bloch, M., and M. R. Hayden, 1990. Opinion: Predictive Testing for Huntington Disease in Childhood: Challenges and Complication. *American Journal of Human Genetics* 46 (1): 1–4.

Bloom, Alan. 1987. *The Closing of the American Mind*. New York: Simon and Schuster.

Bluglass, Kerry. 1984. Early Infant Loss and Multiple Congenital Abnormalities. In *Psychological Aspects of Genetic Counselling*, ed. Alan Emery, 55–74. London: Academic Press.

Blumberg, Bruce. 1984. The Emotional Impact of Prenatal Diagnosis. In *Psychological Aspects of Genetic Counselling*, ed. Alan Emery, 201–17. London: Academic Press.

Blumberg, Bruce, Mitchell Golbus, and Karl Hanson. 1975. The Psychological Sequelae of Abortion Performed for a Genetic Indication. *American Journal of Obstetrics and Gynecology* 122 (7): 799–808.

Bok, Sissela, 1976. The Unwanted Child: Caring for the Fetus Born Alive after an Abortion. *Hastings Center Report* 6 (Oct.): 10–11.

———. 1981. Ethical Problems of Abortion. In *Bioethics*, ed. Thomas A. Shannon, 45–71. Ramsey, N.J.: Paulist Press.

Bonilla, M. S., M. Sampaio, C. Simon, Z. Serra, J. Strasser. 1990. Pathology of the Yolk Sac: Endosonographic Results. *Ultraschall in der Medizin* 11, no. 1 (Feb.): 24–28.

Borg, Susan, and Judith Lasker. 1981. *When Pregnancy Fails: Coping with Miscarriage, Stillbirth and Infant Death*. New York: Bantam.

Botstein, David, Raymond White, Marc Skolnick, and Ronald Davis. 1980. Construction of a Genetic Linkage Map Using Restriction Fragment Length Polymorphism. *American Journal of Human Genetics* 32 (3): 314–31.

Boué, J., A. Boué, and P. Lazar. 1975. Retrospective and Prospective Epidemiological Studies of 1500 Karyotyped Spontaneous Human Abortions. *Teratology* 12:11.

Boulot, P., F. Deschamps, G. Lefort, P. Sarda, P. Mares, B. Hedon, F. Laffargue, and J. L. Viala. 1990. Pure Fetal Blood Samples Obtained by Cordocentesis: Technical Aspects of 322 Cases. *Journal of Prenatal Diagnosis* 10 (2): 93–100.

Brambati, Bruno, A. Oldrini, E. Ferrazzi, A. Lanzani. 1985. Chorionic Villi Sampling: General Methodology and Clinical Approach. In *First Trimester Fetal Diagnosis*, ed. Marco Fraccaro, Giuseppe Simoni, and Bruno Brambati, 7–18. Berlin: Springer-Verlag.

Brambati, Bruno, and B. Simon. 1983. Diagnosis of Fetal Trisomy 21 in First Trimester. *Lancet* 1 (March 12): 586.

Brandt, Richard. 1978. Defective Newborns and the Morality of Termination. In *Infanticide and the Value of Life*, ed. Marvin Kohl, 46–57. Buffalo, N.Y.: Prometheus Books.

Brennan, William. 1983. *The Abortion Holocaust: Today's Final Solution*. St. Louis: Landmark Press.

Brock, David J. H. 1982. *Early Diagnosis of Fetal Defects*. Edinburgh: Churchill Livingstone.

———. 1990. A Consortium Approach to Molecular Genetic Services. Scottish Molecular Genetics Consortium, *Journal of Medical Genetics* 27 (1): 8–13.

Brock, David J. H., and R. G. Sutcliffe. 1972. Alpha-fetoprotein in the Antenatal Diagnosis of Anencephaly and Spina Bifida. *Lancet* 2 (July 29): 197–99.

Brock, J. F. 1976. A Medical Paradox: Curative versus Preventive Medicine. *South African Medical Journal* 50 (Aug. 7): 1327–33.

Brody, Baruch, 1982. The Morality of Abortion. In *Contemporary Issues in Bioethics*, 2nd ed., ed. Tom Beauchamp and LeRoy Walters, 240–50. Belmont, Calif.: Wadsworth Publishing Co.

Buck, Pearl S. 1968. *Forward to the Terrible Choice: The Abortion Dilemma*. Edited by Robert Cook, ix–xi. New York: Bantum Books.

Bundy, Sarah, and Elizabeth Boughton. 1989. Are Abortions More or Less Frequent Once Prenatal Diagnosis is Available? [letter]. *Journal of Medical Genetics* 26 (12): 794–96.

Buresh, Marjorie Ann. 1981. Mongolism. In *New Perspectives on Human Abortion*, ed. Thomas Hilgers, Dennis Horan, and David Mall, 60–68. Frederick, Md.: University Publications of America.

Burton, Barbara. 1988. Elevated Maternal Serum Alpha-fetoprotein (MSAFP): Interpretation and Follow-up. *Clinical Obstetrics and Gynecology* 31 (June): 293–305.

Burton, Lindy. 1975. *The Family Life of Sick Children*. London: Routledge and Kegan Paul.

Callahan, Daniel. 1970. *Abortion: Law, Choice and Law*. New York: Macmillan.
———. 1971. *Who Should Be Born? Is Procreation a Right?* Symposium on Human Rights, Retardation and Research. Washington, D.C.: Joseph P. Kennedy, Jr. Foundation.
———. 1973. *The Tyranny of Survival and Other Pathologies of Civilized Life*. New York: Macmillan Co.
———. 1986. How Technology Is Reframing the Abortion Debate. *Hastings Center Report* 16 (Feb.): 33–42.

Callahan, Sidney, and Daniel Callahan (eds.). 1984. *Abortion: Understanding the Differences*. New York: Plenum Press.

Campbell, A. V. 1984. Ethical Issues in Prenatal Diagnosis. *British Medical Journal* 288 (June 2): 1633–34.

Campbell, Stuart, and J. Malcolm Pearce. 1983. Ultrasound Visualization of Congenital Malformations. *British Medical Bulletin* 39 (Oct.): 322–31.

Carmenisch, Paul. 1976. Abortion: For the Fetus's Own Sake? *Hastings Center Report* 6 (April): 38–41.

Carter, C. O., K. Evans, and A. Norman. 1973. Cystic Fibrosis: Genetic Counseling Follow-up. In *Fundamental Problems of Cystic Fibrosis and Related Diseases*, ed. J. A. Mangos and R. C. Talamo, 79–102. New York: Intercontinental.

Cassel, Eric J. 1982. The Nature of Suffering and the Goals of Medicine. *New England Journal of Medicine* 306 (March 18): 639–45.

Chervenak, Frank A., M. A. Farley, L. Walters, John Hobbins, and Maurice Mahoney. 1984. When is Termination of Pregnancy During the Third Trimester Morally Justifiable? *New England Journal of Medicine* 310 (Feb. 23): 501–4.

Chervenak, Frank A., and Laurence B. McCullough. 1985. Perinatal Ethics: A Practical Method of Analysis of Obligations to Mother and Fetus. *Obstetrics and Gynecology* 66 (Sept.): 442–46.
———. 1990. An Ethically Justified, Clinically Comprehensive Management Strategy for the Third-Trimester Pregnancies Complicated by Fetal Anomolies. *Journal of Obstetrics and Gynecology* 75 (March): 311–16.

Childs, James. 1985. Genetic Screening and Counseling. In *Questions about the Beginning of Life: Christian Appraisals of Seven Bioethical Issues*, ed. Edward Schneider, 97–119. Minneapolis: Augsburg Publishing House.

Churchman, John. 1989. The Ethics of Using Modern Technology for Detecting Down's Syndrome. *Radiography Today* 55 (July): 25.

Clayton-Smith, J., P. A. Farndon, C. McKeown, and D. Donnai. 1990. Examination of Fetuses after Induced Abortion for Fetal Abnormalities. *British Medical Journal* 300 (Feb. 3): 295–97.

Cohen, Felissa. 1984. *Clinical Genetics in Nursing Practice*. Philadelphia: J. B. Lippincott Co.

Cole, William. 1971. The Right to Be Well-born. *Today's Health* 49 (Jan.): 42–44, 68.

Colen, B. D. 1986. *Hard Choices: Mixed Blessing of Modern Technology*. New York: G. P. Putnam Sons.

Connor, J. M. 1989. Genetic Aspects of Prenatal Diagnosis. *Journal of Inherited Metabolic Disorders* 12 (Suppl. 1): 89–96.

Cook, Rebecca. 1985. Legal Abortion: Limits and Contributions to Human Life. *Ciba Foundation Symposium* 115:211–27.

Crawford, Martin. 1983. Ethical and Legal Aspects of Early Prenatal Diagnosis. *British Medical Bulletin* 39 (4): 310–14.

Creasy, Robert K., and Robert Resnik (eds.). 1989. *Maternal-Fetal Medicine: Principles and Practice*. 2nd ed. Philadelphia: W. B. Saunders and Co.

Cuckle, H., K. Nanchahal, and N. Wald. 1991. Birth Prevalence of Down's Syndrome in England and Wales. *Prenatal Diagnosis* 11 (1): 29–34.

Cuckle, H., N. Wald, J. D. Stevenson, H. M. May, M. A. Ferguson-Smith, A. M. Ward, H. M. Barbour, K. M. Laurence, B. and B. Norgaard-Fendersen. 1990. Maternal Serum Alpha-fetoprotein Screening for Open Neural Tube Defects in Twin Pregnancies. *Prenatal Diagnosis* 10 (2): 71–77.

Curlender v. Bio-Science Laboratories. 1980. 106, Cal. App. 3d 811.

Damme, Catharine. 1978. Infanticide: The Worth of an Infant under Law. *Medical History* 22:1–24.

Danforth, David, ed. 1974. *Textbook of Obstetrics and Gynecology.* 2nd edition. New York: Harper and Row.

Danks, D. M. 1990. Disorders of Copper Metabolism. In *Principles and Practice of Medical Genetics,* vol. 2, ed. Alan E. H. Emery and David L. Rimoin, 1771–81. New York: Churchill Livingstone.

D'Arcy, Elizabeth. 1968. Congenital Defect: Mother's First Reactions to First Information. *British Medical Journal* 3 (Sept. 28): 796–800.

Darling, Rosalyn B. 1979. *Families against Society: A Study of Reactions to Children with Birth Defects.* London: Sage Publications, Ltd.

Davis, B. D. 1990. Limits to Genetic Intervention in Humans: Somatic and Germlike. *Ciba Foundation Symposium* 149:81–86.

Davis, Jessica G. 1981. Ethical Issues Arising from Prenatal Diagnosis. *Mental Retardation* 19 (Feb.): 12–15.

Dechecchi, M. C., E. Girella, G. Borgo, and G. Mastella. 1989. Prenatal Diagnosis of Cystic Fibrosis: Analytical Evaluation of Microvillar Enzyme Determination in Amniotic Fluid. *Enzyme* 42 (4): 209–18.

de George, Richard. 1981. Do We Owe the Future Anything? In *Values in Conflict,* ed. Burton Leiser, 202–12. New York: Macmillan Co.

de Grouchy, Jean, and Catherine Turleau. 1984. *Clinical Atlas of Human Chromosomes.* 2nd ed. New York: John Wiley and Sons.

Denayer, L., G. Evers-Kiebooms, and H. Van den Berghe. 1990. A Child with Cystic Fibrosis. Part I: Parental Knowledge about the Genetic Transmission of Cystic Fibrosis and about DNA-Diagnostic Procedures. *Clinical Genetics* 37 (March): 198–206.

Denes, Magda. 1976. *In Necessity and Sorrow: Life and Death in an Abortion Hospital.* New York: Basic Books.

Department of Obstetrics and Gynecology, Tietung Hospital of Anshan Iron and Steel Co., Anshan, China. 1975. Fetal Sex Prediction by Sex Chromatin of Chorionic Villi Cells during Early Pregnancy. *Chinese Medical Journal* 1:117.

DeSpelder, Lynne Ann, and Albert Strickland. 1987. *The Last Dance.* Palo Alto, Calif.: Mayfield Publishing Co.

de Vries, Johanna, Gerard Visser, and Heinz Prechtl. 1984. Fetal Motility in the First Half of Pregnancy. In *Continuity of Neural Functions from Prenatal to Postnatal Life,* ed. Heinz Prechtl, 46–64. Philadelphia: J. B. Lippincott Co.

Didache. 1948. In *Ancient Christian Writings*. Translated by James Kleist. Westminister, Md.: Newman Press.

Dicke, J. M., D. L. Gray, G. S. Sonster, and J. P. Crane. 1989. Fetal Biometry as a Screening Tool for the Detection of Chromosomal Abnormal Pregnancies. *Journal of Obstetrics and Gynecology* 74 (Nov.): 726–29.

Dickens, Bernard. 1982. Ethical and Legal Issues in Medical Management of Sex Chromosome–Abnormal Adolescents. *Birth Defects* 18 (4): 227–46.

————. 1986. Prenatal Diagnosis and Female Abortion: A Case Study in Medical Law and Ethics. *Journal of Medical Ethics* 12 (Sept.): 143–44.

Dictionary of Medical Syndromes. 2nd ed. 1981. Philadelphia: J. B. Lippincott Co.

Diseases and Disorders Handbook. 1988. Springhouse, Pa.: Springhouse Corp.

Donnai, P., N. Charles, and N. Harris. 1981. Attitudes of Parents after "Genetic" Termination of Pregnancy. *British Medical Journal* 282 (Feb. 21): 621–22.

Dougherty, Charles. 1985. The Right to Begin Life with Sound Body and Mind: Fetal Patients and Conflicts with Their Mothers. *University of Detroit Law Review* 63 (89): 89–117.

Drotar, D., A. Baskiewicz, N. Irvin, J. Kennell, and M. Klaus. 1975. The Adaptation of Parents to the Birth of an Infant with a Congenital Malformation: A Hypothetical Model. *American Journal of Pediatrics* 56:710–17.

Drugan, A., F. C. Koppitch, J. C. Williams, M. P. Johnson, S. Moghissi, and M. I. Evans. 1990. Prenatal Genetic Diagnosis Following Recurrent Early Pregnancy Loss. *Journal of Obstetrics and Gynecology* 75 (3 Pt 1): 381–84.

Dubois, Rene, 1974. *Beast or Angel? Choices That Make Us Human*. New York: Charles Scribner's Sons.

Duff, Raymond, and A. G. M. Campbell. 1973. Moral and Ethical Dilemmas in the Special Care Nursery. *New England Journal of Medicine* 289 (Oct. 25): 890–94.

————. 1976. On Deciding the Care of Severely Handicapped or Dying Persons: With Particular References to Infants. *Pediatrics* 57 (April): 487–93.

Dyke, Arthur. 1977. *On Human Care*. Nashville: Abingdon Press.

Edmonds, D. K., K. S. Lindsay, J. F. MIller, E. Williams, and P. J. Wood. 1982. Early Embryonic Mortality in Women. *Fertility and Sterility* 38:447–53.

Edwards, Janice, William Rothstein, and S. Robert Young. 1989. Elective Termination of Chromosomally Abnormal Pregnancies: Psychosocial Effects and Experience in Genetic Counseling. *Loss, Grief & Care* 3 (3/4): 21–36.

Edwards, Paul (ed.). 1967. *The Encyclopedia of Philosophy*. Vol. 5. New York: Macmillan Co. S.v. "Persons" by Arthur Danto.

Einstein, Albert. 1949. *The World as I See It*. New York: Philosophical Library.

Elejalde, B. R., M. M. Elejalde, and T. Heitman. 1985. Visualization of the Fetal Genitalia by Ultrasound: A Review of the Literature and Analysis of Its Accuracy and Ethical Implications. *Journal of Ultrasound Medicine* 4 (Dec.): 633–39.

Elias, Sherman, and George J. Annas. 1987. *Reproductive Genetics and the Law*. Chicago: Year Book Medical Publishers.

Elias, Sherman, and Joe Leigh Simpson. 1986. Amniocentesis. In *Genetic Disorders and the Fetus*, 2nd ed., ed. Aubrey Milunsky, 31–52. New York: Plenum Press.

Elkins, Thomas, Diane Crutcher, Joseph Spinnato, Garland Anderson, and P. V. Dilts, Jr. 1985. Baby Doe: Is There Really a Problem? *Obstetrics and Gynecology* 65 (April): 492–95.

Elshtain, Jean Bethke. 1984. Reflections on Abortion, Values, and the Family. In *Abortion: Understanding the Differences*, ed. Sidney Callahan and Daniel Callahan, 47–72. New York: Plenum Press.

Engelhardt, H. Tristam. 1973. Euthanasia and Children: The Injury of Continued Existence. *Journal of Pediatrics* 83:70–71.

———. 1982a. Bioethics in Pluralistic Societies. *Perspectives in Biology and Medicine* 26:64–77.

———. 1982b. Ethical Issues in Aiding the Death of Young Children. In *Beneficent Euthanasia*, ed. Marvin Kohl, 180–92. Buffalo, N.Y.: Prometheus Books.

————. 1982c. Medicine and the Concept of Person. In *Contemporary Issues in Bioethics*, 2nd ed., ed. Tom Beauchamp and LeRoy Walters, 94–101. Belmont, Calif.: Wadsworth Publishing Co.

————. 1983. Viability and the Use of the Fetus. In *Abortion and the Status of the Fetus*, ed. William Bondeson, H. Tristam Engelhardt, Stuart Spicker, and Daniel Winship, 183–208. Dordrecht, Netherlands: D. Reidel Publishing Co.

————. 1986. *The Foundations of Bioethics*. New York: Oxford University Press.

English, Jane. 1975. Abortion and the Concept of Person. *Canadian Journal of Philosophy* 5 (Nov. 2): 233–43.

Erbe, Richard. 1974. Mass Screening and Genetic Counseling in Mendelian Disorders. In *Ethical, Social and Legal Dimensions of Screening for Human Genetic Disease*, ed. Daniel Bergsma, 85–100. Miami: Symposia Specialists.

EUROCRAT Working Group. 1991. Prevalence of Neural Tube Defects in 20 Regions of Europe and the Impact of Prenatal Diagnosis, 1980–1986. *Journal of Epidemiology and Community Health* 45 (1): 52–58.

Faden, R. R., A. J. Chwalow, and K. Quaid. 1987. Prenatal Screening and Pregnant Women's Attitudes toward the Abortion of Defective Fetuses. *American Journal of Public Health* 77 (3): 288.

Farrant, Wendy. 1985. Who's for Amniocentesis? The Politics of Prenatal Screening. In *The Sexual Politics of Reproduction*, ed. Hilary Homas, 96–122. London: Gower.

Farrer, L. A. 1986. Suicide and Attempted Suicide in Huntington Disease. *American Journal of Medical Genetics* 24 (June): 305–11.

Ferguson-Smith, M. A. 1983. Early Prenatal Diagnosis. *British Medical Bulletin* 39 (4): 301–4.

Fiedler, Leslie A. 1984. The Tyranny of the Normal. *Hastings Center Report* 14 (April): 40–42.

Finegan, Jo-Anne K., Bruce J. Quarrington, Helen E. Hughes, and Terence A. Doran. 1987. Infant Development following Midtrimester Amniocentesis. *Infant Behavior and Development* 10 (3): 379–83.

Fineman, Robert, and David Gordis. 1982. Occasional Essay: Jewish Perspective on Prenatal Diagnosis and Selective Abortion of Affected Fetuses, Including Some Comparisons with Prevailing Catholic Beliefs. *American Journal of Medical Genetics* 12 (July): 355–60.

Finley, Sara, Pamela Varner, Paula Vinson, and Wayne Finley. 1977. Participants' Reaction to Amniocentesis and Prenatal Genetic Studies. *Journal of the American Medical Association* 238 (Nov. 28): 2377–79.

Fletcher, John. 1972. The Brink: The Parent-Child Bond in the Genetic Revolution. *Theological Studies* 33 (Sept.): 457–85.

———. 1974. Attitudes toward Defective Newborns. *Hastings Center Report* 2 (Jan.): 21–32.

———. 1975. Moral and Ethical Problems of Prenatal Diagnosis. *Clinical Genetics* 9 (Oct.): 251–57.

———. 1979. Prenatal Diagnosis, Selective Abortion, and the Ethics of Withholding Treatment from the Defective Newborn. *Birth Defects* 15 (2): 239–54.

———. 1981a. Abortion, Euthanasia and Care of Defective Newborns. In *Bioethics*, ed. Thomas Shannon, 121–28. Ramsey, N.J.: Paulist Press.

———. 1981b. Ethical Issues in Genetic Screening and Antenatal Diagnosis. *Clinical Obstetrics and Gynecology* 24 (Dec.): 1151–68.

———. 1981c. The Fetus as Patient: Ethical Issues. *Journal of the American Medical Association* 246 (Aug. 14): 772–73.

———. 1983a. Emerging Ethical Issues in Fetal Therapy. *Progress in Clinical Biological Research* 128:293–318.

———. 1983b. Ethics and Public Policy: Should Sex Choice Be Discouraged? In *Sex Selection of Children*, ed. Neil Bennett, 213–52. New York: Academic Press.

———. 1983c. Ethics and Trends in Applied Human Genetics. *Birth Defects* 19 (5): 143–58.

———. 1986. Moral Problems and Ethical Guidances in Prenatal Diagnosis: Past, Present and Future. In *Genetic Disorders and the Fetus*, 2nd ed., ed. Aubrey Milunsky, 819–59. New York: Plenum Press.

Fletcher, John, Kare Berg, and Knut Tranoy. 1985. Ethical Aspects of Medical Genetics: A Proposal for Guidelines in Genetic Counseling, Prenatal Diagnosis and Screening. *Progress in Clinical Biological Research* 177:511–23.

Fletcher, John, and M. I. Evans. 1983. Maternal Bonding in Early Fetal Ultrasound Examinations. *New England Journal of Medicine* 308 (Feb. 17): 392–93.

Fletcher, John, and Dorothy Wertz. 1987a. Ethical and Human Genetics: A Cross-Cultural Perspective. *Seminars in Perinatology* 11 (July): 224–28.

————. 1987b. Ethical Aspects of Prenatal Diagnosis: Views of U.S. Medical Institutes of Health. *Clinical Perinatology* 14 (June): 293–312.

Fletcher, Joseph. 1971. Ethical Aspects of Genetic Controls: Designed Genetic Changes in Man. *New England Journal of Medicine* 285 (Sept. 30): 776–83.

————. 1972. Indicators of Humanhood: A Tentative Profile of Man. *Hastings Center Report* 2 (Nov.): 1–4.

————. 1973. Ethics and Euthanasia. In *To Live and to Die*, ed. Robert Williams, 113–22. Buffalo, N.Y.: Springer-Verlag.

————. 1979. Our Duty to the Unborn. In *Humanhood: Essays in Biomedical Ethics*, ed. Joseph Fletcher, 106–31. Buffalo, N.Y.: Prometheus Books.

Flew, Anthony. 1979. *A Dictionary of Philosophy*. New York: St. Martin's Press.

Ford, C. E., O. J. Miller, P. E. Polani, J. C. Almeida, and J. H. Briggs. 1959. A Sex-chromosome Anomaly in a Case of Gonadal Dysgenesis (Turner's Syndrome). *Lancet* 1 (March 14): 711–13.

Fost, Norman. 1976. Ethical Problems in Pediatrics. *Current Problems in Pediatrics* 6 (Oct.): 1–31.

————. 1981. Counseling Families Who Have a Child with a Severe Congenital Anomaly. *Pediatrics* 67 (March): 321–25.

Fox, Matthew. 1983. *Original Blessing*. Sante Fe, N. Mex.: Bear and Co.

Fuchs, Fritz. 1971. Amniocentesis: Techniques and Complications. In *Early Diagnosis of Genetic Defects: Scientific and Ethical Considerations*, ed. Maureen Harris, 11–16. Fogarty International Center Proceedings, no. 6. Washington, D.C.: U.S. Government Printing Office.

Fuchs, Fritz, and Povl Riis. 1956. Antenatal Sex Determination. *Nature* 117:330.

Fuhrmann, W. 1989. The Impact, Logistics and Prospects of Traditional Prenatal Diagnosis. *Journal of Clinical Genetics* 36 (5): 378–85.

Furlong, Regina, and Rita Black. 1984. Pregnancy Termination for Genetic Indications: The Impact on Families. *Social Work in Health Care* 10 (Fall): 17–34.

Gallup, George. 1978. *The Gallup Poll: Public Opinion 1972–1977.* Wilmington, Del.: Scholarly Resources.

———. 1989. *The Gallup Poll: Public Opinion 1988.* Wilmington, Del.: Scholarly Resources.

———. 1992. *The Gallup Poll: Public Opinion 1991.* Wilmington, Del.: Scholarly Resources.

Geertz, Clifford. 1960. *The Religion of Java.* Glencoe, Ill.: Free Press.

Gentile, Gwen, and Richard Schwarz. 1986. Elective Abortion: Techniques, Risks, and Complications. In *Genetic Disorders and the Fetus,* 2nd ed., ed. Aubrey Milunsky, 723–39. New York: Plenum Press.

Gilligan, Carol. 1982. *In a Different Voice: Psychological Theory and Women's Development.* Cambridge, Mass.: Harvard University Press.

Glantz, Leonard. 1983. Is the Fetus a Person? A Lawyer's View. In *Abortion and the Status of the Fetus,* ed. William Bondeson, H. Tristam Engelhardt, Stuart Spicker, and Daniel Winship, 107–17. Dordrecht, Netherlands: D. Reidel Publishing Co.

Glasser, John. 1985. *Caring for the Special Child: Ethical Decision Making.* Kansas City, Mo.: Leaven Press.

Glendon, Mary Ann. 1989. A World without *Roe:* How Different Would It Be? *Hastings Center Report* 19 (July–August): 30–31.

Golbus, Mitchell, Felix Conte, Edward Schneider, and Charles Epstein. 1974. Intrauterine Diagnosis of Genetic Defects: Results, Problems and Follow-up of One Hundred Cases in a Prenatal Genetic Detection Center. *American Journal of Obstetrics and Gynecology* 118 (7): 897–905.

Golbus, Mitchell, William Loughman, Charles Epstein, Giesela Halbasch, John Stephens, and Bryan Hall. 1979. Prenatal Genetic Diagnosis in 3000 Amniocenteses. *New England Journal of Medicine* 300 (Jan. 25): 157–63.

Goldenberg, R. L., and S. C. Finley. 1978. Prenatal Diagnosis of the 47, XYY Karyotype. *Lancet* 2 (Aug. 26): 465–66.

Gorman, Michael. 1982. *Abortion and the Early Church.* New York: Paulist Press.

Gosden, Christie. 1983. Amniotic Fluid Cell Types and Culture. *British Medical Bulletin* 39 (4): 348–54.

Grannum, Peter A., and Joshua A. Copel. 1990. Invasive Fetal Procedures. *Journal of Fetal Ultrasound* 28 (1): 217–24.

Green, Harold, and Alexander Capron. 1974. Issues of Public Policy in Compulsory Genetic Screening. *Birth Defects: Original Article Series* 10 (6): 57–84.

Green, J. 1990. *Calming or Harming? A Critical Review of Psychological Effects of Fetal Diagnosis on Pregnant Women.* London: Galton Institute, 2nd Series.

Green, Jeffrey, Andrew Dorfmann, Shirley Jones, Samuel Bender, Laurel Patton, and Joseph Schulman. 1988. Chorionic Villus Sampling: Experience with an Initial 940 Cases. *Obstetrics and Gynecology* 71 (Feb.): 208–12.

Green, Josephine. 1990. Prenatal Screening and Diagnosis: Some Psychological and Social Issues. *British Journal of Obstetrics and Gynaecology* 97:1074–76.

Gregory, Hamilton. 1983. *The Religious Case for Abortion: Protestant and Catholic Perspectives.* Asheville, N.C.: Madison and Polk.

Grimes, David, Kenneth Schulz, Willard Cotes, Jr., and Carl Taylor, Jr. 1980. The Safety of Midtrimester Abortion. In *The Safety of Fertility Control,* ed. Louis Keith, 198–210. New York: Springer Publishing Co.

Grobstein, Clifford. 1988. *Science and the Unborn.* New York: Basic Books.

Gusella, J. F., N. S. Wexler, P. M. Conneally, S. L. Naylor, M. A. Anderson, R. E. Tanzi, P. C. Watkins, K. Ohira, M. R. Wallace, A. Sakaguchi, A. B. Young, I. Shoulson, E. Bonilla, and J. B. Martin. 1983. A Polymorphic DNA Marker Genetically Linked to Huntington's Disease. *Nature* 306:234–38.

Gustafson, James. 1971. What Is Normatively Human? *American Ecclesiastical Review* 165:192–207.

———. 1973. Mongolism, Parental Desires, and the Right to Live. *Perspectives in Biology and Medicine* 16:529–57.

———. 1974. Genetic Screening and Human Values: An Analysis. In *Ethical, Social and Legal Dimensions of Screening for Human Genetic Disease,* ed. Daniel Bergsma, 201–24. Miami: Symposia Specialists.

Guttenback, M., and M. Schmid. 1990. Determination of Y Chromosome Aneuploidy in Human Sperm Nuclei by Nonradioactive in Situ Hybridizaiton, *American Journal of Human Genetics* 46 (3): 553–58.

Hagay, Z. J., J. R. Leiberman, R. Picard, and M. Katz. 1989. Uterine Rupture Complicating Midtrimester Abortion: A Report of Two Cases. *Journal of Reproductive Medicine* 34 (11): 912–16.

Hahnemann, Niels. 1974. Early Prenatal Diagnosis: A Study of Biopsy Techniques and Cell Cultured from Extraembryonic Membranes. *Clinical Genetics* 6 (4): 294–306.

Hamerton, J., A. Boué, and M. Ferguson-Smith. 1982. Workshop in Collaborative Studies in Prenatal Diagnosis of Chromosome Disease. In *Human Genetics: Medical Aspects*, ed. B. Bonne-Tamin, T. Cohen, and R. M. Goodman, 369–73. New York: Alan R. Liss.

Haring, Bernard. 1971. *Morality Is for Persons.* New York: Farrar-Straus and Giroux.

Harris, Henry. 1974. *Prenatal Diagnosis and Selective Abortion.* London: Nuffield Provincial Hospital Trust.

Harrison, Beverly. 1983. *Our Right to Choose.* Boston: Beacon Press.

Hauerwas, Stanley. 1986. *Suffering Presence: Theological Reflections on Medicine, the Mentally Handicapped and the Church.* Notre Dame, Ind.: University of Notre Dame Press.

Heckerling, Paul S., and Marion S. Verp. 1991. Genetic Risk and Early Versus Late Prenatal Testing. *Lancet* 337 (Nov. 24): 363.

Heidrich, Susan M., and S. Cranley-Mecca. 1989. The Effect of Fetal Movement, Ultrasound Scans, and Amniocentesis on Maternal-Fetal Attachment. *Journal of Nursing Research* 38 (2): 81–84.

Henshaw, Stanley K., Nancy J. Binkin, Ellen Blaine, and Jack C. Smith. 1985. A Portrait of American Women Who Obtain Abortions. *Family Planning Perspectives* 17 (2): 90–96.

Hern, Warren, and Billie Corrigan. 1978. What about Us? Staff Reactions to the D&E Procedure: A paper presented at the October 26 meeting of the Association of Planned Parenthood Physicians, San Diego, Calif. Photocopy.

Heymann, Philip, and Sara Holtz. 1975. The Severely Defective Newborn: The Dilemma and the Decision Process. *Public Policy* 23 (Fall): 381–412.

Hilgers, Thomas, and Dennis Horan (eds.). 1973. *Abortion and Social Justice.* New York: Sheed and Ward.

Hilgers, Thomas, Dennis Horan, and David Mall. 1981. *New Perspectives on Human Abortion.* Frederick, Md.: University Publications of America.

Hilton, Bruce. 1972. Will the Baby Be Born Normal? And What Is the Cost of Knowing? *Hastings Center Report* 2 (June): 8–9.

Hodge, Susan. 1989. Waiting for the Amniocentesis. *New England Journal of Medicine* 320 (Jan. 5): 63–64.

Hollerbach, Paula. 1979. Parental Choice and Family Planning: Four Methods. In *Counseling Genetics,* ed. Y. Edward Hsia, 198–222. New York: Alan R. Liss.

Holmes, Helen, Betty Hoskins, and Michael Gross. 1981. *The Custom-made Child? A Women-centered Perspective.* Clifton, N.J.: Humana Press.

Holtzman, Neil A. 1990. Prenatal Screening: When and for Whom? *Journal of General Internal Medicine* 5 (Sept.–Oct. Supplement): S42–S46.

Hook, Ernest. 1973. Behavioral Implications of the Human XYY Chromogenotype. *Science* 179 (Jan. 12): 139–50.

———. 1977. Exclusion of Chromosome Mosaicism: Tables of 90%, 95% and 99% Confidence Limits and Comments on Use. *American Journal of Human Genetics* 29 (1): 94–97.

Hook, Ernest, Philip Cross, and Dina Schreinemachers. 1983. Chromosomal Abnormality Rates at Amniocentesis and Live-born Infants. *Journal of the American Medical Association* 249 (April 15): 2034–38.

Hook, Ernest, B. B. Topol, and P. K. Cross. 1989. The Natural History of Cytogenetically Abnormal Fetuses Detected at Midtrimester Amniocentesis Which Are Not Terminated Electively: New Data and Estimates of the Excess and Relative Risk of Late Fetal Death Associated with 47, +21 and Some Other Abnormal Karyotypes. *American Journal of Human Genetics* 45 (6): 855–61.

Hoskins, Betty, and Helen Holmes. 1984. Technology and Prenatal Femicide. In *Test-tube Women*, ed. Rita Arditti, Renate Klein, and Shelly Minden, 237–55. London: Pandora Press.

Hsia, Y. Edward (ed.). 1979. *Counseling in Genetics.* New York: Alan R. Liss.

Hsieh, T. T., J. D. Lee, D. M. Kuo, L. M. Lo, C. C. Hsieh, T. H. Chiu, J. D. Liou, and Y. K. Soong. 1989. Perinatal Outcome of Chorionic Sampling versus Amniocentesis. *Taiwan I Hsueh Hui Tsa Chih* 88 (9): 894–99.

Hsu, Lillian. 1986. Prenatal Diagnosis of Chromosomal Abnormalities. In *Genetic Disorders and the Fetus*, 2nd ed., ed. Aubrey Milunsky, 115–83. New York: Plenum Press.

Hubbard, Ruth. 1982. Some Practical and Ethical Restraints on Genetic Decision-making about Childbearing. In *Science and Morality*, ed. Doris Teicher-Zallen and Colleen Clements, 37–48. Lexington, Mass.: Lexington Books.

———. 1985. Prenatal Diagnosis and Eugenic Ideology. *Women's Studies International Forum* 8 (6): 567–76.

Humphries, Stephen, and Robert Williamson. 1983. Application of Recombinant DNA Technology in Prenatal Detection of Inherited Defects. *British Medical Bulletin* 39 (4): 343–47.

Ireys, Henry. 1981. Health Care for Chronically Disabled Children and Their Families. In *Better Health for Our Children: A National Strategy, The Report of the Select Panel for the Promotion of Child Health*, 321–53. Washington, D.C.: U.S. Department of Health and Human Services.

Jackson, Robert. 1987. Ethics and Prenatal Testing. *American Family Physician* 36 (Aug.): 49.

Jacobs, P. A., M. Burton, and M. Melville. 1965. Aggressive Behavior, Mental Subnormality and the XYY Male. *Nature* 208:1351.

Jacobs, P. A., and J. A. Strong. 1959. A Case of Human Intersexuality Having a Possible XXY Sex-determining Mechanism. *Nature* 183:302–3.

Jahoda, M. G., L. Pijpers, A. Reuss, F. J. Los, J. W. Wladimiroff, and E. S. Sachs. 1989. Evaluation of Transcervical Chorionic Villus Sampling with a Completed Follow-up of 1550 Consecutive Pregnancies. *Prenatal Diagnosis* 9 (9): 621–28.

Jerome Biblical Commentary, The. 1968. Vol. 1, ed. Raymond Brown. Englewood Cliffs, N.J.: Prentice-Hall.

Johnson, A., R. J. Wapner, G. H. Davis, and L. G. Jackson. 1990. Mosaicism in Chorionic Villus Sampling: An Association with Poor Perinatal Outcome. *Obstetrics and Gynecology* 75 (April): 573–77.

Johnson, Anthony, and Lynn Godmilow, 1988. Genetic Amniocentesis at 14 Weeks or Less. Clinical *Obstetrics and Gynecology* 31 (June): 345–52.

Johnson, JoAnn, and Sherman Elias, 1988. Prenatal Treatment: Medical and Gene Therapy in the Fetus. Clinical *Obstetrics and Gynecology* 31 (June): 390–407.

Johnson, Susan, and Thomas Elkins. 1988. Ethical Issues in Prenatal Diagnosis. *Clinical Obstetrics and Gynecology* 31 (June): 408–16.

Jonas, Robert, and John Gorby. 1976. West German Abortion Decision: A Contrast to *Roe v. Wade? John Marshall Journal of Practice and Procedure* 9 (Spring): 605–84.

Jones, Clifton. 1982. Prenatal Diagnosis of Cystic Fibrosis and Other Genetic Diseases. *Journal of the Kansas Medical Society* 83 (Nov.): 571–78, 592.

Jones, Oliver. 1989. Basic Genetics and Patterns of Inheritance. In *Maternal-Fetal Medicine: Principles and Practice,* 2nd ed., ed. Robert K. Creasy and Robert Resnik, 3–77. Philadelphia: W. B. Saunders and Co.

Jones, Oliver, Nolan Penn, Stephen Schucter, Claire Stafford, Teri Richards, Colleen Kernahan, Jennifer Gutiérrez, and Patricia Cherkin. 1984. Parental Response to Mid-trimester Therapeutic Abortion Following Amniocentesis. *Prenatal Diagnosis* 4 (July–Aug.): 249–56.

Jones, Shirley. 1988. Decision Making in Clinical Genetics: Ethical Implications for Perinatal Nursing Practice. *Journal of Perinatal Nursing Practice* 1 (Jan.): 11–23.

Jonsen, A. R., and Michael Garland (eds.). 1976. *Ethics of Newborn Intensive Care.* Berkeley, Calif.: University of California Institute of Government Studies.

Jorgensen, Connie, Nils Uddenberg, and Ingrid Ursing. 1985. Ultrasound Diagnosis of Fetal Malformation in the Second Trimester: The Psychological Reaction of the Women. Journal of *Psychosomatic Obstetrics and Gynecology* 4 (1): 31–40.

Kan, Yuet, Mitchell Golbus, and Andree Dozy. 1976. Prenatal Diagnosis of Alpha-thalassemia: Clinical Application of Molecular Hybridization. *New England Journal of Medicine* 295 (Nov. 18): 1165–67.

Kan, Yuet, Mitchell Golbus, Richard Trecartin, and Roy Filly. 1977. Prenatal Diagnosis of ß-thalassemia and Sickle Cell Anemia: Experience with 24 Cases. *Lancet* 1 (Feb. 5): 269.

Kant, Immanuel. 1956. *The Metaphysics of Morals*. Translated by Lewis Beck. New York: Liberal Arts Press.

Kantrowitz, Barbara. 1987. How to Protect Abused Children. *Newsweek*, Nov. 23, 70–71.

Kaplan, Paige, Jean Normandin, Jr., Golder N. Wilson, Henri Plauchu, and Abby Lippman. 1990. Malformations and Minor Anomalies in Children Whose Mothers Had Prenatal Diagnosis: Comparison between CVS and Amniocentesis. *American Journal of Medical Genetics* 37 (Nov.): 366–70.

Kass, Leon. 1973. Implications of Prenatal Diagnosis for the Human Right to Life. In *Ethical Issues in Human Genetics*, ed. Bruce Hilton, Daniel Callahan, and Maureen Harris, 185–89. New York: Plenum Press.

———. 1985. *Toward a More Natural Science*. New York: Free Press.

Kazazian, Haig. 1980. Prenatal Diagnosis for Sex Choice: A Medical View. *Hastings Center Report* 10 (Feb.): 17–18.

Kazy, Z., I. S. Rozovsky, and V. A. Bakharev. 1982. Chorionic Biopsy in Early Pregnancy: A Method of Early Prenatal Diagnosis for Inherited Disorders. *Prenatal Diagnosis* 2:39–45.

Kenen, Regina. 1981. A Look at Prenatal Diagnosis within the Context of Changing Parental and Reproductive Norms. In *The Custom-made Child? A Woman-centered Perspective*, ed. Helen Holmes, Betty Hoskins, and Michael Gross, 67–73. Clifton, N.J.: Humana Press.

Kenyon, Edward. 1986. *The Dilemma of Abortion*. London: Farber and Farber, Ltd.

Kerenyi, Thomas, and Usha Chitkara. 1981. Selective Birth in Twin Pregnancy with Discordancy for Down's Syndrome. *New England Journal of Medicine* 304 (June 18): 1525–27.

Kett, Joseph. 1984. The Search for a Science of Infancy. *Hastings Center Report* 14 (April): 34–39.

Kevles, Daniel. 1985. *In the Name of Eugenics.* New York: Alfred A. Knopf.

Klaus, M. H., and J. H. Kennell. 1976. *Maternal Bonding.* St. Louis: C. V. Mosby Co.

Kleinberg, Susan. 1982. *Educating the Chronically Ill Child.* Rockville, Md.: Aspen Systems Corp.

Knight, George, Glenn Palomaki, and James Haddow. 1988. Use of Maternal Serum Alpha-fetoprotein Measurements to Screen for Down's Syndrome. *Clinical Obstetrics and Gynecology* 31 (June): 306–25.

Koenig, M., E. P. Hoffman, C. J. Bertelson, A. P. Monaco, C. Feener, and L. M. Kunkel. 1987. Complete Cloning of the Duchenne Muscular Dystrophy (DMD) DNA and Preliminary Genomic Organization of the DMD Gene in Normal and Affected Individuals. *Cell* 50:509–17.

Kohl, Marvin. 1978. Vountary Death and Meaningless Existence. In *Infanticide and the Value of Life,* ed. Marvin Kohl, 206–18. Buffalo, N.Y.: Prometheus Books.

Kohlberg, Lawrence. 1981. *The Psychology of Moral Development.* San Francisco: Harper and Row.

Kolata, G. B. 1980. Mass Screening for Neural Tube Defects. *Hastings Center Report* 10 (Dec.): 8–10.

Kolker, Aliza, and B. Meredith Burke. 1987. Amniocentesis and the Social Construct of Pregnancy. *Marriage and Family Review* 11 (3–4): 95–116.

Kushnick, T. 1985. An Overview of Prenatal Screening and Genetic Counseling. In *Human Prenatal Diagnosis,* ed. Karen Filkins and Joseph R. Russo, 1–12. New York: Marcel Dekker.

Lamanna, Mary Anne. 1984. Social Science and Ethical Issues: The Policy Implications of Poll Data on Abortion. In *Abortion: Understanding the Differences,* ed. Sidney Callahan and Daniel Callahan, 1–23. New York: Plenum Press.

Lampe, Joseph, 1973. The World in Perspective. In *Abortion and Social Justice*, ed. Thomas Hilgers and Dennis Horan, 89–103. New York: Sheed and Ward.

Langer, J. C., N. S. Adzick, R. A. Filly, and M. S. Golbus. 1989. Gastrointestinal Tract Obstruction in the Fetus. *Archives of Surgery* 124 (10): 1183–86.

Langer, Martin, Marianne Ringler, and E. Reinold. 1988. Psychological Effects of Ultrasound Examinations: Changes of Body Perception and Child Image in Pregnancy. *Journal of Psychosomatic Obstetrics and Gynecology* 8 (3): 199–208.

Lappé, Marc. 1972. Moral Obligations and the Fallacies of "Genetic Control." *Theological Studies* 33 (Sept.): 411–27.

———. 1973. How Much Do We Want to Know about the Unborn? *Hastings Center Report* 3 (Feb.): 8–9.

———. 1987. The Limits of Genetic Inquiry. *Hastings Center Report* 17 (Aug.–Sept.): 5–10.

Lappé, Marc, James Gustafson, and Richard Robin. 1972. Ethical and Social Issues in Screening for Genetic Disease. *New England Journal of Medicine* 286 (May 18): 1129–32.

Laurence, K. M., and Ann Beresford. 1976. Degree of Physical Handicap and Occupation of 51 Adults with Spina Bifida. *British Journal of Preventive Socialized Medicine* 30:197–202.

Lebacqz, Karen. 1972. Mongoloid Children and the Burden on the Family: Self-fulfilling Prophecy (editorial correspondence). *Hastings Center Report* 2 (Feb.): 12–13.

———. 1973. Prenatal Diagnosis and Selective Abortion. *Linacre Quarterly* 40 (May): 109–27.

Lebel, Robert. 1978. *Ethical Issues Arising in the Genetic Counseling Relationship*. No. 14 of Birth Defects Original Article Series. New York: March of Dimes Birth Defects Foundation.

———. 1989. Trends, Threads, Themes, and Thoughts. *Loss, Grief & Care* 3 (3/4): 215–20.

Leibman, Monte, and Jolie Zimmer. 1979. The Psychological Sequelae of Abortion: Facts and Fallacies. In *The Psychological Aspects of Abortion*, ed. David Mall and Walter Watts, 127–38. Washington, D.C.: University Publications of America.

Lejeune, Jerome. 1970. On the Nature of Man. *American Journal of Human Genetics* 22 (March): 121–28.

Lejeune, Jerome, R. Turpin, and M. Gautier. 1959. Le Mongolisme: premier example d'aberration autosomique humain. *Ann.-de Genet.* 1:41.

Lemna, W. K., G. L. Feldman, B. Kerem, S. D. Fernbach, E. P. Zevkovich, W. E. O'Brien, J. R. Riordan, F. S. Collins, L. C. Tsue, and A. L. Beaudet. 1990. Mutation Analysis for Heterozygote Detection and the Prenatal Diagnosis of Cystic Fibrosis. *New England Journal of Medicine* 322 (Feb. 1): 291–96.

Lenoski, E. F. 1976. Translating Injury Data into Preventive Health Care Services: Physical Child Abuse. Department of Pediatrics, University of Southern California. Photocopy.

Levine, Katharine. 1979. What I Thought During My Abortion. *Mademoiselle,* May, 110, 114, 118, 129.

Levi-Setti, P. E., M. Buscaglia, E. Ferrazzi, G. Zuliani, L. Ghisoni, and F. Pardo. 1989. Evaluation of the Fetal Risk after Echo-guided Blood Sampling from the Umbilical Cord in the Second Trimester of Pregnancy. *Annali di Obstetrica, Ginecologia, Medicini Perinatale* 100 (2): 98–104.

Liley, Albert W. 1963. Intrauterine Transfusion of Foetus in Haemolytic Disease. *British Medical Journal* 2 (Nov. 2): 1107–9.

———. 1973. The Fetus in Control of His Environment. In *Abortion and Social Justice,* ed. Thomas Hilgers and Dennis Horan, 27–36. New York: Sheed and Ward.

Lippman, Abby. 1991. Prenatal Genetic Testing and Screening: Constructing Needs and Reinforcing Inequities. *American Journal of Law and Medicine* 17:15–50.

Littlefield, John W. 1969. Prenatal Diagnosis and Therapeutic Abortion. *New England Journal of Medicine* 280 (March 27): 722–23.

Lorber, John. 1973. Early Results of Selective Treatment of Spina Bifida Cystica. *British Medical Journal* 4 (Oct. 7): 201–4.

Lubowe, Stephen. 1989. Suffering and Its Amelioration in the Genetic Disease Muscular Dystrorophy: A Comprehensive Psychosocial View. *Loss, Grief & Care* 3 (3/4): 87–104.

McCormick, Richard. 1981. To Save or Let Die. In *Bioethics*, ed. Thomas A. Shannon, 157–68. Ramsey, N.J.: Paulist Press.

McCormick, Thomas. 1974. Ethical Issues in Amniocentesis and Abortion. *Texas Reports on Biology and Medicine* 32 (Spring): 299–309.

Macklin, Ruth. 1984. Personhood and the Abortion Debate. In *Abortion*, ed. Jay L. Garfield and Patricia Hennessey, 82–102, Amherst, Mass.: University of Massachusetts Press.

McKusick, Victor. 1975. *Mendelian Inheritance in Man*. Baltimore: John Hopkins University Press.

————. 1988. *Mendelian Inheritance in Man: Catalogs of Autosomal Dominant, Autosomal Recessive, and X-linked Phenotypes*. Baltimore: Johns Hopkins University Press.

Mahowald, Mary. 1984. Abortion and Equality. In *Abortion: Understanding the Differences*, ed. Sidney Callahan and Daniel Callahan, 177–96. New York: Plenum Press.

————. 1989. Is There Life after *Roe v. Wade? Hastings Center Report* 19 (July–August): 22–29.

Maia, M., D. Alves, G. Rigeiro, R. Printo, and M. C. Miranda. 1990. Juvenile GM2 Gangliosidosis Variant B1: Clinical and Biochemical Study in Seven Patients. *Neuropediatrics* 21 (1): 18–23.

Maidman, Jack E. 1989. Pregnancy Termination in Genetic Disease. *Loss, Grief & Care* 3 (3/4): 15–20.

Maloy, Kate. 1988. A Matter of Life and Love. *New Woman*, Sept., 66–71.

Mandelbaum, Arthur, and Mary Ella Wheeler. 1960. The Meaning of a Defective Child to Parents. *Social Casework* 41:360–67.

Mandell, J., C. A. Peters, and A. B. Retik. 1990. Current Concepts in the Perinatal Diagnosis and Management of Hydronephrosis. *Urologic Clinics of North America* 17 (2): 247–61.

March of Dimes. 1985. *Genetic Counseling*. New York: March of Dimes Birth Defects Foundation.

Margolis, Joseph. 1978. Human Life: Its Worth and Bringing It to an End. In *Infanticide and the Value of Life*, ed. Marvin Kohl, 180–91. Buffalo, N.Y.: Prometheus Books.

Marsh, Frank. 1982. Prenatal Screening and "Wrongful Life": Medicine's New "Catch-22"? *American Journal of Obstetrics and Gynecology* 143 (7): 745–48.

Marteau, Theresa M., Marie Johnson, Robert W. Shaw, and Susan Michie. 1989. The Impact of Prenatal Screening and Diagnostic Testing upon the Cognitions, Emotions and Behavior of Pregnant Women. *Journal of Psychosomatic Research* 33 (1): 7–16.

Martinius, J. 1986. Psychological and Ethical Problems Arising for Physicians and Parents from the Prenatal Diagnosis of Malformations. *Progress in Pediatric Surgery* 19:197–202.

Mattison, Donald, and Teresita Angtuaco. 1988. Magnetic Resonance Imaging in Prenatal Diagnosis. *Clinical Obstetrics and Gynecology* 31 (June): 353–89.

Mecklenburg, Fred. 1973. The Indications for Induced Abortions: A Physician's Perspective. In *Abortion and Social Justice,* ed. Thomas Hilgers and Dennis Horan, 37–56. New York: Sheed and Ward.

Medical Research Council. 1978. An Assessment of the Hazards of Amniocentesis. *British Journal of Obstetrics and Gynaecology* 5: Supplement 2.

Medical Research Council Working Party on the Evaluation of Chorionic Villus Sampling. 1991. Medical Research Council European Trial of Chorionic Villus Sampling. *Lancet* 337 (June 22): 1491–99.

Meehan, Mary. 1984. More Trouble Than They're Worth? Children and Abortion. In *Abortion: Understanding the Differences,* ed. Sidney Callahan and Daniel Callahan, 145–70. New York: Plenum Press.

Mercer, Jane R. 1965. Social Systems Perspective and Clinical Perspective: Frames of Reference for Understanding Career Patterns of Persons Labelled as Mentally Retarded. *Social Problems* 13 (1): 18–34.

Merkatz, Irwin, Harold Nitowsky, James Macri, and Walter Johnson. 1984. An Association between Low Maternal Serum Alpha-fetoprotein and Fetal Chromosomal Abnormalities. *American Journal of Obstetrics and Gynecology* 148 (7): 886–94.

Metzler, Karen. 1978. If There's Life Make It Worth Living: The Quality of Life for the Infant Born with a Birth Defect. In *Infanticide and the Value of Life*, ed. Marvin Kohl, 172–79. Buffalo, N.Y.: Prometheus Books.

Mikkelsen, M., G. Fischer, J. Hansen, B. Pilgaard, and J. Nielsen. 1983. The Impact of Legal Termination of Pregnancy and of Prenatal Diagnosis on the Birth Prevalence of Down Syndrome in Denmark. *Annals of Human Genetics* 47, pt. 2 (March–April): 317–20.

Milunsky, Aubrey. 1973. *The Prenatal Diagnosis of Hereditary Diseases*. Springfield, Ill.: Thomas.

————. 1986. The Prenatal Diagnosis of Neural Tube and Other Congenital Defects. In *Genetic Disorders and the Fetus*, 2nd ed., ed. Aubrey Milunsky, 453–519. New York: Plenum Press.

Miringoff, Marc L. 1989. *The Index of Social Health 1989: Measuring the Social Well-Being of the Nation*. Tarrytown, N.Y.: Fordham Institute for Innovation in Social Policy.

Modell, Bernadette. 1985. Some Social Implications of Early Fetal Diagnosis. In *Chorionic Villus Sampling*, ed. Marco Fraccaro, Bruno Brambati, and Giuseppe Simoni, 341–51. Berlin: Springer-Verlag.

Mohr, J. 1968. Foetal Genetic Diagnosis: Development of Techniques for Early Sampling of Foetal Cells. *Acta Pathologica et Microbiologica Scandinavica* 73:73.

Mohr, James. 1978. *Abortion in America*. Oxford: Oxford University Press.

Monteleone, Patricia, and Albert Moraczewski. 1981. Medical and Ethical Aspects of the Prenatal Diagnosis of Genetic Disease. In *New Perspectives on Human Abortion*, ed. Thomas Hilgers, Dennis Horan, and David Mall, 45–59. Frederick, Md.: University Publications of America.

Moore, Keith. 1983. *Before We Are Born: Basic Embryology and Birth Defects*. Philadelphia: W. B. Saunders and Co.

Mosse, George. 1964. *The Crisis of German Ideology: Intellectual Origins of the Third Reich*. New York: Grosset and Dunlap.

Motulsky, Arno G. 1989. Societal Problems in Human and Medical Genetics. *Genome* 31 (2): 870–75.

Muller, F., M. C. Aubrey, B. Gasser, F. Duchatel, J. Boué, and A. Boué. 1985. Prenatal Diagnosis of Cystic Fibrosis. Part 2: Meconium Ilcus in Affected Fetuses. *Prenatal Diagnosis* 5 (2): 109–17.

Murray, Robert. 1972. Problems behind the Promise: Ethical Issues in Mass Genetic Screening. *Hastings Center Report* 2 (April): 10–13.

————. 1974. The Practitioner's View of the Values Involved in Genetic Screening and Counseling: Individual vs. Societal Imperatives. In *Ethical, Social and Legal Dimensions of Screening for Human Genetic Disease,* ed. Daniel Bergsma, 185–200. Miami: Symposia Specialists.

Murray, Robert, Naomi Chamberlain, John Fletcher, Ernest Hopkins, Rudolph Jackson, Patricia King, and Tabitha Powledge. 1980. Special Considerations for Minority Participation in Prenatal Diagnosis. *Journal of the American Medical Association* 243 (March 28): 1254–56.

Nathanson, Bernard, and Richard Ostling. 1979. *Aborting America.* Toronto: Life Cycles Books.

Navon, R., E. H. Kolodny, H. Mitsumoto, G. H. Thomas, and R. L. Proia. 1990. Ashkenazi-Jewish and Non-Jewish Adult GM2 Gangliosidosis Patients Share a Common Genetic Defect. *American Journal of Human Genetics* 45 (4): 817–21.

Neel, James. 1971. Ethical Issues Resulting from Prenatal Diagnosis. In *Early Diagnosis of Human Genetic Defects: Scientific and Ethical Considerations,* ed. Maureen Harris, 219–29. Fogarty International Proceedings, No. 6. Washington, D.C.: Government Printing Office.

Nemeti, M., A. Bolodar, K. Horvath, and Z. Papp. 1989. Sex Determination of the Embryo by DNA Studies of Chorionic Villi Samples. *Orvosi Hetilap* 130 (49): 2629–30, 2633.

New Oxford Annotated Bible. 1977. Revised Standard Edition. New York: Oxford University Press.

Ney, Philip. 1979. Infant Abortion and Child Abuse: Cause and Effect. In *The Psychological Aspects of Abortion,* ed. David Mall and Walter Watts, 25–38. Washington, D.C.: University Publications of America.

————. 1983. A Consideration of Abortion Survivors. *Child Psychiatry and Human Development* 13:168–79.

Nicholson, Susan. 1981. Abortion: On Fetal Indications. In *Bioethics,* ed. Thomas A. Shannon, 73–93. Ramsey, N.J.: Paulist Press.

Nicolaides, K. H., and Stuart Campbell. 1986. Diagnosis of Fetal Abnormalities by Ultrasound. In *Genetic Disorders and the Fetus*, 2nd ed., ed. Aubrey Milunsky, 521–70. New York: Plenum Press.

Nielsen, J. 1989. What More Can Be Done for Girls and Women with Turner's Syndrome and Their Parents? *Acta Paediatrica Scandinavica*. 356 (Supplement): 92–100.

Noonan, John. 1970. An Almost Absolute Value in History. In *The Morality of Abortion*, ed. John Noonan, 1–59. Cambridge, Mass.: Harvard University Press.

Okado, Nobuo, and Tobuzo Kojima. 1984. Ontogeny of the Central Nervous System, Neurogenesis, Fibre Connection, Synaptogenesis and Myelination in the Spinal Cord. In *Continuity of Neural Functions from Prenatal to Postnatal Life*, ed. Heinz Prechtl, 31–45. Philadelphia: J. B. Lippincott Co.

Oken, Donald. 1961. What to Tell Cancer Patients. *Journal of the American Medical Association* 175:1120–28.

Ooms, Theodora. 1984. A Family Perspective on Abortion. In *Abortion: Understanding the Differences*, ed. Sidney Callahan and Daniel Callahan, 81–108. New York: Plenum Press.

Palomaki, O. E., G. J. Knight, M. S. Holman, and J. E. Haddow. 1990. Maternal Serum Alpha-fetoprotein Screening for Fetal Down Syndrome in the United States: Results of a Survey. *American Journal of Obstetrics and Gynecology* 162 (2): 317–21.

Paris Conference. 1972. Standardization in Human Cytogenetics. *Birth Defects Original Article* 8 (7): 1–46.

Patrick, A. D. 1983. Inherited Metabolic Disorders. *British Medical Bulletin* 39 (4): 378–85.

Paul VI, Pope. 1968. *Humanae Vitae* (encyclical issued July 29). *American Ecclesiastical Review* 159:290–300.

Pearn, J. H. 1973. Patient's Subjective Interpretation of Risks Offered in Genetic Counseling. *Journal of Medical Genetics* 10 (2): 129–34.

Peterson, Susan. 1981. The Politics of Prenatal Diagnosis. In *The Custom-made Child? A Women-centered Perspective*, ed. Helen Holmes, Betty Hoskins, and Michael Gross, 95–104. Clifton, N.J.: Humana Press.

Polani, P. E. 1982. Pairing of X and Y Chromosomes, Non-inactivation of X-linked Genes, and the Maleness Factor. *Human Genetics* 60 (3): 207–11.

Powledge, Tabitha. 1974. Genetic Screening as a Political and Social Development. In *Ethical, Social and Legal Dimensions of Screening for Human Genetic Disease,* ed. Daniel Bergsma, 25–56. Miami: Symposia Specialists.

———. 1981. "Unnatural Selection": On Choosing Children's Sex. In *The Custom-made Child? A Women-centered Perspective,* ed. Helen Holmes, Betty Hoskins, and Michael Gross, 193–99. Clifton, N.J.: Humana Press.

———. 1983. Toward a Moral Policy for Sex Selection. In *Sex Selection of Children,* ed. Neil Bennett, 37–40. New York: Academic Press.

Powledge, Tabitha, and John Fletcher. 1979. Guidelines for the Ethical, Social and Legal Issues in Prenatal Diagnosis. *New England Journal of Medicine* 300 (Jan. 25): 168–72.

Prechtl, Heinz (ed.). 1984. *Continuity of Neural Functions from Prenatal to Postnatal Life.* Philadelphia: J. B. Lippincott Co.

Prenatal Surgery Advances Struggle over Fetal Rights. 1986. *Providence Journal,* Oct. 12, 1(B).

President's Commission for the Study of Ethical Problems in Medicine and Biomedical and Behavioral Research. March 1983. Washington, D.C.: United States Government Printing Office.

Ramsey, Paul. 1970a. *Fabricated Man: The Ethics of Genetic Control.* New Haven, Conn.: Yale University Press.

———. 1970b. Reference Points in Deciding about Abortion. In *The Morality of Abortion,* ed. John Noonan, 60–100. Cambridge, Mass.: Harvard University Press.

———. 1972. Genetic Therapy: A Theologian's Response. In *The New Genetics and the Future of Man,* ed. Michael Hamilton, 157–75. Grand Rapids, Mich.: William B. Eerdman's Publishing Co.

———. 1973. Screening: An Ethicist's View. In *Ethical Issues in Human Genetics,* ed. Bruce Hilton, Daniel Callahan, and Maureen Harris, 158–60. New York: Plenum Press.

———. 1978. *Ethics at the Edge of Life.* New York: Columbia University Press.

Rapp, Rayna. 1984. The Ethics of Choice: After My Amniocentesis Mike and I Faced the Toughest Decision of Our Lives. *Ms.* 12 (April): 97–100.

Rawls, John. 1971. *Theory of Justice.* Cambridge, Mass.: Harvard University Press.

Reading, Anthony E., David N. Cox, and Stuart Campbell. 1988. A Controlled Prospective Evaluation of the Acceptability of Ultrasound in Prenatal Care. *Journal of Psychosomatic Obstetrics and Gynecology* 8 (3):191–98.

Reardon, David. 1987. *Aborted Women: Silent No More.* Chicago: Loyola University Press.

Report of the Collaborative Acetylcholinesterase Study. 1981. Amniotic Esterase Electrophoresis as a Secondary Testing in the Diagnosis of Anencephaly and Open Spina Bifida in Early Pregnancy. *Lancet* 2 (Aug. 15): 321–24.

Rhoads, George, Laird Jackson, Sarah Schlesselman, Felix de la Cruz, Robert Desnick, Mitchell Golbus, David Ledbetter, Herbert Lubs, Maurice Mahoney, Eugene Pergament, Joe Simpson, Robert Carpenter, Serman Elias, Norman Ginsberg, James Goldberg, John Hobbins, Lauren Lynch, Patricia Shiono, Ronald Wapner, and Julia Zachary. 1989. The Safety and Efficacy of Chorionic Villus Sampling for Early Prenatal Diagnosis of Cytogenetic Abnormalities. *New England Journal of Medicine* 320 (March 9): 609–17.

Rhoden, Nancy. 1989. A Compromise on Abortion. *Hastings Center Report* 19 (July–August): 32–37.

Riccardi, Vincent. 1977. *The Genetic Approach to Human Disease.* New York: Oxford University Press.

Richards, M. P. M. 1989. Social and Ethical Problems of Fetal Diagnosis and Screening. *Journal of Reproductive and Infant Psychology* 7:171–85.

Robertson, John. 1975. Involuntary Euthanasia of Defective Newborns. *Stanford Law Review* 27:213–14, 251–61.

Robinson, Arthur. 1986. Genetic Screening: Medical Progress Prompts Ethical Questions. *AORN Journal* 43 (May): 1137, 1140, 1142.

Rodeck, C. H., and J. M. Morsman. 1983. First-Trimester Chorion Biopsy *British Medical Bulletin* 39, no. 4 (Oct.): 338–42.

Rodeck, C. H., and K. H. Nicolaides. 1983. Fetoscopy and Fetal Tissue Sampling. *British Medical Bulletin* 39 (4): 332–37.

Rodman, Hyman, Betty Sarvis, and Joy Walker Bonar. 1987. *The Abortion Question.* New York: Columbia University Press.

Roe v. Wade. 1973. Decision on Abortion by the United States Supreme Court. 410 U.S. 116.

Rogers, David, and Larry Shapiro. 1986. X-Linked Disease and Disorders of the Sex Chormosomes. In *Genetic Disorders and the Fetus,* 2nd ed., ed. Aubrey Milunsky, 342–68. New York: Plenum Press.

Roggencamp, Viola. 1984. Abortion of a Special Kind: Female Sex Selection in India. In *Test-tube Women,* ed. Rita Arditti, Renate Klein, and Shelley Minden, 266–77. London: Pandora Press.

Romero, Roberto, John Hobbins, and Maurice Mahoney. 1986. Fetal Blood Sampling and Fetoscopy. In *Genetic Disorders and the Fetus,* 2nd ed., ed. Aubrey Milunsky, 571–98. New York: Plenum Press.

Romero, Roberto, Gianluigi Pilu, Philippe Jeanty, Alessandro Ghidini, and John Hobbins. 1988. *Prenatal Diagnosis of Congenital Anomalies.* Norwalk, Conn.: Appleton and Lange.

Rossi, Nicolini, Paola Avveduti, Nicola Rizzo, and Raffaele Lorusso. 1989. Maternal Stress and Fetal Motor Behavior: A Preliminary Report. *Pre- and Perinatal Psychology Journal* 3 (4): 311–18.

Rothman, Barbara. 1985. The Products of Conception: The Social Context of Reproductive Choices. *Journal of Medical Ethics* 11 (Dec.): 188–92.

———. 1986. *The Tentative Pregnancy.* New York: Viking Press.

Rowley, Peter. 1984. Genetic Screening: Marvel or Menace? *Science* 225 (July 13): 138–44.

Rue, Vincent. 1984. The Forgotten Fathers: Men and Abortion? *Heartbeat,* Fall, 19–21.

Rush, Curt. 1983. Genetic Screening, Eugenic Abortion and *Roe v. Wade:* How Viable is *Roe's* Viability Standard? *Brooklyn Law Review* 50 (Fall): 113–42.

Sachdev, Paul (ed.). 1988. *International Handbook on Abortion.* Chicago: Greenwood Publishing.

Salholz, Eloise. 1988. The Abortion Battlefield. *Newseek,* Nov. 28, 44.

Sandberg, A. A., G. F. Koeph, R. Ishihara, and T. S. Hauschka. 1961. An XYY Male. *Lancet* 2 (Aug. 26): 488–99.

Santurri, Edmund. 1985. Prenatal Diagnosis: Some Moral Considerations. In *Questions about the Beginning of Life: Christian Appraisals of Seven Bioethical Questions,* ed. Edward Schneider, 120–50. Minneapolis: Augsburg Publishing House.

Schwarz, Stephen. 1990. *The Moral Question of Abortion.* Chicago: Loyola University Press.

Schweitzer, Albert. 1987. *The Philosophy of Civilization.* Buffalo, N.Y.: Prometheus Books.

Seller, Mary. 1976. Congenital Abnormalities and Selective Abortion. *Journal of Medical Ethics* 2 (Sept.): 138–41.

————. 1982. Ethical Aspects of Genetic Counselling. *Journal of Medical Ethics* 8 (Dec.): 185–88.

Serre, J. L., B. Bouy-Simon, E. Mornet, B. Jaume-Roig, A. Balasso-poulou, M. Schwartz, A. Tailandier, J. Boué, and A. Boué. 1990. *Human Genetics* 84 (5): 446–54.

Shah, Y. G., C. J. Eckl, S. K. Stinson, and J. R. Woods, Jr. 1990. Biparietal Diameter/Femur Length Ratio, Cephalic Index, and Femur Length Measurements: Not Reliable Screening Techniques for Down Syndrome. *Obstetrics and Gynecology* 75 (Feb.): 186–88.

Shapiro, Harry. 1977. *The Birth Control Book.* New York: St. Martin's Press.

Shaw, Anthony. 1978. Who Should Die and Who Should Decide? In *Infanticide and the Value of Life,* ed. Marvin Kohl, 102–14. Buffalo, N.Y.: Prometheus Books.

Shaw, Anthony, Judson G. Randolf, and Barbara Manard. 1977. Ethical Issues in Pediatric Surgery: A Nationwide Survey of Pediatricians and Pediatric Surgeons. *Pediatrics* 60 (Oct.): 588–99.

Sherlock, Richard. 1987. *Preserving Life: Public Policy and the Life Not Worth Living.* Chicago: Loyola University Press.

Silver, Marc. 1986. After Our Abortion, No One Said "I'm Sorry." *The Washington Post,* Jan. 4, Second-opinion section.

Simpson, Joe Leigh. 1990. Incidence and Timing of Pregnancy Losses: Relevance to Evaluating Safety of Early Prenatal Diagnosis. *American Journal of Medical Genetics* 35 (Feb.): 165–73.

Simpson, Joe Leigh, and Sherman Elias. 1989. Prenatal Diagnosis of Genetic Disorders. In *Maternal-Fetal Medicine: Principles and Practice*, 2nd ed., ed. Robert K. Creasy and Robert Resnik, 78–107. Philadelphia: W. B. Saunders and Co.

Singer, Peter. 1988. All Animals Are Equal. In *Contemporary Moral Problems*, 2nd ed., ed., James White, 318–26. St. Paul, Minn.: West Publishing Co.

Sjogren, Berit, and Nils Uddenberg. 1987. Attitudes toward Disabled Persons and the Possible Effects of Prenatal Diagnosis. *Journal of Psychosomatic Obstetrics and Gynecology* 6 (3): 187–96.

————. 1988. Prenatal Diagnosis and Maternal Attachment to the Child-to-be. *Journal of Psychosomatic Obstetrics and Gynecology* 9 (2): 73–87.

————. 1990. Prenatal Diagnosis for Psychological Reasons: Comparison with Other Indications, Advanced Maternal Age and Known Genetic Risks. *Prenatal Diagnosis* 10 (2): 111–20.

Smidt-Jensen, S., N. Hahnemann, P. Jensen, and A. Therkelsen. 1984. Experience with Transabdominal Fine Needle Biopsy from Chorionic Villi in the First Trimester. *Clinical Genetics* 26 (Sept.): 272–74.

Smith, Adam. 1976. *The Theory of Moral Sentiments*, ed. D. D. Raphael and A. C. MacFie. Oxford: Oxford University Press.

Smith, Hamilton, and K. W. Wilcox. 1970. Purification and General Properties. Part 1: A Restrictive Enzyme from Hemophilus Influenzae. *Journal of Molecular Biology* 51:379–91.

Somerville, Margaret. 1981. Selective Birth in Twin Pregnancy. *New England Journal of Medicine* 305 (Nov. 12): 1218.

Sorenson, James. 1974. Some Social and Psychological Issues in Genetic Screening. In *Ethical, Social and Legal Dimensions of Screening for Human Genetic Disease*, ed. Daniel Bergsma, 165–84. Miami: Symposia Specialists.

Southern, Edward. 1975. Detection of Specific Sequences among DNA Fragments Separated by Gel Electrophoresis. *Journal of Molecular Biology* 98:503.

Speckhard, Anne. 1987. *The Psychosocial Aspects of Stress Following Abortion*. Kansas City, Mo.: Sheed and Ward.

Spurdle, Amanda, Jennifer Kromberg, Jennifer Rosendorff, and Trefor Jenkins. 1991. Prenatal Diagnosis for Huntington's Disease: A Molecular and Psychological Study. *Prenatal Diagnosis* 11 (3): 177–85.

The Status of Fetoscopy and Fetal Tissue Sampling. 1984. *Prenatal Diagnosis* 4 (1): 79–81.

Steele, Mark, and W. Roy Berg. 1966. Chromosomal Analysis of Human Amniotic Fluid Cells. *Lancet* 1 (Feb. 19): 383–85.

Steinberg, Terry Nicole. 1989. Abortion Counseling: To Benefit Maternal Health. *American Journal of Law and Medicine* 15 (4): 483–517.

Stetten, G., and H. I. Meissner. 1981. Unusual and Rapid Amniotic Fluid Cell Growth. *American Journal of Obstetrics and Gynecology* 140 (6): 719–21.

Strauss, R. P., and J. U. Davis. 1990. Prenatal Detection and Fetal Surgery of Clefts and Craniofacial Abnormalities in Humans: Social and Ethical Issues. *Cleft Palate Journal* 27 (2): 176–82.

Streifler, J., M. Golomb, and N. Gadoth. 1989. Psychiatric Features of Adult GM21 Gangliosidosis. *British Journal of Psychiatry* 155: 410–13.

Strong, Carson. 1983. Defective Infants and Their Impact on Families: Ethical and Legal Considerations. *Law, Medicine and Health Care* 13 (Sept.): 10–15.

———. 1984. The Neonatologist's Duty to Patient and Parents. *Hastings Center Report* 14 (Aug.): 10–16.

Stubbins, Joseph. 1988. The Politics of Disability. In *Attitudes toward People with Disabilities*, ed. Harold Yuker, 22–32. New York: Springer Publishing Co.

Sugino, S., S. Fujishita, N. Kamimura, T. Matsumoto, M. C. Wapenaar, H. X. Deng, N. Shibuya, T. Miike, and N. Niikawa. 1989. Molecular-Genetic Study of Duchenne and Becker Muscular Dystrophies: Deletion Analysis of 45 Japanese Patients and Segregation Analyses in Their Families with RFLPs Bases on the Data Normal Japanese Females. *American Journal of Medical Genetics* 34 (Dec.): 555–61.

Swavely, Steven M., and Arthur Falek. 1989. Huntington's Disease: The Prototype for Late Onset Terminal Genetic Disorders. *Loss, Grief & Care* 3 (3/4): 111–24.

Taber's Cyclopedic Medical Dictionary. 1989. Philadelphia: F. A. Davis Co.

Tedgard, E., R. Ljung, T. McNeil, and M. Schwartz. 1989. How Do Carriers of Hemophilia Experience Prenatal Diagnosis (PND)? *Acta Paediatrica Scandinavica* 78 (5): 692–700.

Tennes, K., M. Puk, and K. Bryant. 1975. A Developmental Study of Girls with Trisomy X. *American Journal of Human Genetics* 27 (1): 71–80.

Tertullian. 1950. Apologetic Works. In *The Fathers of the Church*, vol. 10, ed. Roy Joseph Deferrari, 3–126. New York: Fathers of the Church.

Thomas Aquinas, St. 1963. *Summa Theologica.* Translated by the Blackfriars. New York: McGraw-Hill.

Thomson, Judith Jarvis. 1971. A Defense of Abortion. *Philosophy and Public Affairs* 1:47–66.

Thoulon, J. M. 1990. Amniocentesis versus Choicentesis and Cordocentesis. *Revieue Française Gynecologie et Obstetriques* 85 (2): 101–14.

Tietz, Christopher, and Stanley Henshaw. 1986. *Induced Abortion: A World Review.* New York: Alan Guttmacher Institute.

Tijo, H. J., and A. Levan. 1956. The Chromosome Numbers of Man. *Hereditas* 42:1–6.

Tonnesen, T., and N. Horn. 1989. Prenatal and Postnatal Diagnosis of Menkes Disease: An Inherited Disorder of Copper Metabolism. *Journal of Inherited Metabolic Disorders* 12 (Suppl. 1): 207–14.

Tooley, Michael. 1973. A Defense of Abortion and Infanticide. In *The Problem of Abortion*, ed. Joel Feinberg, 51–91. Belmont, Calif.: Wadsworth Publishing Co.

Touwen, Bert. 1984. Primitive Reflexes—Conceptual or Semantic Problem? In *Continuity of Neural Functions from Prenatal to Postnatal Life*, ed. Heinz Prechtl, 115–25. Philadelphia: J. B. Lippincott Co.

Turnbull, A. C., and I. Z. MacKenzie. 1983. Second-Trimester Amniocentesis and Termination of Pregnancy. *British Medical Journal* 39 (Oct.): 315–21.

Tuskegee Syphilis Study: Final Report of the Ad Hoc Advisory Panel. 1973. Washington, D.C.: United States Public Health Service.

Twiss, Sumner. 1974. Ethical Issues in Genetic Screening: Models of Genetic Responsibility. In *Ethical, Social and Legal Dimensions of Screening for Human Genetic Disease*, ed. Daniel Bergsma, 225–62. Miami: Symposia Specialists.

Tyler, Carl. 1981. Epidemiology of Abortion. *Journal of Reproductive Medicine* 26 (9): 459–69.

Van Hasselt, Vincent. 1988. *Handbook of Family Violence*. New York: Plenum Press.

Van Riper, Marcia, and Florence E. Selder. 1989. Parental Responses to the Birth of a Child with Down Syndrome. *Loss, Grief & Care* 3 (3/4): 59–76.

Verny, Thomas. 1981. *The Secret Life of the Unborn Child*. New York: Dell Publishing.

Verp, Marion S., A. T. Bombard, Joe L. Simpson, and Sherman Elias. 1988. Parental Decision Following Prenatal Diagnosis of Fetal Chromosome Anomalies. *American Journal of Medical Genetics* 29 (March): 613–22.

Verp, Marion S., and Joe Leigh Simpson. 1985. Prenatal Diagnosis of Cytogenetic Disorders. In *Prenatal Diagnosis*, ed. K. Filkins and H. Kaminestsky, 13–48. New York: Dekker.

Volpe, E. Peter. 1984. *Patient in the Womb*. Macon, Ga.: Mercer University Press.

Wald, N., H. Cuckle, and K. Nanchahal. 1989. Amniotic Fluid Acetylcholinesterase Measurement in the Prenatal Diagnosis of Open Neural Tube Defects. Second Report of the Collaborative Acetylcholinesterase Study. *Prenatal Diagnosis* 9 (12): 813–29.

Walters, LeRoy. 1982. Concepts of Personhood. In *Contemporary Issues in Bioethics*, 2nd ed., ed. Tom Beauchamp and LeRoy Walters, 87–89. Belmont, Calif.: Wadsworth Publishing Co.

Ward, R., B. Modell, M. Petrov, R. Karagozlu, and E. Douratsos. 1983. Method of Sampling Chorionic Villi in First Trimester of Pregnancy under Guidance of Real Time Ultrasound. *British Medical Journal* 286 (May 14): 1542–44.

Warren, Mary Anne. 1973. On the Moral and Legal Status of Abortion. *Monist* 57 (Jan.): 43–61.

———. 1978. Commentary on "Can the Fetus Be an Organ Farm?" *Hastings Center Report* (Oct.): 23–24.

Watson, James D., John Touze, and David T. Kurtz. 1983. *Recombinant DNA: A Short Course.* New York: Scientific American Books.

Weaver, David. 1988. A Survey of Prenatally Diagnosed Disorders. *Clinical Obstetrics and Gynecology* 31 (June): 253–69.

Weber, Leonard J. 1978. In Defense of the Legal Prohibition of Infanticide. In *Infanticide and the Value of Life*, ed. Marvin Kohl, 130–36. Buffalo, N.Y.: Prometheus Books.

Webster's New World Dictionary. 1987. New York: Warner Books.

Wein, P., B. Robertson, and G. J. Ratten. 1989. Cardiorespiratory Collapse and Pulmonary Oedema Due to Intravascular Absorption of Prostaglandin F2 Alpha Administered Extraamniotically for Midtrimester Termination of Pregnancy. *Australian–New Zealand Journal of Obstetrics and Gynecology* 29 (3 Pt 1): 261–63.

Weiner, Anita, and Eugene Weiner. 1984. The Aborted Sibling Factor. *Clinical Social Work Journal* 12: 209–13.

Weiner, Carl. 1988. The Role of Cordocentesis in Fetal Diagnosis. *Clinical Obstetrics and Gynecology* 31 (June): 285–92.

Weir, R. 1984. *Selective Non-Treatment of Handicapped Newborns.* New York: Oxford University Press.

Weiss, L., L. Frischer, and J. Richman. 1989. Parental Adjustment to Intrapartum and Delivery Room Loss: The Role of a Hospital-Based Support Program. *Clinical Perinatology* 16 (Dec.): 1009–19.

Weissman, Rita. 1972. Mongoloid Children and the Burden of the Family: Cold Realities (editorial correspondence). *Hastings Center Report* 2 (Feb.): 12.

Wertz, D. C., J. M. Rosenfeld, S. R. Janes, and R. W. Erbe. 1991. Attitudes toward Abortion among Parents of Children with Cystic Fibrosis. *American Journal of Public Health* 81 (8): 992–96.

Wertz, Dorothy, and John Fletcher. 1988. Ethics and Medical Genetics in the United States. *American Journal of Medical Genetics* 29 (April): 815–27.

———. 1989. Fatal Knowledge? Prenatal Diagnosis and Sex Selection. *Hastings Center Report* 19 (May–June): 21–27.

Wertz, Dorothy, John Fletcher, and J. J. Mulvihill. 1990. Medical Geneticists Confront Ethical Dilemmas: Cross-cultural Comparisons among 18 Nations. *American Journal of Human Genetics* 46 (6); 1200–1213.

Wertz, Dorothy, John Fletcher, and Caroline J. Whitbeck. 1983. Women as People: Pregnancy and Personhood. In *Abortion and the Status of the Fetus,* ed. William Bondeson, H. Tristam Engelhardt, Stuart Spicker, and Daniel Winship, 247–72. Dordrecht, Netherlands: D. Reidel Publishing Co.

Wertz, Dorothy, J. R. Sorenson, and T. C. Heeren. 1984. Genetic Counselling and Reproductive Uncertainty. *American Journal of Medical Genetics* 18 (May): 79.

White-Van Mourik, J. C. A., J. M. Connor, and M. A. Ferguson-Smith. 1990. Patient Care before and after Termination of Pregnancy for Neural Tube Defects. *Prenatal Diagnosis* 10 (8): 497–505.

Wilke, J. C., and M. Wilke. 1981. *Life or Death.* Cincinnati, Ohio: Hayes Publishing Co.

Williams, George Huntston. 1970a. Religious Residues and Presuppositions in the American Debate on Abortion. *Theological Studies* 31 (March): 10–75.

———. 1970b. The Sacred Condominium. In *The Morality of Abortion: Legal and Historical Perspectives,* ed. John Noonan, Jr., 146–71. Cambridge, Mass.: Harvard University Press.

Williamson, Roger, and Jeffrey Murray. 1988. Molecular Analysis of Genetic Disorders. *Clinical Obstetrics and Gynecology* 31 (June): 270–84.

Wilson, R. Douglas, V. Kendrick, B. K. Wittmann, and B. McGillivray. 1986. Spontaneous Abortion and Pregnancy Outcome after Normal First-Trimester Ultrasound Examination. *Obstetrics and Gynecology* 67 (March): 352–55.

World Medical Association. 1949. Declaration of Geneva. *World Medical Association Bulletin* 1:109–11.

Wright, Beatrice. 1988. Attitudes and the Fundamental Negative Bias. In *Attitudes toward Persons with Disabilities,* ed. Harold Yuker, 3–21. New York: Springer Publishing Co.

Wulff, K., F. H. Herrmann, M. C. Wapenaar, and M. Wehnert. 1989. Deletion Screening in Patients with Duchenne Muscular Dystrophy. *Journal of Neurology* 8 (Dec.): 470–73.

Yuker, Harold E. 1988. Perceptions of Severely and Multiply Disabled Persons. *Journal of the Multihandicapped Person* 1 (March): 5–16.

Zachary, R. B. 1982. Life with Spina Bifida. In *Contemporary Issues in Bioethics,* ed. Tom Beauchamp and Leroy Walters, 355–58. Belmont, Calif.: Wadsworth Publishing Co.

Zuk, G. H. 1959. The Religious Factor and Role of Guilt in Parental Acceptance of the Retarded. *American Journal of Mental Deficiencies* 64:139–49.

Zunich, M., and B. Ledwith. 1969. Self-concepts of Visually Handicapped and Sighted Children. *Perceptual and Motor Skills* 21:771–74.

Zuskar, Deborah M. 1987. The Psychological Impact of Prenatal Diagnosis of Fetal Abnormality Strategies for Investigation and Intervention. *Women's Health* 12 (1): 91–103.

Author/Title Index

Subject Index

Abortion. *See also* Elective abortion; Selective abortion
  child abuse and, 218, 246
  decision bias, 12
  demographic factors and, 7
  laws, 1, 5–6. *See also* Roe v. Wade
  procedures, 93, 94–98. *See also* Dilation and curettage (D&C); Dilation and evacuation (D&E)
  rates, 5–6, 91–93, 94
  therapeutic, 173. *See also* Selective abortion, as therapy
  timing of, 92–93
Acetylcholinesterase (AChE) testing, 44, 63
Achondroplasia, 32
Albinism, 32
Allele, 31
Alpha-fetoprotein (AFP) testing, 44, 48, 59–63, 78, 185. *See also* MSAFP screening
  disorders that can be diagnosed by, 60–61
Amniocentesis, 8–9, 11, 60, 88, 141–42, 151, 157, 185, 206
  accuracy rate of, 48
  as cause for anxiety, 81–84, 134
  chorionic villus sampling (CVS), comparison with, 55
  consent form for, 271
  etymology of word, 160
  first use of, 19
  genetic indication for, 49, 87
  limitations and risks of, 48, 50–51, 204–5

maternal age and, 29, 46
maternal-fetal bonding and, 50–51, 84–85, 86
procedure of, 46–48
psychological effects of, 50–51, 135
quantity performed, 45–46
reasons for, 29, 30, 46, 79
sex selection and, 48
timing of, 46, 91
Amniography, 68
Anencephaly, 41, 42, 43, 61, 63, 65, 77
Aneuploidy, 22, 23, 24
Anthropocentricism, 103
Autonomy, 80, 123, 143–45, 196
  maternal/parental, 13, 73, 123, 144, 145, 196, 211, 221
  in Western society, value of, 1, 4–5, 10, 11, 129, 166, 210
Autosomes, 19, 23

Baby, "perfect," 220–22
Beneficence, obligation of, 13–14, 248

Carrier screening, 35, 37, 58, 76, 154, 192
Child. *See* Baby; Fetus
Child abuse, 40, 218, 246
Chorionic villus sampling (CVS), 95
  accuracy of, 52, 54
  amniocentesis, comparison with, 55
  disorders that can be diagnosed with, 53–54
  genetic indication for, 52
  history of, 52